# Kundalini and Self-Realization

*The Journey Back To Our True Home Through Spiritual Energy*

"Thou hast made us for Thyself, and our hearts are restless until they rest in Thee."

Ravindra Kumar

# KUNDALINI AND SELF-REALIZATION

## The Journey Back To Our True Home Through Spiritual Energy

New Age Books

New Delhi (India)

**KUNDALINI AND SELF-REALIZATION**

*Published by*
**NEW AGE BOOKS**
A-44, Naraina Industrial Area, Phase-I
New Delhi–110 028 (INDIA)
E-mail: nab@newagebooksindia.com
Website: www.newagebooksindia.com

ISBN: 978-81-7822-423-7
Reprint: Delhi, 2014

**DEDICATED TO**

*Inner Satguru—My High Self*
*My Grandmother, the Late Bhagwati Devi,*
*My Father, the Late Ganga Singh,*
*My Mother Lakshmi Devi*
*Who nourished the seed of spirituality in me right from my early childhood*
*and*
*Puchchi Babu-Mata*

# Contents

# Abbreviations

| | | |
|---|---|---|
| ARPR | : | Academy of Religion and Psychical Research |
| JRPR | : | Journal of Religion and Psychical Research |
| n d | : | no date given |

# Foreword

In the opening paragraphs of his famous *Confessions*, St. Augustine (354-430) writes

> ***...nos ad te et inquietum est cor nostrum, donec requiescat in te.***
> ("Thou hast made us for Thyself, and our hearts are restless until they rest in Thee.")

All human beings are on a journey back home—back to God, from Whom their journey originated. In spiritual terms, we have left our Father's heavenly house and fallen into this world of matter, in all its lower manifestations: physical, emotional, and mental. This journey is depicted in the parable of the Prodigal Son (Luke 15:11-32), in which the younger son takes his portion of the inheritance and squanders it all in riotous living. In despair, he repents and finally turns back toward home, where he is met by the open arms of his father.

Likewise, we human beings waste the substance of our lives in search of unworthy goals: pleasure, wealth, power, and prestige. But we cannot give up what we have never experienced. Only after these goals are attained and found to be empty and not ultimately satisfying do we give them up for more worthy goals: to serve others and to come to love them unconditionally; to express fully our own talents and capacities, and to encourage and assist others to do the same. Finally, we come to the ultimate purpose of our journey: to know and to love the Divine, and in the end to allow the Divine to live *in* us, *through* us, and ultimately *as* us.

In the West, this journey takes many literary forms. One of the earliest is Homer's *Odyssey*, the story of Odysseus who leaves the battlefield of defeated Troy and heads home where his beloved wife and father are waiting. In a tale full of adventure, Odysseus loses his entire crew to various mishaps, symbolising the dangers along the journey. Some of his men are seduced by the lotus-eaters and become so drunk that they forget about home. Such is the danger of drugs, whether cocaine or pleasure, heroin or power. Other men of Odysseus's crew fall victim to the Cyclops, symbolic of wild animal nature. Still others are bewitched by Circe, who turn them into pigs, wolves, and lions. Echoing this image more than two millennia later, Richard Bach has Sullivan tell Jonathan Livingston Seagull:

> Do you have any idea how many lives we must have gone through before we even got the first idea that there is more to life than eating, or fighting, or power in the Flock? A thousand lives, Jon, ten thousand! And then another hundred lives until we began to learn that there is such a thing as perfection, and another hundred again to get the idea that our purpose for living is to find that perfection and show it forth.

The journey of the human soul is the descent or "Fall" from our heavenly Source into the mental, the emotional, and finally the physical plane of matter. Our evolution is the ascent out of these lower realms, learning, along the way, to master our energies and to give expression to beauty, truth, and goodness. In the end, we come to wisdom: the wisdom of expression, the wisdom of living, the wisdom of knowledge and love of the Divine.

Dr. Kumar outlines this journey of the human soul, from its awakening to its ultimate salvation, in a path which he calls "Integral Yoga". "Yoga" means "union" and so connotes a path whose culmination is union with the Divine. Within each of us is the energy of the Divine, known in the East as *Kundalini.* This energy lies, as a coiled serpent, at the base of the spine, and moves up the body through wheel-like energy centres called *chakras*, which are themselves associated with the endocrine system of glands. As the divine energy moves successively up its pathway through the *chakras,* we are guided back to our Father's house.

An ancient Hindu prayer begins with the words, "Lead me, O Lord, from darkness into light, from mortality to immortality." From the darkness of our ignorance, we need to awaken to the existence of the Presence of the Divine in our soul. When the conscious phenomenal self or ego becomes aware of the soul, the journey back home has begun.

As we move toward union of our own soul with the Absolute or God, we must free ourselves from identification with the three lower vehicles and their energies: the mind, with its thoughts and opinions; the emotional body, with its negative feelings; and the physical body, with its appetites. Blocking our path to union with God are five "enemies": lust, anger, attachment, greed, and ultimately the ego itself, all of which must be conquered during the journey home. As Jesus taught, "No man can serve two masters" (Matthew 6:24):. either we do according to our own will, or we follow God's; either we live for ourselves, or we live for God. If we are to achieve union with God, we must empty ourselves of these five impediments. Only an empty self can be filled with God.

As we move closer to the goal, we will achieve the bliss, joy, peace, love, and knowledge which characterize the enlightened state of self-realization. We will overcome the *karma* which binds us to the wheel of continuous reincarnations. When the five enemies of lust, anger, attachment, greed, and ego are finally overcome, we will find ourselves exhibiting compassion and kindness, benevolence and love, while all the time being detached both from ego and from the effects of our actions. For we will have come to realize that it is the Divine which acts in and through us.

Integral Yoga, which is Dr. Kumar's own path, is the shortest path for a person who must live a life of work and family. Integral Yoga involves yogic exercises, meditation, scripture reading, and a regulated sex life. The desire for sex, the desire to express love for another, is an expression of a deeper desire: the love of the Soul for God. So recognized, sexual love can lead us on our pathway back to God. Dr. Ravindra Kumar explicates this pathway, and we are the more fortunate for sharing the journey back home.

**Dr. John F. Miller, III**
*President, Academy of Religion and Psychical Research*
Tampa, Florida

# Preface

Besides living in India for the major part of my life, I had the fortune of residing in various parts of the world, teaching mathematics at numerous universities. This included spending a minimum of two years in each of the following countries: United Kingdom, United States of America, Iraq, Nigeria, Zimbabwe, Ethiopia, Fiji Islands and Tanzania. In addition to these, I have travelled to other countries for shorter durations to participate in conferences, seminars and lectures.

Although a mathematician, I have also had an equal interest in the field of spiritual research. Over the years, my enthusiasm for mathematics has gradually diminished. Currently, I am fully devoted to exploring spiritual concepts being practised worldwide. Interacting with people of various religions has provided an opportunity to gather data supporting the theory that there is a common thread woven through all of them, which eventually leads one in search of inner peace and God. As I became enlightened about the true meaning of "Truth", I wrote a series of papers on what I discovered for publication. Thus, this book is virtually a collection of these published papers as originally written. Due to limited periodical space, it was necessary for some of my papers to be edited for their publications, thereby omitting pertinent information. The list of references in each paper is reproduced without change.

The search for a common ground has been going on for quite some time and there have been some pleasant outcomes. Huston Smith (1) talked about the "Human Unanimity" and the "Primordial Tradition" in his book *Forgotten Truth.* Aldous Huxley has said that "...happily there is the Highest Common Factor of all religions, the Perennial Philosophy which has always and everywhere been the metaphysical system of the prophets, saints and sages. It is perfectly possible for people to remain good Christians, Hindus, Buddhists, or Moslems and yet to be united in full agreement on the basis of doctrines of the Perennial Philosophy. The *Bhagavad Gita* is perhaps the most systematic scriptural statement of the Perennial Philosophy (Prabhavananda and Isherwood, 2).

As found by Aldous Huxley, the Perennial Philosophy of the *Bhagavad Gita* has four fundamental doctrines:

> *First:* The phenomenal world of matter and individualised consciousness — the world of things and animals and men and even gods — the manifestation of a Divine Ground within which all partial realities have their being, and apart from which they would be non-existent.
>
> *Second:* Human beings are capable not merely of knowing about the Divine Ground by inference; they can also realize its existence by direct intuition, superior to discursive reasoning. This immediate knowledge unites the knower with that which is known.
>
> *Third:* Man possesses a double nature, a phenomenal ego and an eternal Self, which is the inner man, the spirit, the spark of divinity within the soul. It is possible for a man, if he so desires, to identify himself with the spirit and therefore with the Divine Ground, which is of the same or like nature with the spirit.
>
> *Fourth:* Man's life on earth has only one end and purpose: to identify himself with his eternal Self and so to come to intuitive knowledge of the Divine Ground.

In Hinduism the Divine Ground is Brahman, who is reincarnated as Lord Krishna who spoke the words of the *Bhagavad Gita.* Accordingly, He is the *Om* in all the *Vedas,* the Word that is God, the only doer, the womb of all beings and the creator of everything that exists. He is the *Atman* that dwells in the heart of every mortal creature and is capable of reunion through meditation upon Himself. According to Krishna, it is perfectly natural that different people should have diverse methods and even distinctive individual objects of worship. All roads lead to Rome—provided, of course, that it is Rome and not some other city which the traveller wishes to reach. A similar attitude of charitable inclusiveness, somewhat surprising in a Moslem, is beautifully expressed in the parable of Moses and the shepherd, told by Jalaluddin Rumi in the second book of the *Masanavi.* In Mahayana Buddhism the Divine Ground is called "Mind" or the "Pure Light of the Void" and the place of the High Gods is taken by the Dhyani Buddhas (Aldous Huxley (Prabhavananda and Isherwood, 2).

The well-known quote from the *Bible* says, "In the beginning was the Word, and the Word was with God, and the Word was God, and everything that was made was made with the Word, and there was nothing that was not made with the Word." There are three things that are quite clear from this passage:

- — the first thing that came to exist in the universe was the Word (or Logos)
- — the Word was nothing but God Itself
- — everything else, whatsoever appeared in the universe, was created by the WORD-GOD.

The Word-God is unique, self-existent and the cause of all causes. It is the only doer, to the exclusion of anyone else.

The well-known Saint, Guru Nanak, said the following words soon after his Self or God-realization: *"Eck Onkar Satnam, Karta Purukh Nirbhau Nirvair, Akal Murat Ajuni Saibham, Guru Parsad jap, Aadi such jugadi such hai vi such, Nanak ho si vi such."* This means that there is only one God in the form of the "Sound of Onkar (*Aum*)" called Satnam, It is the only doer of all things. It is fearless and does not have enmity with anyone, It is the timeless personality. It has no sex and is established in Itself or is self-existent. It can bless us as the blessing of the Guru in meditation. It was true in the beginning, It was true before the counting of any time period (*yuga*) had begun, It is true today and Nanak says that It will be true in the future also. The three points stated in the previous paragraph from the *Bible* are confirmed: The very first thing to exist in the Universe was the Word or Onkar, the

Word or Onkar is God Itself and It is the only creator of everything that has come to exist in the cosmos—in conformity with Hinduism.

The definition of the Absolute given by Nanak is quite remarkable. It covers the basic attributes of God that should be known to an average man or woman. The main additional point given in his definition is that God is appearing as the blessing of the Guru in meditation on God Itself. It is worth pointing out that early Christianity/Judaism advocated meditation which was eventually eradicated by the later-day priests and ministers of the church.

David Frawly (3), director of the American Institute of Vedic Studies in Santa Fe, New Mexico, writes: "However, given the connections between ancient European and Indian culture, we must conclude that ancient Europe also had a yoga tradition like the Hindu that included devotional worship of various gods and goddesses, the use of sacred sounds or *mantras,* a belief in *karma* and rebirth, the practice of meditation, and the idea of self-realization or enlightenment. These ideas and practices were similarly shared by other cultures throughout the world, though India possessed yet more specific cultural affinities, particularly similar languages."

Merwan Sheriar Irani, popularly known as Meher Baba (4), was a Sufi saint of this century. According to him, "Human psyche has two parts, one part falls within the range of consciousness and the other part falls beyond it. The unconscious part, in its full extent, is identical with the power which is behind matter. It is referred to as God by the orthodox religions. The Ultimate Reality which is symbolically represented through such concepts can be known fully only by *bringing the unconscious into the conscious*" (Vol. I, 39). And again, "The finding of God is a coming to one's own self. The whole process of attaining God-realization is just a *game in which the beginning and end are identical...* . Though the God-realized soul does not possess anything new, its explicit knowledge of all that really is, has been and will ever be, makes God-realization all important. The soul which is not God-realized experiences itself as being finite and is constantly troubled by the opposites of fleeting joys and sorrows; but the soul which has realization is lifted out of them and experiences *"the infinite knowledge and the unlimited bliss of being God-conscious"* (Vol. II, 17 and 41). Meher Baba achieved God-realization through sustained meditation and has devoted most parts of Vol. II to describing various forms of meditation. In confirmation with the Sufi saint Meher Baba, the Hindu saint Nisargadatta Maharaj says, "If you expect any benefits from your search, material, mental or spiritual, you have missed the point. Truth gives no advantage. It gives you no higher status, no power over others; all you get is truth and the freedom from the false" (5, 313).

Quoting Aldous Huxley once again, on the *Bhagavad Gita*, "...the spark within is akin to the Divine Ground. By identifying ourselves with the first we can come to intuitive knowledge of the second. These empirical facts of the spiritual life have been variously rationalised in terms of the theologies of the various religions. The Hindus categorically affirm that *thou art that* — that the indwelling *Atman* is the same as Brahman. The Sufi Mansur was executed for giving to the words "union" and "deification" the literal meaning which they bear in the Hindu tradition...the significant fact is that these words are actually used by Christians and Mohammedans to describe the empirical facts of metaphysical realization by means of direct, super-rational intuitions....In regard to man's final end, all the higher religions are in complete agreement" (Prabhavananda and Isherwood 2, preface).

In the words of Saint Asaramji (5, 5), "*Paramatma* is the source of cosmic energy which activates our consciousness. That consciousness makes the world of dreams in Hita nerve. That consciousness in paralytic state is converted into deep sleep. Attainment of *Atman-Paramatma* or awareness or knowledge of It for a period of even three minutes by someone will not let one suffer the agony of being in the womb of a mother again, one becomes a liberated soul".

It gives one a feeling of great satisfaction that most religions of the world have the following common beliefs:

— The Divine Being or Absolute is self-existent and Its nature has two aspects: Potential and Kinetic.
— The Kinetic aspect is called Word, *Aum,* etc. and It is the creator of all living and non-living entities in the universe. The potential aspect is the unmanifest Absolute.
— Either by inference or by direct intuition one can realize the existence of the Absolute.
— Human psyche has two divisions: the conscious or phenomenal self and the unconscious or eternal Self called the Soul.
— The Soul is akin to the Absolute, and hence, if one can identify oneself with the Soul, it is an identification with the Absolute.
— Meditation can develop the intuition to the extent of identification with the Absolute.

The purpose of this book is twofold: first, to confirm the above grounds of common belief through my personal experiences; second, to show that Kundalini or Sleeping Serpent Power is the common denominator in most cases of awakening, irrespective of the religion or faith of the aspirant. The most important point, however, is to understand that our real home exists on a higher realm where we initially existed in the formless and infinite state as the Soul. This will be elaborated upon in later chapters. As the Soul we are akin to the Absolute, and this is the beginning and the end of the journey.

Chapter 1 defines the Spiritual Energy, Kundalini, the seven *chakras,* cosmic consciousness and the purpose of the human incarnation.

The central theme of Chapter 2 is that most religions show the way through a short path for achieving Self-realisation in a single life time, similar to the experience of Kundalini and repetition of the names of God or the chanting of *mantras.* Chapters 2,3, and 4, are concerned with the suggestion that the Kundalini awakening brings an overall change in the personality which is not brought about by methods like NDE (Near Death Experience), LSD, etc. The awakening takes place when the masculine and feminine aspects in the aspirant have reached a balance. This means that the person is equally intellectual and emotional. This state is best achieved by the fusion of opposite sexes. Consequently, married persons around the globe have been more successful in their spiritual quest, than the single ones. A large variety of examples, both from the East and the West, are given in Chapter 3. Chapter 4 shows the universality of the Kundalini journey.

An autobiographical integration of the Exceptional Human Experiences is presented in Chapter 5. A continuous transformation in the personality is witnessed as the Kundalini passes from the first to the sixth and seventh *chakras.* It is on arrival at the sixth centre that Self-realization takes place.

Chapter 6 shows that everyone within the frame of Euclidean or three-dimensional space has a fixed destiny. The "psychic sense" flashes some important events in advance which could be turning points in the life of a person. Although the exercise of "free will" can change the course of events, more often than not, we fall in the predicted pattern of happenings. However, for some, this is the beginning of the spiritual journey. They have a chance of achieving Self-realization, if other factors are taken care of.

Until the Self-realization is experienced, the soul always wants to return to earth either as an apparition, a ghost or a proper reincarnation. But after Self-realization the Soul wants to go back to its true home and that is liberation. This is the theme of Chapter 7.

Chapter 8 discusses the points which are helpful in the awakening of the Kundalini. An advanced aspirant finds events in his life are accelerated, enabling him to undergo many experiences, that otherwise would have taken several lifetimes, and at this stage he can realize the Self in this very life. This is an important factor which I have corroborated with the experiences in my own life.

Self-realization and the direct feeling of God are based on two aspects, which are the twin pillars of God: the Holy Sound or Word or *Aum,* and the Blue Light. Various stages towards God, in the ascending order are: ignorant about Him, studying

Him, feeling Him, experiencing Him and becoming Him. Experiences related to these aspects are discussed in Chapter 9.

Once the aspirant is in contact with the Holy Sound and Blue Light of his inner perceptions, he is halfway to God. This is the stage where the role of the guru comes to an end and the seeker builds up his own experiences. Chapter 10 discusses life as it is after awakening.

Chapter 11 elaborates the most important point of balancing the masculine and feminine principles in every individual in the psychic view. When intellect and intuition strike the balance, the inner marriage takes place and the "psychic child" is born. This indicates the completion of the process of Individuation. The stages of development are clearly shown in dreams.

Chapter 12 shows that the awakening of Kundalini automatically results in providing healing power to the practitioner for the self as well as for others. In addition to that, it leads to liberation from falsehood and to discontinuation of further incarnations. The Chapter gives details of the various methods of healing at the quantum level.

At this stage, if it is possible, one should retire from active worldly life and totally devote oneself towards experiencing God. Jewels of intuition are received regularly, allowing one to know, without learning, the secrets of the universe. All questions are answered accompanied by inner peace and tranquillity. Through this process the aspirant becomes a magnet; others coming in contact with him/her are also magnetized just as a piece of iron is irresistibly drawn towards a magnet.

Following the principles of Numerology introduced by the great master Pythagoras, Appendix I endeavours to calculate the major numbers associated with the spiritual giants around the world. Numerology verifies it is not by chance that the saints became what they were renowned for. Their numbers clearly indicate their deep-rooted interest in spirituality. Others, not associated with such numbers, are less likely to take interest in the occult sciences.

Appendix II is a collection of letters written to spiritual friends. These epistles touch deeper points of the spiritual theory, giving some explanations concerning them.

A formula, the "Integral Path", is presented in Chapter 2. It combines important elements from *Hatha Yoga, Bhakti Yoga, Jnana Yoga* and *Tantra Yoga.* A person can achieve the goal following a single path, but this is more difficult. For example, while following the path of selfless action, one has to work like Mother Teresa or Mahatma Gandhi, which is not usually possible for a householder. The integral path, however, can be followed without relinquishing the activities of the world, and the Kundalini can be awakened. Once attained, the state of "affectionate detachment" arrives automatically, without focusing on anything. This is what happened to me in 1987. However, depending on the sincerity of approach and by the grace of God, the Kundalini may be awakened in a short period of months or it may take several lifespans.

Finally, I must record my sincere thanks to William Henry Belk II, for sponsoring this project. Without his help in giving me the facility of access to his extensive library, this book would not have been completed. There are others to whom I must express the gratitude I owe to them. Beverly Hale Watson edited the whole manuscript to shape it to its present form. During my absence from India lots of work and other duties have been shared by my brothers Rajendra Singh, Jitendra Singh and Raghvendra Singh, and my son Atul Singh. My thanks to Jacques Brack for making several corrections in the manuscript, and Genevieve Gantt of Belk Stores for her help and assistance from time to time.

I have freely consulted the works of the authors mentioned in my book. I am grateful to them for the insight I gleaned from their writings.

Lastly, a most important fact is that Master Pythagoras was my guru and initiator in the sixth century B.C. My knowledge of Numerology and the Self has been due to his continual guidance for several lifetimes. The completion of the process of Self/God-realization in this lifetime is due to the backing of Master

Pythagoras, Einstein and Socrates from the higher realms. Beverley Hale Watson deserves thanks for periodic communications in this direction through her paranormal faculties.

The gurus who gave initiations and guidance in physical form are: Dr. B.S. Goel, Saint Asaramji, Dr. B. Bhattacharya and Sri Harold Klemp. I have met these God-realized saints many times over the years. There is no other pleasure greater than bowing my head at the lotus-feet of these spiritual giants from higher realms and the present physical world.

It gives me pleasure to have had a rewarding association with Claire G. Walker, editor, *Journal of Religion and Psychical Research*, USA, who helped me in many ways besides the editing of the papers. Other parapsychologists with whom I had useful discussions are Dr. Bonnie Greenwell, A.D. Holcombe, Prof. John F. Miller III, Boyce Batey and R.A. Riechenbach. Thanks are due to Dr. Sanjay Kaushik for some useful suggestions, including the publication of the book and to K.N. Sudarshan for arranging the publication work so effectively. Maya Misra has helped me in many ways. I also wish to record the name of Jytte Larsen for useful spiritual interactions, for providing space for work and revision of the book, and for the use of computing facilities.

**Ravindra Kumar**

H.No. 138, St.No. 3
Vaishali, Dabri-Palam Road,
New Delhi-110045, India.
Ph. 5034143

Sofus Francks Vaenge 6,6
DK-2000, Frederiksberg
Denmark.
Ph. 36 16 9250

# 1

# Kundalini and Cosmic Consciousness

*The spiritual energy, Kundalini and the seven centres of energy, called chakras, are defined and explained in this Chapter. Characteristics of enlightenment are presented and a comparative study of the terms 'cosmic-consciousness', 'Self-realization' and 'God-realization' is made.*

**1. Defining Kundalini**

Since ancient times it has been observed that all individuals appear to be different. Some people write inspiring prose or poetry and some compose beautiful music while others cannot; some students get very high marks in examinations with little effort while others, in spite of long hours devoted to studies, score poorly; some people fight on the battlefield for days together while others cannot even do their normal work properly; some persons are famous for wonderful discoveries and inventions while others live mediocre lives and die unnoticed. As such, this has raised a perturbing question in the minds of several thinkers—what is the "factor" which is responsible for these outstanding differences?

In the course of time it was found that there is a special form of energy within every individual. In some persons it was found to be dormant, in some it was slowly evolving while in a few it was fully awakened. Although this energy has infinite capabilities, it has no form or dimension and consequently, it has been conceived in different manners under different names in various traditions of the world. Perhaps Hindus have the oldest records of naming this energy "Kundalini" and it has been depicted in various physical forms for the understanding of the common people. The word *kunda* means a deeper place, a cavity; referring to the concave pit in which the human brain nestles in the form of a coiled and sleeping serpent; hence the name *Kundalini.* In males it lies asleep in the perineum, between the excretory and urinary organs. In females it lies at the root of the uterus, in the cervix. It is illustrated as a sleeping serpent coiled three and a half times and closing the opening of the *sushumna* nerve in the centre of the spine by its mouth.

Although God is believed to be formless, the mythological idols play an important role in the physical illustration of the Kundalini. We know that energy is of two kinds: potential and kinetic. In the dormant potential state, Kundalini represents *shakti* or power while in the kinetic form its manifestation is represented by a female deity. When it is newly awakened and one is unable to handle it properly, it is represented by the ferocious female deity Kali, who is naked, dark and wears a rosary of 108 human skulls, the latter representing past lives. The blood-red lolling tongue of Kali represents *rajo guna,* signifying creative activity, and it exhorts the practitioner to have a control on his/her *rajo guna.* The sacrificial sword and the several heads represent dissolution. Darkness and death are, in fact, the origin of life. *The masculine static form of energy* is activated only through the *female kinetic energy of Kali.* Even Lord Shiva could not pacify the ferocious Kali, who threw him down and stood on his chest, with a wide open mouth, thirsty for flesh and blood. Only when the *devas,* the pious ones among the celestial beings, prayed to pacify Kali, did she become calm and quiet. Thus, according to yoga philosophy, Kali, the first manifestation of sleeping Kundalini, is a terrible and uncontrollable power; subduing the individual soul, represented by her standing on the chest of Lord Shiva.

When properly awakened and under the control of the aspirant who can then use it for useful purposes and become powerful on its account; the Kundalini is represented by the female deity Durga, who emerges as the higher, more refined and benevolent form of the unconscious. She is beautiful, charming and seated on a tiger. She has eight hands representing the eightfold elements of the human being. She wears a rosary of human heads, representing her wisdom and power. The heads are normally fifty-two in number, corresponding to 52 letters of the Sanskrit alphabet and representing the external manifestation of the "unstruck holy sound", called *Shabda Brahma*. The manifestation of Kundalini in the form of Durga represents the burning of *karma,* accumulated from several lifetimes. All evil consequences from the life of the aspirant are removed, bestowing power and peace, as a result of the awakening of the root centre of energy, called *mooladhara*. Durga is the superconscious form of Kundalini energy.

The serpent is normally a symbol of efficient consciousness and one can find its representations in various old mystic cults of the world. The three coils of the serpent representing Kundalini symbolise three parts of *Aum* (*Om*)—past, present and future; three *gunas* (virtues)—*tamas* (under inertia), *rajas* (creative activity) and *sattva* (purified form); three states of consciousness—waking, sleeping and dreaming; and three types of experiences—subjective, sensual and absence of an experience. The half-coil represents the state of transcendent consciousness which is beyond waking, sleeping or dreaming. Thus, three-and-a-half coils of Kundalini represent the complete set of experiences of the universe followed by the experience of transcendent consciousness.

**2. The Awakening of Kundalini**

Kundalini is a dormant energy. There is a set of three nerves called *ida, pingala* and *sushumna,* which connect the base of the spine to the brain. When Kundalini awakens, it rises through the central nerve *sushumna* to the brain, which causes an explosion in the brain, since the dormant or sleeping areas begin to blossom like flowers. It represents the future consciousness of mankind. All happenings in the spiritual life and all outstanding works in any walk of life, such as poetry, painting, writing, music, war, science, art, philosophy etc., are related to the awakening of Kundalini. It is the creative energy, the energy of self-expression.

The awakening of Kundalini causes a transformation and transcendence in life. There are visions of God and higher or subtler realms of existence, an awakening of supramental faculties and a dawning of creative intelligence. There is a change in the mind, priorities and attachments. An integration of the *karmas* begins to take place. The cells in the body are charged completely and a process of rejuvenation begins. The voice, the smell of the body and hormonal secretions undergo a change. A speeding up of physical, mental, emotional and spiritual evolution takes place. "Once the great *shakti* awakens, man is no longer a gross physical body operating with a lower mind and low-voltage *prana* (quantum cosmic energy). Instead, every cell of his body is charged with the high voltage *prana* of Kundalini. And when total awakening occurs, man becomes a junior god, an embodiment of divinity" (Saraswati 1, 13).

As the first symptoms of an awakened Kundalini, some people experience violent shaking of different parts of the body, such as a car shudders when starting. Aspirants also feel pleasure of a spiritual kind and the brain becomes hot and heavy as if under intoxication, an experience never undergone before. Six symptoms which come into manifestation are—a feeling of blissful pleasure, trembling of the whole body, a newborn power, intoxication, sleep and merger of consciousness. In fact, one could experience one or several of the eighteen symptoms listed, for example, in "Devatma Shakti" (Tirtha 2, 96-105).

### 3. The Physiology of Kundalini

Kundalini energy does not belong to the physical, astral or mental body and consequently, it cannot be found there. The serpent power belongs to a still higher plane, that is, the causal plane, which is above the concept of object, time and space. It connects the lowest unconscious seat of power at the root centre (*mooladhara*) to the highest centre of consciousness at the crown centre (*sahasrara*). Illumination takes place when Kundalini *shakti* (kinetic form of energy) rises to and meets Lord Shiva (potential form of energy). It passes through the central nerve *sushumna,* which is the psychic passage within the spinal column. From the root centre at the base of the spine to the crown centre on top of the head there are seven centres of energy called *chakras*, through which the Kundalini passes. With the passage of Kundalini through the centres of energy, the transformation and transcendence of personality in the aspirant takes place. The most important is the sixth centre, called *ajna chakra,* also known as the "third eye" and it is the centre of command or intuitive knowledge. The *ajna* centre is internally connected with both the root centre and the crown centre.

In the words of Swami Satyananda Saraswati (1, 15):

> The serpent power is considered to arise from the unconscious state in *mooladhara.* This unconscious awareness of man then has to pass through different phases and becomes one with the cosmic awareness in the highest realm of existence. The supreme awareness of Shiva is considered to be seated in *sahasrara,* the superconscious or transcendental body at the crown of the head. In the *Vedas,* as well as the *Tantras*, this supreme seat is called *hiranyagarbha*, the womb of consciousness. It corresponds to the pituitary body, the master gland situated within the brain. For a Kundalini Yogi, the supreme consciousness represents the highest possible manifestation of physical matter in the body. This psychic, supra-sensory or transcendental power in man is the ultimate point of human evolution.

A *chakra* is a vortex of psychic energy which can be visualized as a circular movement of energy at a particular rate of vibration. Physiologically, *chakras* are like junctions where the nerves meet, and they are situated on the interior walls of the spinal column. They are like poles of electricity through which electrical wires (nerves) run across to supply power at different centres. Through the nerves (*nadis*) *prana* (vital energy) flows forward and backward.

The first of the *chakras* is called *mooladhara* (root centre) which is situated at the pelvic floor and it corresponds to the coccygeal plexus of the nerves. It is at this *chakra* that the consciousness rises above animal nature. Below this *chakra* there are supposed to be lower centres of energy going down to the heels, responsible for developing the animal and human qualities of instinct and intellect. The *Mooladhara chakra* controls the excretory and sexual functions in the body.

The second *chakra,* called *swadhishthan,* lies at the terminal point of the spinal column. It relates to the sacral plexus of nerves and takes care of the unconscious in the person.

The third *chakra,* called *manipura,* lies in the spine just at the navel level. It is related to the solar plexus and takes care of the digestive, assimilative and temperature controlling system of the body.

The fourth *chakra,* called *anahata,* is situated in the vertebral column at the back of the heart near the base and it is at the level of the depression in the sternum. It is related to the cardiac plexus of nerves and takes care of the organs of the body in this region, such as the heart, the lungs, the diaphragm, etc.

The fifth centre, called *vishuddhi,* is situated in the vertebral column at the level of the throat pit. It is related to the cervical plexus of nerves and takes care of the thyroid complex, upper palate, epiglottis, etc.

The sixth *chakra,* called *ajna,* is related to the pineal gland and is situated above the spinal column in the midline of the brain. It is the centre of command and takes care of all the functions of one's life. In particular, it controls the sexual activity in a person.

Between the sixth and the seventh *chakra,* there is an additional *chakra,* called *bindu* (point), situated at the top back of the head, where the Hindus normally leave a tuft of hair. It takes care of the optic system and is the centre wherefrom *amrit* (nectar) emanates on awakening and is responsible for the rejuvenation of the whole body system. It is internally connected to the *vishuddhi chakra* and two centres are believed to be activated simultaneously.

The seventh *chakra,* called *sahasrara,* lies at the top of the head and is related to the pituitary gland which is supposed to take care of all the glands and systems of the body. *Sahasrara* is the seat of cosmic awareness and is the terminal point of the journey of Kundalini *shakti.*

A description of the Kundalini and the *chakras* given in this chapter is sufficient for the scope of this book. However, the subject of Kundalini is very exhaustive and the reader is referred to the works of Gopi Krishna (3), Sir John Woodroffe (4), Swami Shivananda (5), and several other authors who will appear in future discussions.

**4. Cosmic-consciousness or Self-realization**

The arrival of Kundalini at the *sahasrara,* is the union of Shakti with Lord Shiva, and it is the beginning of Cosmic-consciousness or Self-realization. The ego is fragmented into pieces and the death of mundane or individual awareness takes place. The aspirant actually experiences death in a way and a new person is born within. One forgets the idea of 'I' and 'you' and experiences oneness with the whole universe. The experience, the experiencer and the experienced, or the seeing, the seer and the seen become one. This moment of single awareness, in which one passes from the stage of seeking to the stage of having arrived, which is full of unprecedented bliss, is Cosmic-consciousness. It is the moment in which Shakti and Shiva cannot be identified separately and become one. All questions are answered and one lives in a perpetual state of peace, happiness and contentment from then onwards. Attachment to worldly things and relations ceases, yet, one feels greater and fuller affection towards everyone. This is called "affectionate detachment".

To understand that this is Self-realization, we begin with the important quote from the *Kathopanishad*: "The living soul is the master (rider), his physical body is his chariot, his intellect (*buddhi*) is the charioteer, the mind is the rein with which the sense-horses are controlled, the sense attributes (such as, perception, hearing, touch, taste and smell) are the path-ways, and the Soul is thus the experiencer and the enjoyer," so the wise people say (2, 147-148). Thus the Soul is the experience and the physical body, intellect, mind and senses are only the mediums through which the Soul experiences life. This realization that I (Soul, Self or *Atman*) am different from body, intellect, mind and senses, and that I am one with the Universal-Self, is Self-Realization.

Most people in the world feel that any amount of worldly enjoyments and secular achievements cannot give "peace of mind" which everyone feels a lack of; the inner heart craves and hankers after "something unknown" which would pacify it, but one does not know how and where to find the same. That "something unknown" is nothing but Self-realization, which comes when the gap between the individual and universal consciousness has been bridged through the recognition of the Atman living within. And, how to achieve this goal is the subject matter of this book.

Now the next important point to be understood is that the Soul is akin to God, and the knowledge of the Soul or *Atman* leads to the intuitive understanding of God. This fact has been clearly stated in the *Bhagavad Gita* and it has been maintained by most of the world religions, in some form or another. The Sanskrit words "Tat-Tvam-Asi" mean "That-Thou-Art" and it is the same meaning when we say "I Am That I Am". Hence, whenever one sees the Soul through the Soul Itself and no other media; that is when the one who sees, the seeing and the seen become one; one lives and witnesses the properties of the Soul, which are the properties of God in a micro form. This has been the experience of saints and prophets [see for example, Meher Baba (6), Saint Asaramji (7), Aldous Huxley (8), Aurobindo (9), Nisargadatta Maharaj (10), etc.] In the words of Aldous Huxley (8, 2): "The Atman, or immanent eternal Self, is one with Brahman, the absolute principle of all existence; and the last end of every human being is to discover the fact for himself, to find out who he really is."

Svetaketu learned all the *Vedas* by the age of twenty-four. His father asked, "Have you asked for that knowledge by which we hear the unhearable, by which we perceive what cannot be perceived and know what cannot be known?" "What is that knowledge, sir?" asked Swetaketu. His father replied, "As by knowing one lump of clay all that is made of clay is known, the difference being only in name, but the truth being that all is clay—so, my child, is that knowledge, knowing which we know all."

The philosophy of the *Upanishads* was developed and enriched in the *Bhagavad Gita* and was finally systematized in *Vivek-chudamani* (The Crest-Jewel of Wisdom) by Shankara in the ninth century A.D Some of his writings which are relevant in the present context are given below:

> The knowledge that Brahman (the supreme spirit) and *atman* are one and the same is true knowledge and according to the Vedas.
>
> Brahman and *atman* are respectively designated by the terms 'that' and 'thou', are fully proved to be identical when investigated by the light of Vedic teaching.
>
> The wise know the perfect identity of the *atman* with *Parabrahman* by attaining the standpoint of Logos.
>
> Realize that thou art 'That'–Brahman which is untouched by the six human infirmities (hunger, thirst, greed, delusion, decay, and death); it is realized in the heart of yogis (i.e., in *samadhi*), it cannot be perceived by the senses, it is imperceptible by intellect or mind.
>
> By known logical inferences and by intuition realize thyself as *atman,* just as the meaning of a word is understood; the certainty of this truth will be established without doubt just as water (held) in the palm of the hand.
>
> Owing to a person's desire for the things of the world, the scriptures and the body, true knowledge cannot be produced.
>
> This cruel trinity of desire is described by those who know, as the iron chain that binds the feet of one aspiring for liberation; he who is free from this attains liberation.
>
> External attachment is to objects of sense, internal is to egotism and the rest. It is only the dispassionate man, devoted to Brahman, who is able to renounce them.
>
> So long as a man is attached to the corpse form (physical body), he is impure (in a levitical sense) through enemies (lust, anger, greed, delusion, pride and jealousy), there is suffering associated with birth, death and disease. When he perceives

the pure *atman* which is bliss and is immovable, then only (he) becomes free from these—so the *Vedas* declare.

He who is perfectly at rest (in his wisdom) is said to be firm in wisdom. He who is firm in wisdom, whose bliss is uninterrupted and by whom the objective universe is well-nigh forgotten, is regarded as *jivanmukta* (liberated while living).

Want of enquiry into the past, absence of speculation about the future, and indifference (as to the present), are the characteristics of a *jivanmukta*.

To one who knows the nature of the *atman* and who enjoys self-bliss, there is nothing but silence, a void of desire, causing the greatest happiness.

He who is liberated from the body and is himself perfect, abides in enjoyment like a worldly man full of desires created by the past *karma* (does). But he lives quietly as a spectator, free from desires and changes, like the centre of a wheel.

Neither the relinquishment of the body, nor of the staff, nor of the water-pot (the wooden water-pot used by ascetics) is *moksha* (liberation); but *moksha* is the happiness (that results from) untying the knot of ignorance in the heart.

The ascetic, free from the idea of desires, always self-satisfied, himself abiding in the all-pervading *atman* lives and wanders alone.

**5. Conclusion**

Shankar in the above writings has defined fully the life of a successful person who has graduated from the school of earth, has cut off the chain of death and rebirth, and has qualified to live on higher realms of psychic worlds. Witnessing *atman* through the eyes of *atman* is always possible, if and when we have qualified (read for example, the writings of Meher Baba, Saint Asaramji and Ramana Maharshi in the recent years). However, there are experiences of saints from different religions all over the world for several millenniums, see for example, *Cosmic-consciousness* by Dr. R.M. Bucke (11). I have described my own experiences in the following chapters.

William Wordsworth also saw his *Atman* (Soul) and the True Home at the point of Self-realization. The passage from his poem "Intimations of Immortality" makes it quite clear (Zemke 12, 156):

> Our birth is but a sleep and a forgetting;
> The Soul that rises with us, our life star,
> Hath had elsewhere, its setting,
> And cometh from afar.
> Not in entire forgetfulness
> And not in utter nakedness,
> But trailing clouds of glory do we come
> From God, who is our home.

And in the words of Nisargadatta Maharaj,

> Until one becomes self-realized, attains to the knowledge of the self, transcends the self, until then, all these cock-and-bull stories are provided, all these concepts (10, X).

The marks of cosmic sense are briefly and explicitly stated by Bucke (11, 65, 66) as follows:

a) The subjective light.
b) The moral elevation.
c) The intellectual illumination.
d) The sense of immortality.
e) The loss of the fear of death.
f) The loss of the sense of sin.
g) The suddenness, instantaneousness of awakening.
h) The previous character of the man—intellectual, moral and physical.
i) The age of illumination.
j) The added charm of the personality so that men and women are usually strongly attracted to the person.

k) The transfiguration of the subject of the change as seen by others when the cosmic sense is actually present.

There are several methods of achieving the goal, and one has to choose one's own path which depends on several personal factors and circumstances. However, the method of Kundalini-yoga following the Integral Path has been proposed in Chapter 2 and it appears to be a *short path* to Self-realization.

A mention has to be made about *shaktipat,* which is in a way an injection of *shakti* by a Guru, the process of spiritualising a person with the charge of psychic force. This transmission of power tends to raise the Kundalini in the disciple in the course of time, which leads to Self-realization. However, the person should be prepared to receive the power, through a self-disciplined life; otherwise, it can result in many disorders, such as, paralysis, brain haemorrhage, etc. As it appears, the words illumination, Cosmic-consciousness, and Self-realization are synonymous and they carry more or less the same meaning. Each term leads to God-realization through intuitive knowledge, and for that reason, most authors consider Cosmic consciousness/ Self-realization/ Illumination/ God-realization as synonymous words. Enlightenment, perhaps, is the stage that precedes "illumination" (Bucke 11, 236).

There are a few more points which should be clarified at this juncture. The first of them is about the similarities and dissimilarities of the experience. There are several aspects which would appear to be similar, such as, the feeling of bliss, loss of the fear of death, etc. Yet, there would be some parts of experiences which could differ in nature as well as description. This could be due to the difference in faiths and orientations. Furthermore, ten people who have seen a tree or a landscape a few hours ago will describe it differently and no two writings may match exactly.

The second point is about the wrong belief that a Self-realized person should be perfect in everything. There is no doubt that a new faculty has opened up in him/her; we call it the opening of the third eye in Hinduism; yet, one has just obtained the visitor's visa to the new kingdom and it might take some time to become a citizen. The person with cosmic consciousness may, to some extent and under some circumstances, be above a person with self-consciousness only, however, he may still be endeavouring for being better and better, according to the new perception.

None the less, there is a stage when everything comes to an end, every drop merges in the ocean, all interests are lost and one does not see the point of continuing to live on earth and the physical body is cost aside. One goes to live on a psychic realm in perfect peace and bliss with no further chance of manifestation (Sri Aurobindo 9, 92). When Swami Ramakrishna was asked about his keen interest in delicious food everyday despite his Self-realization, he said that through that interest he was still keeping himself on earth, giving himself some reason. Perhaps on that day he became conscious of some inner call and he lost interest in food too. His wife and disciples were alarmed and worried. And, as destiny would have it, he died on the third or the fourth day. The reader is referred to the book *From Sweeper to Saint*, by Ḥaridass Baba; presently settled in the Mount Madonna Yoga Center, California; where you find real-life stories of some Indian spiritual perfectionists who announced the day of their death much in advance and later relinquished their bodies as they had predicted.

### References


1. Saraswati, Swami Satyananda; *Kundalini Tantra,* Bihar School of Yoga, Munger, Bihar, India, 1984.
2. Tirtha, Swamin Vishnu; *Divine Shakti-Kundalini,* Yogshree Peeth Trust, Muni-ki-Reti (Rishikesh), India, 1993.
3. Krishna, Gopi; *The Awakening of Kundalini,* New York, N.Y.: Kundalini Research Foundation, 1975.
4. Woodroffe, Sir John; *The Serpent Power,* Ganesh & Co., Madras, India, 1981.
5. Radha, Swamin Sivananda; *Kundalini Yoga,* Motilal Banarsidass Publishers, Delhi, India, 1992.

6. Baba, Meher; *Discourses by Meher Baba,* San Francisco, 1967.
7. Ram, Saint Asa; *Atma Yoga,* Sri Yoga Vedanta Seva Samiti, Ahmedabad, India, 1995.
8. Huxley, Aldous; *The Perennial Philosophy,* Harper & Row Publishers, U.S.A., 1970.
9. Aurobindo, Sri and Mother, The; *The Psychic Being,* Sri Aurobindo Ashram, Pondicherry, 1989.
10. Maharaj, Sri Nisargadatta; *I Am That,* The Acorn Press, Durham, N.C., USA, 1973.
11. Bucke, Richard Maurice; *Cosmic Consciousness,* The Citadel Press, New Jersey, 1961.
12. Zemke, LeRoy E.; *Thoughts for Transformation,* Emberlight Publishers, Florida, 1996.

# 2

# Kundalini—A Common Basis of Most Religions

*There are three basic points in this Chapter: (1) As in the old proverb "All roads lead to Rome", all religions are preparations in their own way for the journey back to the higher realms from which we came. (2) Most of them have shown a short path for achieving the result in a single lifetime, similar to the experience of Kundalini and repetitions of the names of God or the chanting of a mantra. (3) The Kundalini yoga brings an overall change in the personality which is not brought about by methods like NDES (Near Death Experiences), LSD, etc.*

### 1. Introduction

Every religion has a single purpose for understanding and approaching God in its own way. Saints representing various worldwide religions have talked about higher realms of existence beyond this physical world, which in reality is where our true origin and home are located. However, there are variations in details and differences in the vocabulary depending on assorted factors. This Chapter endeavours to show that most religions have a "short path" for achieving the result in a single lifetime, similar to the experience of the Kundalini and repetition of the names of God or chanting of a *mantra.* Furthermore, Kundalini *yoga* brings an overall change in the personality which is not brought about by other methods, i.e., NDE, LSD, etc.

**2. One Goal for All**

Parapsychologist and religionist Robert Winterhalter (1) published his work *New Thought and Vedanta* in 1993. He pointed out the remarkable similarity between ancient Hinduism and the teachings of Jesus of Nazareth. Swami Ramakrishna Paramahansa of India said all religions are different means to the same end. The questioning of people on the differences are empty arguments over external forms only. Certainly there are diversities in rituals and the way prayers are offered to God according to the variances in cultures and backgrounds, etc. Yet collectively *their aim is identical, that is, to please, understand and get closer to God.* Acharya Rajneesh said that the approach of a saint is like a bullet which hits the target and he becomes one with God. Like a master marksman, he aims his weapon, pulls the trigger and watches the bullet hit the target dead-centre. The result of his persistence to obtain perfection is self-evident. The followers of the saint likewise may not have seen his self-discipline, hours of meditation or chanting as he focused his attention on God. However, because of the saint's determination, he reached/hit his target/God. Upon the firing of his gun/body, his consciousness changed when it/bullet merged with the Source. The after-effects are physically visible. A religion is formed to imitate the aforementioned, which can be triggered by different methods. The principle of "firing" and its result will be the same in each case in spite of external dissimilarities in the mechanism.

Hindu saint Kabir equally respected Hindus, Muslims, Christians and others and recited verses from the *Bhagavad Gita,* the *Quran,* the *Bible* and other scriptures with equal mastery. The Bahai way of approaching God, initiated by Bahaullah Khan of Iran, is very much in line with the universal approach. In a Bahai temple verses are recited from the *Bhagavad Gita,* the *Quran,* the *Bible* and other scriptures with equivalent importance. There is no image of God in any form displayed in or around the temple. You may simply enter and meditate, there is nothing to see or talk about. Swami Vivekananda showed equal interest in praying in a Muslim mosque, a Christian church, and in a Buddhist or a Hindu temple to see the light which enlightens the heart of everyone. Joseph Campbell, in whose name a chair in comparative mythology was established at Sarah Lawrence in 1988, consistently quoted from the *Vedas:* "Truth is one; the sages speak of it by many names". ***Religions in general share three major ideas: (1) belief in a supreme absolute Source of all, (2) humankind's immortal nature as a radiation from the Source, and (3) the possibility of learning spiritual secrets by making oneself as pure as the Source.***

Somebody rightly said that if Krishna, Buddha, Jesus, Mohammed, Nanak and Zoroaster were sitting round a table, they would have complete concurrence between them. In fact, there would be nothing to argue, agree or disagree about. It is only their followers who built religions based on bullets and external objects, finding differences between themselves because they have not witnessed or understood the actual firing and its result, which is the same in each case. Hence, anyone who gives any kind of importance to the variances in religions and their goals, is actually millions of miles away from the truth. There cannot be a dozen gods in the sky, just one. The same electric current can operate a fan, a heater, a cooker, a refrigerator or any kind of motor. Likewise, one source of infinite energy is responsible for running every function of the universe; call it by any name you desire. The purpose is to recognise the source and get united with it.

American mythologist Joseph Campbell (2) talked of three stages to attain bliss: first is being full, second, consciousness and third, rapture. St. John of the Cross (Bede (3)) categorized the three phases of mystical union as ***purgation, illumination*** and ***union.*** These three processes are analogous to those pointed out and followed in ancient Hinduism and Buddhism: ***dharna, dhyana*** and ***samadhi***, or purification and concentration, meditation and contemplation, and absorption with the Absolute. The Kabbalist within the framework of traditional Judaism, follows three mystical steps to unity with God called *Sephirot:* ***understanding, wisdom*** and ***humility.*** In Sufism, a branch of Islam, a Sufi passes through the stages of *Fana*, meaning annihilation through intoxication with divine love; ***Baca,*** meaning permanency, having stabilized his knowledge; and the Sufi's third *journey entitled a spiritual guide* in accordance with his ability. In the fourth stage, a Sufi is called the perfect man and he guides others about the transition upon death from physical to invisible realms. Spanish mystic St. Teresa of Avila, one of the best- loved Christian Saints, described four stages like the Sufis for prayer: *recollection,* implying concentration and withdrawal, *quiet,* implying the falling away of desires for material things and opening to the divine for union; *tumescence,* implying inspiration leading to wisdom; and finally, *union* with the divine. From the above we conclude that almost all religions have three milestones on the spiritual path to God: *purgation, illumination* and *union.* The fourth stage, again common to most religions, is the individual being called the perfect man or Guru, who guides others about the transition upon death from physical to higher, invisible realms of existence.

**3. The Quest of God in Two Basic Traditions**

Understanding religion as the way of life to know the ultimate reality, there have been two basic traditions: Western and Eastern. The Western tradition stems from the Semitic group which includes Judaism, Christianity, Islam and their offshoots. The Eastern tradition stems from the parent Indian root which includes Hinduism, Buddhism, Jainism and their offshoots like Taoism, Zen and Shintoism. The Western tradition is based on the prophetic revelation of God to men from outside the human spirit. The Eastern tradition is based on mysticism, emphasizing the finding of God by men from within the human spirit.

Finding of God from within lays emphasis on *meditation* and related disciplines. Several millenniums ago, Krishna asked Arjun to become a *Yogi* and meditate on Him. The whole *Bhagavad Gita* elaborates this point. Starting from Buddha almost all the individuals in India realized the truth through *yoga* and *meditation.* In the same way, a large number of individuals from different faiths and religions all over the world have taken to *meditation* and *yogic* disciplines in one form or the other. According to Plato (Umen, 4), every doctrine was considered to be a shell for a spiritual truth that could only be discovered through *meditation* and mystical exercises. The corporeal bodies of religion and philosophy had little value, and material science was not emphasized at all. Plato, Rudolf Steiner and G. I. Gurdjief maintained that man remains asleep through life and only *meditation* and *mystical exercises* can wake him up. Bernard of Clairvaux, William Blake, Aleister Crowley, Paul Twitchell, Julian of Norwich, Arthur Augustus Ford, Grace Cooke, Milarepa, Richard Alpert alias Ram Dass, Pythagoras, Paracelsus, St. Teresa of Avila are only a few who underwent regular and sustained meditation and had mystical experiences which were not possible by any other means.

It is worth noting that a sudden upsurge of various religious leaders took place around the world in or around the sixth century B.C. Confucius of China was born in 551 B.C. Buddha of India was born in 563 B.C., Pythagoras of Greece was born in 590 B.C. and Taoism was born in China with the birth of Lao Tzu in 604 B.C. Although born in the seventh century B.C. Lao Tzu reportedly lived for 200 years, meaning thereby that his impact was seen in sixth century B.C. Zoroaster of Persia existed in the sixth century B.C. Mahavira, the founder of Jain religion in India, was born in the sixth century B.C. and the Druids, the priestly caste of Celts, a Germanic tribe which spread in Europe and Asia Minor, came up in the sixth and fiftth century B.C. This was no ordinary happening. Perhaps the universal Mind wanted humanity on earth to start the search for God. Since then the spiritual *avatars* like Jesus, Pluto, Plutonius, Socrates, Plato, Mohammed, Nanak and hundreds of lesser known personalities like Richard Maurice Bucke and Gopi Krishna have emerged in the recent years. Thousands of people around the globe have been getting enlightenment and the numbers are increasing. The last decade of the twentieth century seems to have the human mind on top of the evolutionary process. Teilhard de Chardin (5), renowned French philosopher of this century, has had much impact on New Age thoughts for his concept that the universe has its own evolutionary history. According to him, humanity is at a biological turning point, where it has to decide either to fully lose interest in the universe or quite resolutely worship it. He stressed the need for greater psychic energy than what is available in this century for the process of evolution. Gopi Krishna (6) also said that the human mind is at the final stages of evolution in this century. Who knows, the prediction of Nostradamus and several others might come true and the end of the twentieth century might see a catastrophic division between spiritualists and materialists. According to Uri Geller (7), a Israeli psychic born in Tel Aviv, the aliens have been watching the world and are afraid of its imminent destruction. Jose Arguelles (8) said that the modern age is at a turning point and if the earth's spiritual energy did not make a positive shift, a twenty-five year period of disasters and catastrophes would start, and the world would come to an end in 2012.

**4. The Short Path to God**

Repetition of the names of God constantly during meditation is called "chanting of *mantras*" in Hinduism and Buddhism. Chanting of a *mantra* continuously serves two purposes: first, it slowly tires the mind from thinking about many things and wandering aimlessly, thereby bringing about the desired concentration; secondly, the hidden power of *mantra,* which is an intelligently woven garland of effective words, evokes the forces of nature around and finally arouses the Kundalini. Arousal of the Kundalini opens the third eye and a contact with the higher realms is established. Understanding of God then starts as an ongoing process. There are marked symptoms of Kundalini arousal from which the process is recognized.

Most Hindu and Buddhist saints have passed through this procedure. Nevertheless, almost all major religions in the world have a clear description of the process in their terminology and their saints and prophets appear to have passed through it as a prelude to realization or revelation. For example, St. Teresa sometimes experienced the heat, energy, spontaneous body movements and pain, which are the symptoms of Kundalini awakening. Juliana of Norwich (10) fell gravely ill, experienced death, reportedly felt the lower part of her body die away and had such extreme pain that if she had known before, she would not have asked for it. However, she saw God in the twinkling of an eye and later meditated for twenty years. Similar happenings have been reported by King Bushman of Africa, Sufism, Taoism and Shamanism. On the road to Damascus, St. Paul was blinded by a brilliant light from heaven for about three days, and he lived without food and water. On recovering his sight, he was converted to Christianity. The founder of Islam, Mohammed, was awakened one night by an overwhelming light which opened his paranormal eye and the revelation of the *Quran* began. Such experiences with light in the Kundalini process have been described vividly by Swami Muktananda (11). Later on, visits to higher planes in soul form by Muktananda are similar to those of Mohammed. It is with a reference to these realms that master Jesus said, "There are many mansions in my Father's house." Swami Prabhupad (12), founder of the International Society for Krishna Consciousness in the United States, gives similar details in *An Easy Journey to Other Planets.* Taoism and Vajrayan Buddhism have elaborate techniques for manipulating the enormous heat generated by the awakening of Kundalini.

In Sufism, a branch of Islam, a *short path* to God is taken through *faqr* (pious poverty), studying religious literature and prayer with *dhikr*, that is, endless repetition of the holy names of God and sacred passages from the *Quran*, leading to self-hypnosis, like the chanting of *mantras.* People use prayer beads which are similar to the rosaries of Hindus. Rhythmic drum beating and dancing sometimes accompany *dhikr* to bring on the state of trance. According to Idries Shah (13), Freemasonry began with the teachings of Spanish Sufi Iba Masarra and the three tools in the Masonic emblem symbolize the three Sufi postures of prayer. He further said that Boaz and Solomon, builders of King Solomon's temple in Jerusalem, were Sufi architects. An unfinished tower and an eye on a dollar bill of America represent incomplete humanity being watched by the overall eye of God. Clearly, Freemasonry had a great influence on American thoughts.

In Judaism, Kaballah, the *short path* to God, is supposed to have been taught by God to angels, then to Noah, Abraham and Moses, who finally initiated seventy elders. The *Merkabah* mystics endeavoured to reach the "God's Throne Chariot" after passing through *seven heavenly mansions*. The process includes fasting with repeated recitations of hymns and prayers to induce the state of trance. It is similar to meditation with the chanting of *mantras* leading to *samadhi*. Practical Kabalism introduced by Aaron Ben Samuel (Bloom, 14) in Italy further spread to Germany and became the basis of Hasidism. It involved prayer, contemplation and meditation leading to witnessing the Divine Fire, Shekinah (likened to Shakti of Hindus), the mother or female aspect of God. Classical Kaballah was born in France and moved to Spain in the thirteenth century. The *Sefer ha-Zohar*, meaning, the book of splendour, was written by Spanish Kabbalist, Moses de Leon. Another *short path*, named *Tzeruf*, was developed by Abraham Ben Samuel Abulafia (Bloom, 14) in Spain. It was performed at midnight and involved breathing techniques, pronunciation of sacred names of God and meditation. The ecstasy, called *shefa*, meaning divine influx, would occur in a short time. Experiences are similar to the awakening of the Kundalini, including the unlocking of the holy sound leading to enlightenment and, perhaps illumination. Luria (Ponce 15) stressed the need of letter combinations *(mantra)* as the effective way to mystical prayers and meditation. Dion Fortune (16) called Kaballah the "Yoga of the West". The Christian Kaballah was introduced by Cornelius Agrippa Von Nettesheim in his *De Occult a Philosophia* written in 1531.

The *short path* in Hinduism, Buddhism and Zen practices is often called *Tantra* which includes *yoga*, meditation and recognition of the sex drive. Not only in the East but in the West too, a large number of practitioners have achieved higher consciousness, such as Alexandra David-Neel, Alan Watts, Alister Crowley and others—through *Tantra*.

Experiences of the Kundalini type are also found in the esoteric teachings of Egyptians, Chinese and some native Americans. In the *Bible* it is interpreted as "the solar principle in man". Similar references can be found in the *Quran,* and in the work of Greek philosophers, especially Plato, Rosicrucian and Masonic writings.

Alchemy was popular in most parts of the ancient world. Its process was similar to Taoist meditation in which the universal life force *chi* was created and purified in the body. Nutritious elements of food combined with the secretions of glands and organs created blood and *ching* (sexual energy). Through controlled breathing *ching* was converted into *chi* (sublimation of sex) which was made to circulate up and down the spinal column between the crown and the abdomen. The process is similar to the experience of the Kundalini energy. After many circulations *chi* is purified and is responsible for transforming consciousness into mystical love. Male and female opposites are joined into a whole (physically and spiritually). This is exactly what happens in Indian alchemy—the union of Shiva and Shakti—producing enlightenment and illumination through the awakening of the Kundalini. *Chi* is known as *prana* in Hinduism. In either case, sublimation of sex is the factor either by abstaining from it or refraining from ejaculation. In China and now recently in the West, alchemy deals with the transformation of the soul. C. G. Jung (17) was one who took much interest in Western alchemy. Details of alchemy can be found in several books, such as Cavendish (18), Hall (19), Hoeller (20) among others.

The Caduceus, a wand entwined by two snakes and topped by wings, has been an esoteric symbol of spiritual enlightenment and intuitive wisdom since ancient times. Its shape is derived from the T-shaped cross used in Egyptian initiations. Its origin can be traced in Greco-Roman mythology dating back to 2600 B.C. The Caduceus has been a symbol of earth, water, fire and air in ancient Indian temples. The wand represents the stick of Brahma, called *Brahm danda,* and the snakes represent the Kundalini force, the sleeping serpent power residing on earth. The *pranic energy* transforms the spiritual consciousness through the rising of the Kundalini via higher realms of awareness. This is the significance of the wings on the top of the Caduceus. It represents a balance between negative and positive forces in Freemasonry (Cirlot, 21, Mercatante, 22).

The ancient Masters of India knew the importance of Kundalini. That is why they depicted *seven chakras* of its passage on the Himalayan range, likening it to the spinal column of the human body. The first *chakra* is represented by the temple of Kamakhya Devi in Assam, at the lowest altitude. Kamakhya Devi is worshipped for the power of sex and marital happiness. Going on, the sixth *chakra* representing the *third eye centre* is at the temple of Vaishno Devi in Jammu, the base of Kashmir. The seventh and the final *chakra* is represented by the temple of Lord Shiva at the top of Kashmir. The passage from Vaishno Devi to the Amarnath temple of Shiva is very narrow and risky, making it difficult for all people to survive the journey. This is parallel to the journey of the Kundalini from the *ajna* centre to the crown centre, which is the most difficult one.

**5. The Holy Sound and Personality Transformation**

A. D. Holcombe (23) and Alexander I. Kopytin (24) have very recently argued that the Kundalini alone is not enough and it is only one of the means of spiritual balance. I am contending that the after-effects of Kundalini cannot be created by any other means and it is perhaps the best way towards spiritual perfection. For example, as Holcombe says, an NDE experiencer usually returns to the body with a different view of life, knowing much more about the ultimate values. True, but not enough since an NDE does not bring about the complete transformation of personality that the Kundalini does. Similarly, things like LSD give a temporary glimpse of the ecstasy and higher realms of existence but they do not transform the personality completely. Rather the user gets addicted, and more often than not, his health deteriorates later.

This fact is illustrated through the famous cases of Timothy Leary (25), Richard Alpert and Aldous Huxley (26). Timothy Leary married four times, the last being at the age of fifty-eight, made extensive use of LSD, had problems with the law and was jailed for twenty years. Richard Alpert had a successful introduction to higher realms through LSD but then he moved to India, and became a disciple of Neem Karoli Baba who changed his name to Ram Dass. Thus he was successful in his later days and wrote the book *Grist for the Mill.* Aldous Huxley used LSD in the company of Leary and Alpert, suffered numerous health problems throughout his life and deplored Leary's talks about the drug. However, Huxley was not too influenced by LSD, and he wrote the commendable book *The Perennial Philosophy,* which won him high acclaim. Peter Hurkos had an NDE experience and consequent psychic gifts which troubled him a great deal. He died of heart failure. However, he heard celestial music during his NDE which he wanted to play on the piano (Browning, 27).

Paul Pond (28) in his *The Road Home* writes the last two lines: "To truly hear the sound of *Om* is a miraculous coming home". The sound of *Om* is the after-effect of Kundalini. The most common feature of all religions is the hearing of this *unstruck sound* by the practitioner through the inner ears. Christians call it the Word or Logos, Hindus and Buddhists call it *Om* or *Aum*, Muslims call it *Kalma-i-Ilahi,* Sikhs of India call it *Shabad*, Pythagoras called it the *Music of the Spheres,* Paul Twitchell called it the *Audible Sound Current*; parallel expressions can be found elsewhere. This sound is like the "humming of a swarm of bees" (Gopi Krishna, 6), or like the sound you hear "on opening the door of a refrigerator" (Dr. B. S. Goel, 29), or like the "hissing of a serpent" (Arthur Avlon, 39), or like the "blowing of a conch" (Dr. B. Bhattacharya, 31). It is the sound of instinctual wisdom of the earth and it takes the spirit beyond personal individuality to higher realms of existence. Normally the holy sound is accompanied by the "blue light" or "blue pearl" seen through inner the eyes. This sound and its blue light are the inner Guide or Guru, God living in the human temple. It takes the human soul to higher planes in the states of meditation, trance or sleep. See for example, Swami Sivananda (32), Paul Twitchell (33), and Wilson Terril (34) among others.

After the arousal of the Kundalini there is an experience resembling death and rebirth. The personality starts transforming gradually, and many changes are seen at the offset itself. In fact, it is consciousness turned towards God which makes the individual pray and meditate which in turn arouses the Kundalini. I would say that "meditation" is not the means; rather it is, in a sense, the "end". One who is engaged in meditation is already God-conscious. However, one continues to pray and meditate after the successful awakening of Kundalini, since evolution is a never-ending process. After an initial encounter with some spontaneous bodily effects such as excessive heat, one comes back to normal. The individual is more at peace with oneself. The adversities of the daily life do not upset one, one takes and meets them calmly and accepts the results equally, whether good or bad. More often than not, the person starts withdrawing from the affairs of the world, like an old, successfully retired person. Although daily needs must be satisfied, interest in material things, physical sensations and worldly relations declines. One is constantly engaged in the thought of God, while the holy name or *mantra* keeps on repeating itself ceaselessly in the end.

Physical love-making takes on an opposite course. The frequency and interest reduces considerably, to the extent that the spouse starts complaining about it. Something seems to be going on in the testicles, noticeably at times. Perhaps, the production of seminal fluid increases and it is felt being pumped up towards the brain, as I experienced it for more than a year after the awakening. Similar experiences are described by female practitioners, such as Irina Tweedie, accounted by Bonnie Greenall in her book *The Energies of Transformation.* The state of *samadhi* is quickly achieved in meditation. Either in the state of *samadhi* or during sleep the awakened person visits the higher planes in spirit-soul form. The *blue pearl* and *holy sound* of *Om* are always present. Gradually the sound of *Om* becomes louder and you hear it all the time. Dependence on external relations that is reduced to aloneness does not perturb one.

Interest in matters of daily routine, including one's job, is reduced. The efficiency thereby is not the same and many people take retirement at this stage so that they can fully devote themselves to spiritual pursuits. Dr. B. S. Goel of India and Emanuel Swedenborg of Sweden, both scientists in their fifties, took immediate retirement after the breakthrough. However, awakened people may continue writing about spirituality.

**6. The Experience of Kundalini**

The Vedanta tells us that spontaneous mystical experiences are impure and it is only through *yoga* that one can obtain pure enlightenment. Swami Ramakrishna said that "a man's spiritual consciousness is not awakened unless his Kundalini is aroused." However, it is now obvious that Kundalini-related experiences have been responsible for spiritual uplifting in most religions of the world since ancient times. In the present age we see an increasing number of "Kundalini awakening" cases in the West, developed during the last two decades. I was one of the speakers at the first international conference of KRN (Kundalini Research Network) held in California from June 18 to 22, 1992. I came across several persons in the workshop groups who were suffering from the side-effects of partial awakening of the Kundalini. I listened to their case histories carefully. In another talk Bronwyn Fox, director of the pain and anxiety disorder association in South Australia, spoke of her discoveries related to the correlation between anxiety disorders and faulty Kundalini awakening. According to her, hundreds of thousands of people in Australia were victims of the side-effects of faulty Kundalini awakening. The majority of the cases, both in the US and Australia involved females.

As I have stated earlier in this chapter, ***humanity in this century and especially in this decade is at the climax of evolution.*** The knowledge of Kundalini is now widespread in the West, the Far East and other parts of the developed world. As such, more and more people are following yogic and other spiritual disciplines to activate the lever of Kundalini for enlightenment, and they are able to recognize the symptoms. In my opinion there can be two reasons for these side-effects and anxiety disorders: firstly, the practitioners are not following an integrated discipline for the path of Kundalini; secondly, one-pointed concentration in many walks of life is responsible for the partial awakening of the Kundalini, without the person being aware of it. In the case of women, childbirth often triggers the lever. This is what happened to Christina Groff, who later founded the Spiritual Emergence Network (SEN) in 1980. However, her final awakening of Kundalini came when she got *shaktipat* from Swami Muktananda of India, at his camp in Honolulu. I have made an exhaustive survey of the yogic disciplines followed for the awakening of the Kundalini, especially after my own experience with this energy in 1987. There are basically four areas which need equal attention in the path of the Kundalini: yogic exercises, meditation with or without chanting of *mantras* but with faith in God, reading connected literature and biographies or case histories of spiritually evolved persons, and a regulated sex life with variations of a personal nature; of course, single persons do not have to care about the fourth factor, although this is the requirement for avoiding severe headaches (Saraswati 35, 89-90). When any of these areas are neglected, the energy will have the tendency to shoot in the wrong direction and cause disorders or ill-effects. Yogic exercises are necessary to build up the physical stamina and power of concentration required for long hours of meditation. Those who neglect this part undergo spontaneous yogic postures on arousal of the power. Those who neglect reading and studying are likely to suffer mental disorders, emotional problems and panic attacks or anxieties. Reading case histories of realized people prepares one against pitfalls and shortcomings on the path and brings emotional stability as well. Regulated sex is necessary because it is the fusion of the male and female aspects which brings the transformation of consciousness from the physical to the spiritual level. My study, which is presented in the next chapter, points out that married practitioners have been more successful, and have experienced fewer problems, than single persons. This applies equally to a male and a female aspirant. In the words of Swami Satyananda Saraswati (35):

> Some aspirants experience terrible headaches when Kundalini is awakening, however, this does not mean that

all headaches are related to Kundalini. And not everybody will have headaches. Generally, those who have had married life do not have this experience. It is usually only those who have not had any kind of sexual interactions who experience headaches with the advent of Kundalini awakening.

Dr. B. S. Goel suffered from terrible headaches for several years, and perhaps it was because he remained unmarried for his whole life (29).

Accordingly, there are two kinds of people who need guidance in this matter: first, those who are following yogic disciplines to awaken the Kundalini; secondly, those in whom a partial awakening has already taken place without their knowing it, suffer from side-effects, making them prone to some kinds of anxiety disorders. In either case, I would suggest the following model of the "Integral Path" to be followed every day:

1) Yogic exercises for 30 to 45 minutes.
2) Meditation from 1 to 3 hours, preferably with the chanting of an appropriate *mantra* which acts as a catalytic agent.
3) Reading scriptures and case histories of spiritually realized persons for 2 to 4 hours.
4) Regulated sex life between married partners depending on personal factors and variations. This, however, is optional, since a single man or woman may equally take part in the programme.

If one gets a Guru, it is fine, but it is not necessary. If one starts with determination, guidance will come through books, literature, and the shared experience of others. I never had a Guru, but whenever there was a problem and I sincerely wished for an answer or guidance, I would take a book, open it at random at a page, and find help. Gopi Krishna did not have a Guru either. Several examples of this kind can be found and quoted.

Even for *shaktipat*—the direct transmission of energy from an evolved person—the aspirant has to be prepared in advance in all the four disciplines described above, otherwise the power can misfire. Christina Grof and Da Free John both received *shaktipat* from Swami Muktananda successfully only after they had disciplined themselves in all the four areas for several years. Da Free John is now running an ashram in Fiji, imparting similar training. Sri Aurubindo, Swami Yogananda Paramhansa and Mahesh Yogi (transcendental meditation), have all stressed the need of Integral Yoga, involving basically similar factors. I (36) had a similar preparation for more than fifteen years before experiencing the Kundalini in 1987. Training in Integral Yoga, such as that given at the centre in New Delhi, is a valuable overall preparation for the experience of the Kundalini.

## References

1. Winterhalter, Robert; "New Thought And Vendanta", *JRPR* Jan. 1993, pp. 14-20.
2. Campbell, Joseph; *The Inner Reaches of Outer Space: Metaphor as Myth and as Religion,* New York, Harper & Row, 1988.
3. Frost, Bede; *Saint John of the Cross: Doctor of Divine Love, an Introduction to His Philosophy, Theology and Spirituality,* New York, Vantage, 1980.
4. Umen, Samuel; *The World of the Mystic,* New York, Philosophical Library, 1988.
5. Teilhard de Chardin; *The Future of Man,* New York, Harper & Row, 1968.
6. Krishna, Gopi; *The Awakening of Kundalini,* New York, Kundalini Research Foundation, 1975.
7. Geller, Uri; *My Story,* New York, Praeger, 1975.
8. Arguielles, Jose; *The Mayan Factor,* Santa Fe, NM: Bear & Co., 1987.
9. Whiting, Joshua C. "Sources of Spontaneous Mystical Experience", *JRPR* 10, No. 3, July 1987, pp. 148-157.
10. Julian of Norwich; *Revelation of Divine Love,* translated by James Walsh, New York, Harper & Row, 1961.
11. Muktanada, Swami; *Chitshakti Vilas,* Gurudev Siddhapeeth, Maharashtra, India, 1972.
12. Prabhupad, Swami; *An Easy Journey to Other Planets,* ISKCON, West Virginia, USA
13. Shah, Idris; *The Sufis,* Garden City, NY: Anchor/Doubleday, 1971.
14. Bloom, Harold; *Kabbalah and Criticism,* New York: Continuum, 1984

15. Ponce, Charles; *Kabbalah: An Introduction and Illumination for the World Today,* Wheaton, II: The Theosophical Publishing House, 1973.
16. Fortune, Dion; *The Mystical Kabbalah,* 1934. York Beach, ME; Samuel Wiser, 1984.
17. Jung, C. G.; *Memories, Dreams, Reflections; recorded and edited by Aniela Jaffe,* New York: Random House, 1961.
18. Cavendish, Richard; *The Encyclopaedia of the Unexplained,* New York, McGraw Hill, 1974.
19. Hall, Manly P.; *The Secret Teachings of All Ages,* Los Angeles: The Philosophic Research Society, 1977.
20. Hoeller, Stephen. A.; *C. G. Jung and the Alchemical Revival,* Gnosis 8 Summer 1988: 34-39.
21. Cirlot, J. E.; *A Dictionary of Symbol,* New York: Philosophical Library, 1971.
22. Mercatante, Anthony. S.; *Encyclopaedia of World Mythology and Legnen,* Frenches Forest, Australia: Child & Associates, 1988.
23. Holcombe, A. I.; "Christ-consciousness, Kundalini and Spiritual Energy", *JRPR,* April 1993.
24. Kopytin, A.I.; "Why Kundalini is Not Enough", *JRPR,* Oct. 1992
25. Leary, Timothy; *Flashbacks: An Autobiography,* Los Angeles, Jeremy P. Tarcher, 1983.
26. Huxley, Aldous; *A Biography,* New York: Alfred A. Knop, Harper & Row, 1973.
27. Browning, Norma Lee, *The Psychic World of Peter Hurkos,* Garden City, N Y: Doubleday and Co., 1970.
28. Pond, Paul; "The Road Home", *JRPR,* Jan., 1993.
29. Goel, Dr. B.S.; *Third Eye and Kundalini,* Third Eye Foundation of India, New Delhi, 1985.
30. Avlon, Arthur, *The Serpent Power,* Ganesh & Co., Madras, India, 1981.
31. Bhattacharya, Dr. B; *The Way of Tantra,* Sterling Publications, New Delhi, India, 1985.
32. Sivananda, Swami; *Kundalini Yoga,* The Divine Life Society, Sivananda Nagar, Tehri-Garhwal, India, 1991.
33. Twitchell, Paul; *The Tiger's Fang,* Menlo Park, CA, IWP Publishing Co., 1971.

34. Willson, Terrill; *How I Learned Soul Travel,* ECKANKAR, Minneapolis, MN, USA, 1987.
35. Saraswati, Swami Satyananda, *Kundalini Tantra,* Bihar School of Yoga, Munger, Bihar, India, 1984, pp. 89-90.
36. Kumar, Ravindra; "On Enlightenment and God", *JRPR,* Oct. 1991, pp. 181-193.

# 3

# From Human Marriage to Spiritual Union

*It is not necessary to become a recluse to achieve spiritual goals. Remaining unmarried and relinquishing the world has chances of failure and may elude perfection. On the other hand, living a regulated married life brings a balance between the male and female aspects of nature and may lead to enlightenment. Most of the saints, prophets and realized persons in the East and West have been married persons who harnessed their energy and redirected it towards the brain rather than wasting it for sensual pleasure. In this way the brain is enriched and is made fit to receive enlightenment.*

*A regulated sex life means mating with your spouse with mind focused on God, preferably with the chanting of a mantra. Attention is withdrawn from the sensual pleasure and is redirected towards the spiritual union of the soul with the super-soul. Procreation or raising a family is not at all the purpose. This is the theory behind the well-known term "Tantra".*

*There are yogic postures which prolong the period of coition and hold the ejaculation. This leads to the state of samadhi. Many travellers on the spiritual path marry more than once in order to have a suitable partner for this purpose.*

**1. Introduction**

More and more people around the world are realizing the meaninglessness of materialistic values and worldly relations. Their consciousness has started coaxing and cajoling them to start a search for God and find inner peace and happiness.

Nevertheless, their way of life is woven through material pleasures and human relationships and they find it very difficult to either come out of the web completely or feel unconcerned about things. At such a juncture, when human evolution is at the peak of its development, people need a practical formula which would purify and convert earthly living into spiritual living. There should not be a drastic change in living standards but existing with a different sense of awareness is required. Once we know why we have incarnated on earth, the whole outlook for one's purpose changes.

**2. The Purpose of Earthly Incarnation**

Many millenniums ago Krishna told Arjun that both of them had appeared on earth several times, the difference being that he (Krishna) remembered all the times they happened, but he (Arjuna) did not remember any occurrences. In the course of time, successful yogis like Buddha, Pythagoras and others could see thousands of their past incarnations in a row. And now, in the modern age, psychiatrists and parapsychologists have led people to know their past lives through hypnotic regression. See, for example, Lynn Elwell Sparrow (1), Dr. Raymond Moody (2), Dr. Joel L. Witton and Joe Fisher (3), etc.

The most common feature of all past life research is that a person upon death is shown a complete review of the life lived recently, in the presence of some Masters in their astral bodies. Based on shortcomings or negative doings of the person, one decides to reincarnate on earth to strike a balance. The Masters give their suggestions and help in choosing the next life. The individual has access to the cumulative experience of all his or her past lives lived so far. At the proper time, when the model chosen by the person matches with the coordinates on earth, the next birth takes place for the purpose of learning and achieving the needed balancing. However, just before the soul enters the womb of the mother, a mechanism operates by which the entity forgets all his past lives consciously and a seemingly fresh life begins on a clean slate. Nevertheless, those who have a good intuition subconsciously continue to feel the purpose of their birth, and their way of living is markedly different from the mechanical way of the majority of people. The process of death and rebirth continues until a balance between the male and female principles in the person is accomplished and one has learned the lessons of love, compassion and benevolence. This is what the image of Lord Shiva as half-male, half-female (*ardhanareeshvara)* means. This is the main lesson of *Bhagavad Gita.*

Human birth provides an excellent opportunity for spiritual development, which is not available in the soul form after death. The reason is that on earth we encounter people who are on different stages of development and we are required to learn to have a balanced disposition towards all. In the soul form after death, grouping takes place according to the level of development and there is no knowledge gained through association with a heterogeneous set of people (Stephen O'Brien, 4). Talents, desires and ambitions of a person continue in the same form even after death. Thus the soul looks for an opportunity to express itself. For example, Patience Worth, an English woman born in 1649, could not exploit her literary slant of mind due to her early death. Nearly three centuries later in 1913 she dictated 2,500 poems, six full-length novels, and several plays and short stories through automatic writing via the hands of a St. Louis housewife, Pearl Curran (Gina Covina, 5).

Another and perhaps more important reason for spiritual development possible on earth is that the soul develops a "psychic being" around it which eventually has its own individuality. It guides the person from time to time as *an inner guru* and is the intermediate connecting factor between *Atman* and *Paramatma* or between the Soul and the Absolute. It is called *Chaitya Purusha* in Hinduism, *High Self* in Jungian philosophy and perhaps it is the *Holy Ghost* of Judaism between the Son and the Father. This advantage is available only on earth and in no other realms of higher existence. In the book *The Psychic Being,* Sri Aurobindo and the Mother give the following explanation (p. 37):

> The beings of the Overmind, for instance, and all the beings of the higher regions have no psychic being; the

> "angels" have no psychic being. It is only upon earth that the psychic life begins, and it is just the process by which the Divine has awakened material life to the necessity of rejoining the divine origin. Without the psychic, Matter would never have aspired for the life of its origin, the spiritual life. Therefore, the psychic being in the human being is the manifestation of spiritual aspiration; but there is a spiritual life independent of psychic.

The Hindu *Upanishads* have given the message in clear words: *"ant mati so gati"*, that is, the state of mind at the time of death decides the plane of living for the outcoming soul. Hence, it is on this end-state of mind that the whole life should be dedicated. A materially-inclined person will carry material thoughts and unfulfilled desires in the soul existence and will live with the other comparable souls after physical death. A person used to repeating the name of God most of his life is likely to be reiterating it at the time of death. Hence, they will be elevated to a higher and final plane where similar souls are continuing their lives. Such realms in extreme cases include the conditions from hell to heaven in varying degrees, where the soul is automatically transferred until the next incarnation. If, however, the process of learning on earth has been completed, a soul has the option to return or not to return for another life-time here. Thus, Krishna and Jesus are examples of souls coming back to earth through their past lives (Lynn Elwell Sparrow, 2).

**3. Self/God Realization by Married Persons**

Neither a man nor a woman can singly achieve the perfection of balance between the male and female principles without a proper interaction with the opposite sex. Thus, in Hinduism, marriage is perhaps the most sacred event in the life of a person. It is performed with vows around the sacred fire. The goal, however, is not simply marital happiness, but the realization of the Truth.

Most Hindu Godmen, *avatars* or saints, i.e., Shiva, Rama, Krishna, Buddha, Kabir, Raidąss, Kapila, Gopi Krishna, were all married persons. Some of them wed more than once in the course of their lives. Raja Janak was always surrounded by beautiful ladies.

Other traditions likewise have recorded distinguished leaders who were married. Pythagoras married one of his young disciples in his early sixties and had seven children by her. Mohamad had ten wives and at least two concubines, one after another. His third wife, A'isha, had an innate ability to stimulate his intuition and sense of spiritual immanence. The Islamic laws' limit of four wives per man was waived for the Prophet, according to a revelation in the *Quran* (Emile Dermenghem, 6).

The Sikh religion had a series of ten gurus, starting from Guru Nanak Dev to Guru Gobind Singh. All of them, without exception, were married persons. J. Krishnamurti, although never married officially, had Rosalind of the United States as a companion. Lahiri Mahasaya, the guru of Swami Yogananda Paramhansa, was married and had three or four children. The difference is that a religious person used one's spouse or companion for spiritual perfection with few or no children, while a worldly person used one's spouse for sexual pleasure, fathered many children and generally remained involved in family affairs all his life.

Most Western men and women who achieved Higher Consciousness, married once or several times in the course of their lives. Some of them wed or had partners even after the realization in their late fifties or early sixties. Starting from recent cases, Christina Grof lived a regular married life with her first husband by whom she had two children. She then became attracted to Stanley Grof, and joined him in matrimony. Upon the birth of her third child, her Kundalini was activated. Later she founded the "Spiritual Research Network" (Thompson, 7). Da Free John lived a normal life. After receiving Higher Consciousness he married and currently runs an ashram in Fiji. He now has four young women called "Kumaris of Kanyadan Order" with whom he can cohabit, if and when he desires (Steinberg, 8). Alan Watts (9), in his own words, said: "I have had three wives, seven children and five grandchildren—I cannot make up my mind whether I am confessing or boasting." Watts lived the life of a *Tantric*, even when he had extra marital relations. Gopi Krishna praised Watts as "one of those intellectuals in whom the evolutionary metamorphosis is almost complete" (Kieffer, 10). However, perhaps Watts could not rise to the permanent state of illumination. Chogyam Trungpa (11) married a sixteenyearold woman when he was 31 and died in 1987, leaving behind his widow and five children. He commanded respect as the enlightened one. To his credit he wrote eleven books on meditation and Tibetan Buddhist spiritual teachings.

Madame Helena Petrovna Blavatsky, founder of the Theosophical Society, first married at 17, then at 44 and finally she formed a lifelong friendship with Colonel Henry Steel Olcott, the co-founder of the society (Campbell, 12). St. Hildegard of Bingen (13), the first German mystic, best known for her series of illuminations and the visions she experienced, was one of the most important women of the twelfth century. She celebrated human sexuality as the beautiful, spiritual union of two human beings, not just the means of procreation. Alexandra David-Neel became a mistress of Philip Neel at 32 and later married him, formed a romantic friendship with Maharaj Kumar, the crown prince of Sikkim and later participated in *Tantric* sexual rites of Tibet. Her works include more than thirty titles. She is also famous for her spiritual achievements and lectures (Barbara Foster, 14). Eileen J. Garret (15), a gifted medium, clairvoyant, and founder of the Parapsychology Foundation, was cited by Prof. Rhine, for her experiences as a "turning point in parapsychology". She married three times in her life. She worked with Lawrence Leshan and could shift her awareness into a different reality simply by changing her breathing (Leshan, 16).

Joan Grant (17) saw her seven past lives (4 males, 3 females) in dreams, had out-of-body experiences with another reality, and wrote six biographies. She married first at the age of 20 and after realization, married for a second time at 57. Mary Baker Eddy, founder of the "Church of Christ", experienced a miraculous healing and had a Near Death Experience at the age of 45. She established her own religion, the *Journal of Christian Science* and the *Christian Science Monitor* newspapers in 1908. She had approximately 100,000 followers. She married first at the age of 22, the second time at 32 and for the third time when she was 56 (Melton, 18). Grace Cooke (19), popular British spiritualist, founder of the White Eagle Lodge, learned meditation techniques from an Eastern adept and would rise through the crown *chakra* and read the Akashik Records. She lived a successful married life all through. Jane Roberts (20), American poet and author, had her full-bloom paranormal experience at 34. She remained married all her life. She channelled the famous Seth spirit who said that the past, present and future exist concurrently and we experience all our lives simultaneously. Seth had lived many lives on earth as male and female. He stated that the human concepts of personality are too limiting to comprehend God's multidimensional existence.

Rudolf Steiner of Yugoslavia introduced Anthroposophy, a unique blend of Rosicrucian, Theosophical, and Christian trends. Guided by occult powers behind him, he synthesized science and religion. He passed through profound and concentrated meditation, which enabled him to give more than six thousand lectures on Spiritual Science. He married young, then the second time after realization at the age of 53 (Shepard, 21). Emanuel Swedenborg had his first mystical experience at age 54, after which he retired from official life. Although never married officially, he always indulged in mistresses. Aldous Huxley had his first experience at the age of 60 and then he married at the age of 62. St. Augustine, acknowledged as second only to St. Paul, heard God through inner ears and commented that he need not give an account of the ways God speaks. He took a mistress who bore him a son in A.D. 372; the relation lasted for fifteen years (Simpson, 22). Timothy Leary (23), a professor at Harvard, got enlightened by using LSD, and married four times at ages 24, 44, 45, and 58. He even had an in-between affair while he was jailed for the use of LSD.

Aleister Crowley, the English Occultist, recalled his past lives through yoga, remembering that he had lived as many famous personalities. He not only married at 28 and 54 but was known to have many, extra marital relations (Symonds and Grant, 24). John Donne, an English mystic, fell in love, married at 26, wrote 160 sermons plus much religious poetry containing erotic imagery. He described the ecstatic union of the human soul with God, comparing it with love between human beings (Smith, 25)). Paul Twitchell (26-28), modern founder of ECKANKAR, who authored many books on the realization of God, lived in Yogananda Ashram for five years with his first wife. His second marriage, with a student, was at the age of 50, after he travelled through all the higher realms and talked successfully to God on the nameless plane. He showed the path of God without asceticism.

Arthur Augustus Ford (29) was an American medium who turned to spiritualism. He could hear voices of spirits and gave messages. Arthur learned yoga exercises to control trances from Paramhansa Yogananda and was championed by Sir Arthur Conan Doyle. He founded the Spiritual Frontiers Fellowship. He was an alcoholic, and married twice at ages 25 and 43. Daniel Dunglas Home, a Scottish medium, possessed several supernatural powers, especially out-of-body travels for many hours. He could also stretch the body by 11 inches to become six feet, six inches, and once shrunk it to five feet. He first married at 25 and for the second time at 38 (Hall, 30). Richard Sutphen, born in 1937 in the United States, is known for his work in reincarnation and past life regression. With an ability to see his own Mayan life in the past, he wrote the book *You were born again to be together*. Married first at 25, then at 36, he is currently married and living with his third wife whom he wed at the age of 45 (Carter, 31).

**4. From Human Marriage to Spiritual Union**

There have been a large number of saints, prophets and realized people who remained unmarried throughout their lives. But most of them were attached to and were very respectful to their mothers who lived with them most of their lives. Perhaps, this was the reason why the female aspect of their nature was in balance, making them suitable for the spiritual heights they attained. One can find such examples from the past to the present day, such as, Jesus Christ, Milarepa of Tibet (Evans - Wentz, 32), Dr. B. S. Goel (33) etc. Many an aspirant who pursued the spiritual path all alone was unsuccessful and met failure, unless he was under the strict supervision of an able Guru.

Gautama Buddha reconciled with his family after getting enlightenment. He advocated the middle path between the extremes of asceticism and worldly life. Dr. Joel L. Whitton (3) reports the case of Tony Kalamaris, who, after knowing about his ten most recent incarnations, was trying to integrate the spiritual and erotic aspects of his nature. He was watching himself fluctuate from one extreme to another in different lives and was quite annoyed with the physical life. He then became aware of an incredibly vivid woman's face which told him, "...the erotic element provides the yeast for developing conscience, altruism and benevolent concern. Eroticism, being a rudimentary force that provokes interaction, can therefore initiate and assist in the spiritual development." This is what he had to learn because he had always seen sex and spirituality as separate from one another. He realized that this is what he must now put into practice.

Pak Subuh was a spiritual master of the Sufi order. After illumination people called him Bapak. Highlights of the philosophy of Bapak are given by Anne Bancroft (34) in the following words:

> Bapak believes that the act of sexual union gives man a chance to be influenced by the force which is properly human because, in the moment of orgasm, the innermost self of the man or woman becomes isolated from the lower forces. At this instant, if a man can be free of desire, and of thinking, he will become aware of an inner awakening of his true nature. when his consciousness is raised to a purely human level, as can happen in the sexual act, he can become aware of the behaviour of the lower forces and detach himself from them. Their domination

over, he is then their master and can direct them into their proper paths.

Gopi Krishna, a married man, found that the reproductive and evolutionary mechanism in the human system are so closely related that they are identical. In his own words, "The same life energy produced by the nerves is at the base of erotic excitement on one end, and of passion for the Divine on the other." According to Kenneth Thurston Hurst (35), former president of the Academy of Religion and Psychical Research, the sexual energy, when preserved and properly channelled, can be used to enhance our creative abilities in many areas. A stage comes when the energy is no more directed towards the reproductive organs, but rather it moves upwards to the brain, enriching it for the paranormal and spiritual experiences. The person at this stage is called *Urdhva-reta*. This is what happened to Jiddu Krishnamurti ultimately. Although many women fell in love with him, he seemed to have no need for the physical expression of sex (Lutyens, 36). All the sexual energy was directed upwards for the evolution of the brain and the nervous system, which eventually resulted in the union with the Divine. This is what we mean when we say, "From Human Marriage to Spiritual Union".

In one of the Edgar Cayce readings through past life regression, a young man was not aware that his intense pursuit of spiritual growth was turning him into a recluse until he learned of several past lives as a monk. This knowledge helped him recognize a previously unconscious tendency to pair spirituality with separation from the world. With that understanding, he was better equipped to decide consciously whether monk-like seclusion was a part of his chosen path in his current life, or whether he preferred to blend his spiritual quest with a more secular life (Sparrow, 37).

**5. Conclusion**

Each one of us is free to choose our path for enlightenment—remaining unmarried and relinquishing the world or blending spiritual quest with a secular and worldly life. The first path is difficult and has good chances of failure, I would even call it unnatural and unnecessary. Most of us have heard the story of two monks walking across a river. They found a woman standing on the bank of the river asking for help to be carried across since she was feeling weak. The first monk refused to touch her while the second one quickly picked her up in his arms, crossed the river and deposited her safely on the other side. They walked for quite some time towards their destination. The first monk was feeling uneasy all the way and finally became impatient enough to break the silence and said to the second monk, "You are not worthy of spiritual pursuits since you held that woman so close to your body that you have become impure." The second monk replied, "My friend, I left the woman a long time back but you are still carrying her". So it is the first monk who was impure and not the second one. This is the aspect which we are supposed to blend into our life with respect to every action in the world.

The *Vedas, the Upanishads* and the recent Edgar Cayce readings tell us that we ourselves created the world long ago and got involved in its substance. Materialism and material desires made most of us selfish and aggressive while some of us became weak, emotional and helpless. The purpose of earthly incarnations is to learn the qualities of the pure soul and hence return to our True Home. The earth provides the best means to learn and grow through our interactions with souls at different levels of evolution, since learning is not possible on higher planes where the souls regroup at the same level of evolution and because the Psychic Being or *Chaitya Purusha* or High Self, whatever one may call it, is available only on earth and no other realm.

Love, kindness, tolerance, compassion and benevolence are the qualities of the soul which we have to learn and embed in ourselves as a permanent part of our nature. Once we know about life on higher planes our interest in the affairs of the world will start declining. We will stop accumulating wealth beyond need and will develop a sense of *affectionate detachment* in human relationships. We have to live our lives in the world in all its aspects without getting attached to or involved in any one of them. This is the central message of the *Bhagavad Gita*.

All these things and a *balance* in the nature can be achieved through living a regulated married life by harnessing the potential sexual energy for creativity and not wasting it through sexual pleasure alone. Intellectuality is said to be masculine while emotionality is supposed to be the feminine part of the human nature. Striking a perfect balance between the two is our goal. When realization comes, a woman becomes more intellectual while a man becomes more emotional, thereby getting the desired balance in their nature. By masculinity we do not mean aggressiveness, but intellectuality. Similarly, by femininity we do not mean weakness, but emotionality. This is the balance found in all saints and enlightened persons. Enlightenment comes in various ways to different people as I (38) pointed out in an earlier publication. It is an ever-growing process and the goal is the awareness of the journey, not the end of it.

A word about alcohol. Yogis have been taking regulated quantities of it at proper times to accelerate the process of spiritual development. Robert A. Johnson (39), a Jungian analyst, studied "the psychology of joy" with respect to the myth of Dionysus, the Greek God, "the personification of Divine ecstasy who can bring transcendent joy or madness". He concluded that wine can bring either spiritual transcendence or physical addiction. This was also the finding of the *Tantric* saint, Vimal Anand.

Abraham H. Maslow (40) found that it is the nature of a desire to be replaced by another desire as soon as the first desire is satisfied. The drive for self-actualization (realizing one's fullest potential) can be observed in exceptional individuals in whom all lower needs are satisfied. This is the goal of the *Tantric* pursuits. At the end of the successful culmination of the *Tantric* yoga, all basic desires are conquered. The person loses interest in drinking, love-making and all activities of sensual pleasure. One possesses an *affectionate detachment* towards every person and everything. One lives a life of contentment, bubbling with love of God and like a withdrawn and successfully retired person. One acquires a peacefully glowing face like the Masters—Krishna, Buddha,

Christ, and Nanak. Snakes are representatives of sexual desire, which when conquered, are tamed. That is why you see garlands of live snakes around the neck of the greatest yogi of all times—Lord Shiva.

**References**

1. Sparrow, Lynn Elwell; *Edgar Cayce's Wisdom for the New Age-Reincarnation,* Harper and Row, Publishers, San Francisco, 1988.
2. Moody, Dr Raymond; *Life After life,* Bantom Books, NY, 1986.
3. Whitton, Dr. Joel L. and Fisher, Joe; *Life Between Life,* Grafton, London, 1986.
4. O'Brien, Stephen; *In Touch with Eternity,* A Bantom Book, Great Britain, 1992.
5. Coina, Gina; *The Ouija Book,* New York: Simon and Shuster, 1979.
6. Dermenghem, Emile *Mohammad and the Islamic Tradition,* 1955, Woodstock, New York: The Overlook Press, 1981.
7. Thompson, Keith, *Story of My Search for the Self,* Yoga Journal, July/August, 1990.
8. Steinberg, James; *Divine Distraction,* The Dawn Horse Press, Clearlake, California, 1991.
9. Watts, Alan; *In my Own Way: An Autobiography 1915-1916,* New York: Pantheon Boots/Random House, 1972.
10. Kieffer, Gene; *Kundalini for the New Age: Selected Writings of Gopi Krishna,* New York: Bantom Books, 1988.
11. Trungpa, Chogyam; *Shambhala. The Sacred Path of the Warrior,* 1984, New York: Bantom Books, 1986.
12. Campbell, Bruce F.; *Ancient Wisdom Revealed; A History of the Theosophical Movement,* Berkeley University of California Press, 1980.
13. Hildegard of Bingen's *Scivas*; Translated by Bruce Hozeski, Santa Fe, NM, Bear & Co, 1986.
14. Barbara and Foster, Michael; *Forbidden Journey: The Life of Alexandra David-Neel,* San Francisco; Harper & Row, 1987.
15. Garret, Eilen J., *Many Voices: Autobiography of a Medium,* New York: G. P. Putman's Sons, 1968.

16. Leshan, Lawrence; *The Medium, the Mystic and the Physicist, Toward a General Theory of the Paranormal,* New York: Harper & Row, 1974.
17. Grant, Joan, *Far Memory,* New York: Harper & Row, 1956.
18. Melton, J. Gordon; *Encyclopaedic Handbook of Cults in America,* New York: Garland Publishing Inc., 1986.
19. Cooke, Grace; *The Illumined Ones, New Lands England,* White Eagle Publishing Trust, 1996.
20. Roberts, Jane; *Seth Speaks: The Eternal Validity of the Soul,* Englewood Cliffs, NJ: Prentice Hall, 1972.
21. Shepard, A. P.; *Rudolph Steiner: Scientists of the Invisible,* 1954, Rochester, VT: Inner Traditions International, 1983.
22. Simpson, William, J.; *St. Augustine's Conversion: An Outline of His Development to the Time of His Ordination,* New york: Macmillan, 1930.
23. Leary, Timothy; *Flashbacks: An Autobiography,* Los Angeles: Jeremy P. Tarcher, 1983,
24. Symonds, John and Grant, Kenneth; *The Confessions of Aleister Crowley, An Autobiography,* London: Routledge & Kegan Paul, 1979.
25. Smith, A. J.; *John Donne,* New York: Mettwen, 1985.
26. Twitchell, Paul; *The Spiritual Notebook,* Menlo Park, California: IWP Publishing, 1971.
27. Twitchell, Paul; *The Tiger's Fang,* New York; Lancer Books, 1967.
28. Twitchell, Paul;*Eckankar: The Key to Secret World's,* San Diego, Illumined Way Press, 1969
29. Ford, Arthur and Bro, M. H.; *Nothing So Strange: The Autobiography of Arthur Ford,* New York: Harper & Brother, 1958.
30. Hall, Trevor H.; *The Enigma of Daniel Home,* Buffalo, NY: Prometheus Books, 1984.
31. Carter, Darlene; A Very Outspoken Interview with Dick and Tara Sutphen, *Self-Help Update* Issue 31, 1986,
32. Evans-Wentz, W. Y.; *Tibet's Great Yogi Milarepa: A Biography from the Tibetan,* 2nd ed. London: Oxford University Press, 1951.
33. Goel Dr.B S.; *Third Eye and Kundalini,* Third Eye Foundation of India, 1985.
34. Bancroft, Anne, *Twentieth-Century Mystics and Sages,* Arkana, William Heinemann Ltd., U K., 1976.
35. Hearst, Kenneth Thurston; *FIND's Eighth Annual Conference,* Oct. 1992.
36. Lutyens, Mary; *Krishnamurti—The Years of Awakening,* Avon Books, 1975.

37. Sparrow, Lynn Elwel; *Edgar Cayce's Wisdom for the New Age-Reincarnation,* Harper & Row, Publishers, San Francisco, 1988.
38. Kumar, Ravindra; "On Enlightenment and God", *JPRR,* Oct. 1991.
39. Johnson Robert A., *Ecstasy; Understanding the Psychology of Joy,* San Francisco, Harper & Row, 1987.
40. Maslow, Abraham H.; *Toward a Psychology of Being,* Princeton NJ: Van Nostrand, 1962.

# 4

# Kundalini and Christian Spirit Energy

*Dr. Kopytin has tried to find differences between Kundalini and Christian Spirit Energy, which in my opinion are Eastern and Western names for the same mechanism. However, the text and literature concerning this energy has been more extensively elaborated in the East over the centuries and even millenniums. There are two possible reasons for considering them to be different: First, Christian writers have not thoroughly gone through relevant details about Kundalini available in a very large number of books and documents; second, the writers do not have a personal experience of transformation which automatically follows transcendence in the path, whatever name is given to it. It is high time we should work for unity rather than invent more of the diversities which have already wrecked the world.*

**1. Introduction**

In his two papers (*JRPR* Oct. '92, and July, '93), Alexander Kopytin has tried to find and elaborate the differences between Eastern Kundalini and what he calls Christian Spirit Energy. Dr. Kopytin's 1992 paper argued the insufficiency of Kundalini in regard to scope and perspective of traditional Christian consciousness. As far as this part is concerned, I have already answered (*JRPR* Jan. '94), that the Kundalini phenomenon brings a complete transformation of the personality, whether the aspirant is a Hindu, Muslim or Christian. Several examples from Christian saints were provided.

In his 1992 publication Kopytin has pointed out that two aspects of spiritual reality are not covered by Kundalini: First, psychical mechanism and processes of the external aspect of the human being and social functioning; second, prerequisites of human development and the evolution of man's physical and spiritual nature. His July '93 publication in the journal contends that Kundalini is a transcending power while the Christian spirit energy is a transforming one.

This chapter is an endeavour to prove that Kopytin's observations above are not based on the study of the extensive literature on Kundalini from both Eastern and Western sources. These show that the energy evolution of Kundalini brings such transformation in the personality as is perhaps never known to an average person. And most important of all, transcendence and transformation are not unrelated phenomena; rather transformation invariably follows transcendence as an integral part of the process of evolution, which is neither Eastern nor Western but a biological fact. The pituitary gland, the pineal gland, the solar plexus, and the nervous system have similar effects on an individual whether one is a Hindu, a Muslim, or a Christian.

Most of the people in the West who have experienced this energy, and call it Christian spirit energy, have reported the same symptoms associated with Kundalini. And on the other hand, the people of the East experiencing Kundalini have invariably reported the same transformation described by Kopytin.

**2. Transcendence and Transformation through Kundalini**

Michael Grosso (1985) (1) is quoted as saying that there are two camps of truth seekers, two camps of truth: one confirming, the other transforming. In fact, he dismissed the age-old quotation 'God is Love' as meaningless since it expressed only a confirming truth.

Let me point out that the words 'God is Love' quoted by God-realized men like Krishna, Buddha and Jesus Christ, cannot be understood in their meaning by intelligent but unrealized people of the world. An intelligent man/woman, however learned he or she may be, cannot touch the level of understanding of a "realized person" who has seen and directly experienced truth for him or herself. In the words of B. A. Reichenbach (*JRPR*, July '93), "while individuals who can perceive and actively participate in spiritual events are very rare, their witness nonetheless provides the only possible authentic source of knowledge concerning the mysteries of life 'beyond', which all the efforts of the human mind in science and philosophy have not been able to discover or disprove."

The realized and established saint Swami Satyananda Saraswati (1984)(5) states: "Energy at different levels is known by different names. At the highest level it is called spiritual experience. On the emotional level it is known as love. On the physical level it is known as sex, and at the lowest level it is known as 'ignorance'." Thus a human at the lowest level is said to be ignorant. When evolution transcends this level, the person is transformed to the next or physical level in which he takes interest in sex and is confirmed in it. When evolution further transcends this level of being, the individual is transformed to the emotional level. He lives in love with mankind, not merely involved in animal sex. At this level energy touches the level of Godliness for the first time.

Finally, when evolution transcends this level, the person is transformed to the stage where he sees the energy as a "spiritual experience". It is at this stage that the individual exclaims *Aham Brahmasmi*, meaning, "I am God", because he is full of the love which is God. This level of understanding cannot be possessed by any person, whatever number of books one might have read, at whatever level of intelligence one may be, unless the "ego" has been transcended and the transformation of "self" has taken place, which occurs in a single event.

Swami Sivananda Radha (1978), a German psychiatrist who adopted a Hindu name after spending a major portion of her life as a disciple of Swami Sivananda Saraswati of India, has given a very exhaustive account of the seven *chakras* (centres of energy) with regard to their respective transcendence and the resulting transformation in personality. Kundalini *yoga* provides the best possible integration of the physical and spiritual aspects in a logical manner. The moral lesson of transcending the first *chakra* is the gladness of overcoming selfishness.

As Kundalini leaps into other dimensions, the person is able to tap the source of knowledge in himself and intuitively understands the Eternal Laws, which he puts into the language of his own time for the benefit of others. Thus most of the successful yogis on the path of Kundalini have written volumes of books for the transformation of mankind in general, following their own transformation. To cite some of them, Swami Yogananda, Ramakrishna, Vivekananda, Muktananda, Pundit Gopi Krishna, Sivananda Saraswati have all been living examples of physical and spiritual unification. Another exponent of Kundalini Yoga is Da Free John of the United States, settled now in his ashram in Fiji.

The successful transcendence of the second *chakra* gives many the ability of well-reasoned discourse or the writing of prose or verse reflecting great power of imagination as the basis of beautiful and inspiring words. The aspirant may be transformed into a poet or a writer who at the highest level may be a prophet also.

At the third *chakra* the aspirant creates a great wealth of knowledge and discrimination applied to daily events as they happen. A saintly person, by simply entering the room, can bring a sense of quiet and stillness into a tumultuous group, opening the senses of those present to higher perceptions. The fourth *chakra* promises hearing with the inner ear the cosmic Aum or Word. This is the sound heard without the striking of two objects, as the name *anahata* implies. The aspirant by now has learned through past mistakes, has transcended "sin" which means repetition of past mistakes in yoga, and has a future of harmony and happiness. By elimination of self-will and removal of self-protected screens, one can put oneself in another's shoes and understand the person. In extreme cases, through sustained practice, one can actually enter (as a soul) in another's body (Radha 4, 309-310).

People who have not yet crossed the first and second *chakras* accept their fate as inevitable. As consciousness transcends the third *chakra,* one becomes master over some of the situations of life, but one is still influenced and bound by "accumulated *Karma*" over previous lifetimes. In the fourth *chakra* one realizes that fate is, of course, real, but still one can go totally beyond its dictates. It is like throwing something into the sky beyond the gravitational field. Consciousness is accelerated to the speed of free-will in order to transcend the pull of latent *sanskaras.* In the fourth *chakra* one becomes a yogi, who can shape his own destiny.

After transcending the fifth *chakra* one becomes free of worldly desires, as one's life has served its purpose. The energy that is no longer locked up in the pursuit of worldly desires raises a person to a higher plane which is the Gateway of Liberation. At this stage the secret of eternal youth opens up, regeneration and rejuvenation begin, and the aspirant achieves perfect health and freedom from all diseases. One can look back with a great clarity, see the present and anticipate the future. Thus one knows the past, present and future.

In the sixth *chakra* one acquires pure intellect with a balance between the principles of male and female, intellect and intuition, free of selfish desires. As a process of learning one understands the creation of one's own life with all the pains, problems and difficulties. What has been gained should be preserved and what is no longer necessary must be destroyed to fulfil the Divine Union. The final plunge is taken from his state of wisdom to enter the seventh *chakra,* that is *mahasamadhi.* Whenever the final decision is taken the body drops off within a few days.

I can vouch for all these happenings by sharing a first-hand experience of my own. I clearly remember the night of October 20, 1987 while working at the University of Zimbabwe in Harare. After a sound sleep of about four hours I got up to attend to the call of nature. I became aware of a constant sound of the blowing of a conch without a break. I asked all the persons in the house if they were also hearing such a noise. Everyone replied in the negative. This was apparently the opening of the fourth centre, the *anahata chakra*, and I was hearing the cosmic sound of Aum or the Word through inner ears. Later I was examined by Dr. Kiri of the medical centre at the university and after a few weeks by Dr. Kylee, Head of the Centre of Naturopathy in London. Both of them were amazed at the sound health I possessed at this age. The sound of Aum is permanent and I hear it 24 hours a day.

Since then, a series of chemical reactions have been taking place in my body which I have to account for somewhere else. From being a mathematician, I suddenly turned to writing spiritual articles. My first book was *Secrets of Numerology* (1992) (2); the second one, *Destiny, Science and Spiritual Awakening* was released in March 1997. I have clairvoyantly seen many astral planes and have visited some of them in my spirit body with full consciousness. I have been speaking at conferences around the world on Kundalini and life after death, with no real interest left either in my profession of mathematics or world affairs. Eventually, I resigned as a professor in September 1994.

I can now review the transformation I underwent in 1987. I even had an experience of death similar to that of Dr. Elisabeth Kubler-Ross. I intend to compile and publish all these details separately.

Experiences of the higher order, which an exponent of Kundalini Yoga undergoes at times, can be found in the works of Swami Yogananda Paramhansa (3), Swami Satyananda Saraswati (4), Swami Sivananda Radha (5) and many, many other Indian Yogis. Yogananda could associate with the higher self of Jesus Christ and experience the torture he underwent while carrying the heavy cross on his shoulders and being tormented by the citizens of Jerusalem. Once while moving in a mountainous region toward a meeting with his Guru, he saw a white shining fortress. On entering this astonishing structure he found gold ornaments and real jewels on various tables. Everything was as real as life. After some time he thought of his Guru and everything vanished in a second. After this event his desire to live in a rich palace was transcended forever. In another experience, Yogananda, while mourning the death of his Guru very emotionally, suddenly saw his Guru materializing in flesh and talking to him. He touched his Guru and sat with him for quite some time before the Guru dematerialized. All these details, which are in *The Autobiography of a Yogi* (3), falsify any statement that only Christian energy can manifest itself in external as well as internal dimensions.

**3. Conclusion**

As a matter of fact, there is no process other than Kundalini Yoga which is responsible for the complete human development process, which in my opinion, is the same, whether conceived through Christian, Buddhist, Sufi or any other approach. However, it is the exponents of Kundalini Yoga who have given a step-by-step approach and development of the process, which is not found elsewhere. With the passage of the Kundalini energy from the first to the sixth *chakra,* the aspirant is transformed into a new person step-by-step, until one's final merging with the Divine in the seventh *chakra.*

Through the practice of yoga and chanting of *mantras* a balanced development of the physical, mental, emotional and intuitional aspect of the personality takes place. Such development is not dogma-bound. Swami Vivekananda showed equal interest in praying in a Muslim mosque, a Christian church, or Buddhist or Hindu temple, to see the light which opens the way to Divine Union. One who sees an esoteric difference between various religions and considers one's approach to be better than all others is millions of miles away from God. Through such an approach one might find a particular deity on one of the astral planes but not Supreme Reality above and beyond all of them.

Quoting once again Professor B. A. Reichenbach about *The Book on the Living God* by Bo Yin Ra, the spiritually realized saint of Germany born in the 19th century: "The book also discusses the common origin of all the spiritually influenced religions and underlines the timeless element concealed in myth and dogma." Looking at the comments of the Editor of *JRPR* (July 1993, 161) about *Judaism between Yesterday and Tomorrow* by Hans Kung: "The book is an urgent appeal to Christians, Muslims and Jews to recognize that all three religions stem from Abraham and, to participate in genuine dialogue, working together to all their futures. How else (Kung is quoted as asking) are the pious fanatics to be kept at bay in all camps?"

I conclude by quoting the words of Father Bebe Griffiths (Weber, 6):

> At the deepest level I do not find anything incompatible. The deeper you go into Hinduism or Buddhism, the more you see how there is a fundamental unity with Christianity. On the surface there're many differences and contradictions, and even below the surface there are problems. But the deeper you go, the more you converge on this one.

**References**

1 Grosso, Michael; *The Final Choice,* Walpole, NH: Stillpoint Pub., 1985, pp. 333-334.

2. Kumar, Ravindra; *Secrets of Numerology,* Sterling Publishers (P) Ltd., New Delhi, India 1992.

3. Paramhansa, Swami Yogananda; *The Autobiography of a Yogi,* Bombay, India: Jaico Publishing House, 1946, 1986.

4. Radha, Swami Sivananda; *Kundalini Yoga,* Palo Alto, CA: Timeless Books, 1978.

5. Saraswati, Swami Satyananda; *Kundalini Tantra,* Bihar, India: Bihar School of Yoga, Munger, 1984, p. 161.

6. Weber, Rene; *Dialogues with Scientists and Sages,* London, England: Routledge and Kegan Paul, 1991, p. 170.

# 5

# Personality Transformation with Chakras—The Awakening

*An increasing number of Exceptional Human Experiences (EHEs) are being reported these days. A single incident may appear to be a baffling event, but when it is viewed through the windows of the seven chakras, it can be clearly seen as a particular milestone on the ladder of evolution. And a series of EHEs can be linked and understood in the light of the theory of Kundalini Yoga. Application of the knowledge gained after awakening is automatic since gradual transformation of the personality reflects the manner in which the individual handles day-to-day situations in life. An account of the awakening of the chakras in a systematic and integrated way, supplemented with my personal experiences over the years, is presented in this chapter.*

## 1. Introduction

John Crowley (1, p.90) and Dr. Grace Crowley said: "Let us ask, what possibility can account for these marvellous phenomena, these EHEs, which make a few of us stare in wonder, and many others retreat in sullen rejection?" Dr. Evon Kason (2, p.28) attempted to answer the first part of the question by saying: "After 15 years of clinical and literary research, I have come to the conclusion that the modern Kundalini hypothesis provides a plausible model to explain the biological, psychological and spiritual aspects of EHEs and the often associated spiritual transformation of consciousness." Stanley Kripper (George W. Fisk 3, pp.56-57) said: "...some internally consistent processes are at work."

This chapter attempts to present facts which suggest that the activation of the *chakras* by the passage of Kundalini from the first to the sixth/seventh centre, brings a systematic biological, psychological and spiritual change in the person who undergoes a series of EHEs in a consistent and coherent manner. As an illustration, I have described my own experiences over the years. Any aspirant with some EHEs can identify one's position with a particular *chakra* and know where one stands on the ladder of evolution.

Rhea A. White (4, pp.48 and 53) said that unless one's own self is changed, the investigation for validation will be non-significant. Claire G. Walker (5, p.64) said that "...the nearest we can come to validation is to look at what happens to the life and outlook of the individual in the wake of the event." According to Paul Pond (6, p.75) subjectivity makes the scientific investigation difficult. He further said (6, p.80), "Although the occurrence of the EHE has thousands of years of recorded history on its side the modern mind remains sceptical and confused."

According to Gough and Shacklett (8, pp.197-198) the reality/wholeness cannot be analysed scientifically/objectively because we are a part of it. John Franklin Miller, III (9, p.183) rightly suggests the following steps for validation: (1) the consistency of similar subjective experiences; (2) inter-subjective corroboration by others of the same experience; (3) inter-subjective corroboration of different experiences which give evidence for the experience in question; (4) the ecstatic character and noetic content of the experience; (5) the coherence of the experience within an accepted conceptual framework and; (6) the objective corroboration of the same experience or similar subjective experiences.

**2. Awakening of the Chakras and the Gradual Transformation**

The first and the foremost centre of energy is the *mooladhara chakra* where all the passions, all the guilt and all the agony are stored. As long as the Kundalini *shakti* is dormant in this *chakra*, the five eternal enemies of the man/woman —*kama* (lust), *krodh* (anger), *moha* (attachment), *lobh* (greed) and *ahankar* (ego) —

remain active at the instinctive level of our basic existence. As soon as the *shakti* awakens in *mooladhara* these five negative forces are transcended (to a large extent) and the first stage of personality transformation takes place. In the words of Swami Sivananda Radha (10, p.303):

> Freedom from all sin is achieved at the first stage by recognizing mistakes, by controlling impulse, by learning through reflection, and by making the simultaneous connection between learning and knowledge. Sin is, from a Yogic point of view, the intentional repetition of mistakes that are well known...greed and ambition can deprive the mind of its wonderful potential for creativity and quality in all aspects of living. Quality in living is the first step to bliss. The joy of life is our inherited right. To always be living in the spirit of gladness comes when we are free of selfishness and all that it entails. This process of self-mastery is indeed an experience of bliss that comes once the early stages of learning are past.

Often we catch ourselves when we are just about to make a mistake, even the awareness of it is there, but pride refuses to admit the fault in the decision or action. When pride is under control through the awakening of the *chakra,* the most intelligent level of learning is achieved through intuition, since the level of awareness is greatest. As the animal bonds of body and mind break down, awareness expands and greater possibilities of the "creative potential" are envisioned. The individual then puts into language the intuitive knowledge thus received for benefit of the mankind. Eternal knowledge and power of speech are bestowed on the person as gift from the first *chakra.*

The *mooladhara chakra* is related to the urinary, excretory, sexual and reproductive organs. All the lower *sanskaras* and *karmas* are embedded there. The Lives of schizophrenics, neurotics and insane persons are imbalanced because of the complexes and the feelings of guilt since the energy has not crossed the first *chakra* in them. As Sigmund Freud said, everything is influenced by the sexual awareness of the person. A yogi is concerned with the "awakening of an experience and sublimating it", thereby opening the higher centres. The first experience I had of this was sometime in the middle of 1985 while I was in Nigeria. After about half an hour of chanting, I was completely engrossed in concentration. The worldly sense, even the counting of beads, was forgotten. Suddenly, I heard the sound of lightning as if an electric spark had jumped between two poles. The pitch of the sound was quite high and my eyes were opened. I saw a thick column of white light (2 ´ 6 inches) appearing at a distance of about four feet from my eyes. It was vibrating like a tongue of fire and it started moving to the left. It moved to a distance of about one foot, slowly diminishing in size, and then vanished. I was amazed and looked around expecting to find the source of this spark, thinking that there was some electrical leakage. Slowly my amazement subsided as it became clear that the Light had materialized from nowhere. Its explanation will be discussed.

Besides other minor effects, there are three main phenomena which are noticed with the awakening of the first *chakra*. Levitation of the astral body and clairvoyance or clairaudience are preceded by a tingling sensation at the root of the spine. This tingling feeling as if a small and sharp snake wants to rise through the spine, was repeated many times over the month. Separation of the astral body was also experienced many times while I was engaged in meditation, as if I had risen above my seat. I saw myself sitting from an elevated point, in flashes of seconds. This was followed by a series of clairvoyant visions of non-physical planes, some of which involved actual soul travel out of the body.

The second transformation which clears almost completely the five negative forces—lust, anger, attachment, greed and ego—takes place at the second centre of energy, called the *swadhishthan chakra*. *Swadhishthan* literally means "one's own home" and all the perceptions, experiences and *karmas* over past lives, reside here in the potential state. One of the names of Lord Shiva is Pashupati, meaning the master of all animal instincts and it has complete control over the *mooladhara chakra*—the centre of manifestation of negative forces. *Prarabdha* (collective) *Karmas* over past lives are filed in some layer of the mind and this *chakra* has the key to it. Quarrels and bitter experiences in past lives, for example, colour the activities of the present life with unconscious pessimism. This stage of evolution is rightly named purgatory and the seed of the cycle of death and rebirth is perhaps situated in this centre.

When the Kundalini *shakti* arrives at this centre, most of the sleeping *karmas* are evoked. Sometimes the aspirant becomes excessively angry; sometimes he is fearful of ordinary things, and sometimes is charged with sexual passion beyond control. I remember having seen in dreams and visions an extremely beautiful and naked woman dancing around and trying to arouse the desire in me. Kundalini can pass through this second *chakra* in a successful way only through real *vairagya* (detachment), earned through first-hand experiences in life, and with the understanding of the truth that desires can never be satisfied in any number of lifetimes.

Sexual arousal passes on to other parts of the body as sublimated energy. There is a cooling down and an upsurge of pure love for everyone. This type of experience took place with me three times in a period of one year and now it is over. Swami Muktananda described this experience in detail in his book *Cit Shakti Vilas—The Play of Consciousness.* Female aspirants also pass through this same experience, see for example the case of Irina Tweedy (Greenwell, 11).

In the words of Swami Satyananda Saraswati (12, p.161), "when no sexual desires of any kind manifest in an aspirant anymore, and when there is no more personal attraction, that means Kundalini has passed beyond Swadhishthan Chakra." However, sexual awareness never really dies since it is fuelled by the primal energy which is present all throughout, although its form changes. As mentioned earlier, at the lowest level it is *avidya* (ignorance), at the physical level it is known as sex, at the emotional level it is called love and at the highest level it is called spiritual experience. While Kundalini is still in the *swathishthan chakra,* strong sexual desires can manifest and disturb the aspirant.

As soon as the second *chakra* is crossed, the sublimated energy manifests as pure love, sincere consideration for the highest feelings and needs of others, tolerance, forgiveness and compassion.

With freedom from the five enemies—lust, greed, anger, attachment, and ego—one gets the ability to use well-reasoned discourse and produce prose and verse. Imagination and intuition are sharpened and the writing down of the internal wisdom comes as a natural flow. The sublimated energy may still desire the company of the opposite sex, but in a refined and a balanced way, since disturbance and turbulence have been eradicated forever.

The next junction is the third centre of energy, called *manipura chakra,* meaning literally, "The City of Jewels". In fact, *mooladhara* is the seat of Kundalini, *swadhishthan* is its abode and its arousal takes place in *manipura.* On its awakening, the body of the aspirant becomes free from diseases; it acquires a luminous lustre and an expanded consciousness. This *chakra* is the last of the mortal planes and the beginning of the heavenly planes. Those individuals who are in the stage of persecution, are seriously involved in either intellectual metaphysics or yoga and meditation, (normally a combination of the two in varied proportions) or are in search of a Guru, have their Kundalini residing in *manipura.*

The third *chakra* is very important in the sense that it is the boundary between the mortal and heavenly planes. Once the Kundalini crosses this *chakra* it does not go back, as it does many times from the first and second *chakras.* On crossing this *chakra,* the aspirant acquires a spiritual perspective and gets visions of the higher planes in heavenly realms, which happens for the first time only at *manipura.* After such visions, the thinking of the person is completely transformed. All biases, prejudices and complexes are dropped with the touch of the infinite state of consciousness, since all human differences appear to be trivial now. One's vision of things becomes higher as the beauty and perfection of the heavenly worlds dawn in one's consciousness. Perfect ideas, noble thoughts, bliss and the power to create and destroy worlds with the power of speech are gifts of the *manipura chakra.* Saraswati, the goddess of speech, is said to reside in the tongue of the person at this stage. One no more looks at the world on the basis of personal problems, which, in fact, do not exist anymore.

I can give a brief account of the celestial visions I had at this stage. A bluish-green light was spread everywhere but had no source. There was peace, tranquillity and happiness. People were moving as circles or semicircles of light on green meadows on both sides of a canal of water. On another occasion I saw a transparent fortress in which souls were entering through one gate and coming out of another gate, the queues moving swiftly. Yet on another occasion I could see myself in a formless state, just a dimensionless point of existence. I could see everywhere, and move with the speed of thought as I received telepathic instructions from my Guru on the ground. Once I moved on a very vast ocean of clear blue water over a bridge of hairline breadth in my dimensionless form. Close to a group of mountains, my journey suddenly ended, and I returned to my body. These were also soul travel experiences which are pleasantly stored in my memory for all time to come.

The fourth station on the journey is the *anahata chakra* or heart centre. The word *anahata* means "unstruck or unbeaten" and the centre relates to the ***unstruck sound*** which has different names in different religions, such as *Aum,* Word, Logos, *Kalma-i-Ilahi, Shabad*, Music of Spheres, etc. This point has been widely discussed in Chapter 2. There are two main symbols in this centre—the transcendental unstruck sound and the blue lotus or star. The aspirant on successful awakening of the centre hears this ***sound*** through inner ears like an unbroken continuity of heartbeats and sees the ***blue pearl*** through inner eyes constantly.

I cannot forget that midnight of 1987 at Zimbabwe when I got up for a call of nature and was surprised to hear the sound of a blowing conch which would not subside at all. I checked my ears, asked everyone in the house and saw the doctor next morning, only to be told that there was nothing wrong with me physically. I did not know the meaning of the experience at that time. And after a few days when I got up early there was a shining blue light spread in front of me which I would see whether I closed my eyes or kept them open. However, now I see the blue pearl whenever I close my eyes and concentrate on the centre between my eyebrows.

The most important feature of the heart centre is an access to the "wish-fulfilment tree" called *Kalpataru* or *Chintamani,* meaning "jewel of correct and positive thinking". An aspirant at the first and second *chakras* still believes in fate and the inevitability of destiny. At the third *chakra* you have a mastery over some of the situations of life but you do not know the way to escape the grip of destiny. *Prarabdha* (accumulated) *karma* still influences and bounds the events of your life. But at the fourth *chakra* consciousness is accelerated to the speed of free will and the force of *karma* can be transcended. The aspirant can be called a yogi on reaching the fourth centre because here one shapes one's own destiny. But, according to the rule of *Chintamani*, positive and optimistic thinking must be maintained. At this stage optimism results in positive happenings and pessimism brings negative happenings since the aspirant is standing under the "wish-fulfilment tree". There is a big warning about it in Hindu literature.

Love without expectations, compassion, unselfishness, complete harmony with the self and family, optimism and affectionate detachment are the gifts of *anahata chakra.* One gets the power of entering another's body due to the elimination of self-will and removal of self-protective screens. One can stand in another's shoes and understand the other person. In extreme cases, a yogi as a soul can actually enter the body of another person whose soul has abandoned it (Wood, 13). The individual at *anahata* requires little sleep and feels healthy and active. The person may acquire clairvoyance/clairaudience/psycho-kinetic power or may impress an audience and win their hearts through the power of love. Through affectionate detachment there is peace and freedom from falsehood and one loses interest in the pleasures of the dualistic world. Since the heart is full of love, all the remnants of ego are washed off. One may become an inspired writer, poet or speaker. His/her very presence in the room may bring quietness and stillness among a tumultuous group of persons and evoke a sense of higher perception in them.

The fifth centre of energy is the *vishuddhi chakra* or the "Purification Centre". Purification of the mind, eloquence, wisdom, uninterrupted peace, freedom from disease and pessimism. Physical rejuvenation and eternal youth are the gifts of the *vishuddhi chakra.* Pythagoras, who married a young disciple when he was 63, was still in the prime of his youth at the age of 99 when he was assassinated by non-believers. Most of the yogis in India and other parts of the world have displayed peace of mind and a robust physical body even in their late eighties. A "nectar", called *amrit* or *soma rasa* in the *Vedas*, "madya" in *Tantra*, "sweet wine" in Sufism, and the "sacred wine" in Judaic/Christian rituals flows from the "*bindu* centre" at the back of the head when the fifth *chakra* is evoked.

The yogi attains freedom from worldly desires and the energy is now directed to higher planes and to the "gateway of liberation". The aspirant now understands the real meaning of yoga–the Divine Union. With increased concentration and peace of mind, the yogi can see the past and present, and anticipate the future. False ambitions are removed, clear discrimination shows what should be done and what should be avoided, increased awareness shows that we are the products of our own desires and ignorance, and one is full of compassion and mercy towards all, willing to take greater responsibilities in the world with a clear mind.

The experience of the void—*Shoonyata* (a huge nothingness)—occurs frequently. In December 1989 I was a guest speaker at the University of Malawi at a mathematical conference, fully relaxed and free. In the early hours of the morning I was awakened many times and at least on two occasions I had a vision that I was connected with the infinite somewhere—a strange and unknown feeling with the presence of a huge emptiness. A feeling of fear entered me for a moment, but it vanished as quickly as it came and I sighed pleasantly. I felt suddenly devoid of all thoughts and feelings, my head drooping on one side of my neck.

The most important centre is the sixth centre called *ajna chakra* meaning the "Centre of Command". It is also called the *guru chakra* because *ajna* is the centre of Jupiter, representing Brihaspati—the Guru of gods. The three important nerves—*ida, pingla* and *sushumna*—starting and diverging from the first centre reconverge at the *ajna chakra.* As Swami Satyananda Saraswati (12, pp.132-133) has pointed out:

> In Mythology these three nadis are represented by three great rivers--Ganga, Jamuna and Saraswati. They converge at a place Prayag or Triveni, which is near present-day Allahabad. Hindus believe that every twelve years, when the sun is in Aquarius, if one takes a dip at the point of confluence, one will be purified. This place of confluence corresponds symbolically to the Ajna Chakra.

When the yogi enters the state of the void in deep meditation, the directions of the inner Guru are heard at this very *chakra.* In a large number of cases an experience of death takes place at this stage. Soon after that, the "eye of Shiva" or the *third eye,* that is the "eye of intuition" opens up and the aspirant enters the astral and psychic dimensions of consciousness. It is this "divine eye" or the "eye of knowledge" which looks inward and receives revelation. One gets an insight into the very nature of existence, which cannot come from any kind of bookish knowledge. The intuitive sense comes into full operation with the awakening of the *ajna chakra.* The manifestation of the mind without the aid of the physical body results in astral projection. The vestiges of imperfection are removed and the *karmas* are burnt in the fire of the *divya chakshu* (divine eye).

At this stage the individual achieves pure intellect which is free of selfish desires. A balance between the male and female aspects of nature establishes the *divine union* between the individual Self and the Supreme Self. This is represented by the *ardhanaarishwara* (half male/half female) form of Lord Shiva in

Hindu temples in India. The cause of ignorance and lack of discrimination is attachment which drops away. The individual wakes up from the dream of life and one understands clearly the relation between cause and effect. Each action can be seen both as cause and effect. Different results which correspond to various energy centres are collectively realized with the awakening of the *ajna chakra.* On meditation the yogi sees a flaming lamp shining as brightly as the morning sun.

Some of the *siddhis,* according to the individuals' mental tendencies, may be manifested since the *ajna chakra* is related to extra-sensory perceptions. However, the *siddhis* do not manifest if the Kundalini passes quickly through all the *chakras,* which happens if *ajna chakra* is awakened before other *chakras* of the lower order. Psychic powers usually linger only when the Kundalini gets blocked in one of the *chakras.* I remember having passed through such powers as a brief episode. Once, while out-of-body, I could uproot a big tree, twist a pole and throw a very big stone away merely by gestures of my fingers. However, this never happened again, although clairvoyance continues in variations.

Before the sixth *chakra* is activated, the individual still lives under the delusions of the opposite forces like love and hatred, victory and defeat, gain and loss, etc. But after the awakening, one's whole philosophical attitude and approach to life changes. The person is not disturbed by any kind of happening or experience, good or bad as defined by others. One participates in all the affairs of life and lives fully in them with a sense of *affectionate detachment* as a witness. The events of life flow like a current and the yogi moves with them with total faith and surrender.

Among the series of Exceptional Human Experiences, the most important one happened to me at this stage. In the early hours of the morning in 1987, while I was engaged in deep meditation, I suddenly felt very vulnerable and helpless. I was praying to the Mother Goddess because I had no Guru and no one to guide me, and was continuously sobbing with tears flowing out of my eyes. In the flash of a second I was in a void, followed by an experience of death. I saw my dead body being carried away on the shoulders of friends and relatives and someone was saying continuously, "Ravindra Kumar is dead." The pain suddenly converted to bliss and I was smiling as the state of *samadhi* was broken in a spontaneous way.

Just a month after this occurrence, in a similar situation, I saw clearly through the eyes of the mind, the Mother Goddess clad in a red sari with an extremely beautiful face and a red vermilion *bindi* on her forehead. I clearly saw myself in white clothes bowing down to her and bending my head to her feet. And I saw her hand with colourful bangles on the wrist touching the top of my head while she gave me blessings with a smile on her face. The vision lasted for about fifteen seconds and was repeated in a similar way after a few days. It was during these days that I saw myself from the top of the roof, sitting and meditating quietly. This happened a couple of times in that period. Sometimes I had a strong feeling that someone was watching me through two sparkling eyes, sometimes with one eye. An inner voice kept repeating, "I am being watched". I even felt the touch of gentle hands on my shoulders and I could very clearly feel a non-physical presence around me. However, there was no fear, only a strange happiness. And now whenever I concentrate on the *ajna chakra* I invariably see a flaming light like the morning sun.

The seventh and the final centre is the *sahasrara chakra* meaning, the "thousand petal centre". But in-between the sixth and the seventh centre lies the source of creation, called the *bindu visarga* near the back of the head where Hindus have a lock of hair. Literally, it means the falling of a drop. When this centre awakens, nectar falls from it in drops which assimilate in the body, making it lustrous and vital without depending on the intake of food. This is the reason why yogis eat very little food, often surviving only on fruits and leaves. The metabolism of the body is arrested and rejuvenation takes place. In fact, the *vishuddhi chakra* (fifth centre) and *bindu* are interconnected with nerves and the activation of one causes spontaneous activation of the other in most cases.

The other and important aspect of the *bindu* is that it is the "Gateway to the Cosmic Void". Actually it is the trapdoor that opens in both directions. It is through this centre that the formless energy of the cosmos enters and assumes shape and limitations. On the other hand, the reversal of the process through yoga starts involution, when the individual turns one's face towards the *bindu* and it is through this point that one approaches *sahasrara,* the final destination. There are two aspects of the energy; static and dynamic, male and female, Shiva and Shakti. Lord Shiva is represented by a white point residing in the *bindu* while Shakti is represented by a red point residing in the *mooladhara chakra.* It is worth noting here that the colour of male sperm is white, while the colour of female menses is red. The attempt of all yogic practices is to unite theses two polarities, the world of opposites, and as soon as the union takes place, the Kundalini ascends to *sahasrara.* A confirmatory sign of the passage of Kundalini through the *bindu* is the hearing of the Cosmic *Aum* or Word intermittently through the inner ear.

It was the month of October, in 1987, while I was at the University of Zimbabwe, in the evening around 5 o'clock, at tea-time. Suddenly I felt that my whole body was likely to be twisted like a snake and a very heavy pressure on the top of my head was likely to blow my head off. My face became pale and sucked-in, as I was told by the family members watching me at that time. Some sense worked on me, and I ran out of the house very fast. I kept on running very fast with heavy motions of hands and legs for some time. On returning home I cycled in the room for about 15 minutes and then did some vigorous exercises. This brought the situation under some control. Next day the doctor examined me thoroughly, and said that if I had not been maintaining very good health it could have been a case of paralysis or brain haemorrhage. He warned me to suspend all meditation and heavy brain activities, which I did from then onwards. For one week my head was blocked by heat and I could not think or read and I did not do any lecturing at the university. After a week, slowly, I returned to normality. This was the ascent of Kundalini to *sahasrara.*

On the night of January 1, 1988 around 11 p.m. I was about to fall asleep in my relative's house in London. I was in a state of satisfaction, peace and nullity of thoughts. Suddenly I saw through the eyes of my mind, a very beautiful child with open eyes and a blissful smile on his face. Next morning around 6 a.m. when my sleep was half broken, I saw clearly the same child facing a different direction. This was a vision of Child Brahma, the male aspect of Energy unmanifest (10, 39).

**3. Concluding Remarks**

*Sahasrara* is the culmination of all yogic activities. As the Kundalini ascends various *chakras,* the personality transformation indicates the evolving nature of consciousness. These are the various stages of *Savikalpa Samadhi* (absorption with fluctuations) as classified by Patanjali. The intermediate category is called *asampragyata* (absorption without awareness). And then comes *Nirvikalpa Samadhi* (absorption without any fluctuation). It is difficult to pinpoint the transition from "meditation" to "Samadhi", just as one cannot say when youth ends and old age begins. And in the same way it is difficult to pinpoint the transition from *Savikalpa* to *Asampragyata* to *Nirvikalpa Samadhi.* Swami Satyananda Saraswati (12, 204) has summed up the situation in the following words:

> The whole process occurs in continuity, each stage fusing into the next and transforming in a very graduated way. This seems logical when you consider that it is the same consciousness which is undergoing the experience... .
>
> From *Mooladhara* up to *Ajna Chakra,* the awareness is experiencing higher things, but it is not free from ego. You cannot transcend ego at the lower points of awakening. It is only when Kundalini reaches *Ajna Chakra* that the transcendence begins. There is where the ego is exploded into a million fragments and the ensuing death experience occurs. At this point *Savikalpa* ends and *Nirvikalpa* begins. From here, the energies fuse and flow together up to *Sahasrara,* where enlightenment unfolds.

## References

1. Crowley. J.; *Psychic Surgery - how is such a sensational* EHE *to be validated,* ARPR Proceedings, 1993.
2. Kason, Dr. Evon; *Exceptional Human Experiences, Spiritual Transformation, and Kundalini Awakening: A Clinical Perspective,* ARPR Proceedings, 1993, p. 28.
3. Fisk, George W.; *Response to Rhea White's Exceptional Human Experience as Vehicles of Grace: Parapsychology, Faith and Outlier Mentality,* ARPR Proceedings, 1993.
4. White, Rhea A.; *Exceptional Human Experiences as Vehicles of Grace: Parapsychology, Faith and The Outlier Mentality,* ARPR Proceedings, 1993.
5. Walker, Claire G.; *The Question of Validation in Psychic Surgery,* ARPR Proceedings, 1993.
6. Pond, Paul; *What is the Purpose of Exceptional Human Experience?,* ARPR Proceedings, 1993.
7. Reichenbach, B.A.; "Empirical Accounts of Spiritual Reality: The Enclosed Garden of Bo Yin Ra", *JRPR,* July 1993.
8. Gough, W.C. and Shacklett, "Physics, Parapsychology and Religion", *JRPR,* April '93.
9. Miller, John Franklin; *In Defence of Religion, JRPR,* Oct., 1993.
10. Radha, Swami Sivananda; *Kundalini Yoga,* Motilal Banarsidass Publishers, Delhi, 1992.
11. Greenwell, Bonnie; *The Energies of Transformation,* Shakti River Press, Cupertino, CA, 1990.
12. Saraswati, Swami Satyananda; *Kundalini Tantra,* Bihar School of Yog Munger, India, 1984.
13. Wood, Earnest E.; *Practical Yoga—Ancient and Modern,* NY:, Wilshire Book Co., 1948.

# 6

# Predestination, Psychic Sense and Free Will

*After surveying a large number of cases of intuitively receiving foreknowledge of future events, the following points are suggested: (1) There is predestination and each human being goes on unfolding his or her destiny event by event. (2) The "psychic sense" which is beyond the five normal senses, flashes some important events in advance which could be turning points in the life of a person. (3) With a strong determination, the force of "free will" can change the course of events, thus avoiding catastrophes. It is very difficult, but not impossible.*

### 1. Psychic Sense and Precognition

Claire Walker has observed, "We are psychic beings in transition from animal to spirit, and as such are moving from a five-sensory to a multi-sensory nature (p.12)...a hankering for perceived growth for a feeling of getting somewhere, is something we all have, and I am suggesting that it is the nature of the psychic sense (p.15)... connectedness, identity and level of awareness are psychic senses affiliated with our images, each person is developing an answer to the question, who and what I am? (p.15)...there are among us, saints and sages, but no saviours. Is it not evident that we must be our own saviours, more deliberately attuning ourselves to the all beyond us, and doing our own evolving in an unfolding universe?...This is all taking place now, consciously or not, in thousands of individuals of all religions and races around the world. Is it dawning psychic sense of distant purpose and vast connectedness that, once we begin to recognize and respect it, will save our species from destroying our planet and ourselves?

We do not have to live the Atlantis myth; we may already be started on a different and saving way (p.20)." (ARPR Annual Conference Proceedings, 1994).

Many important instances of this nature have been noticed in the past and they deserve a mention in the present context. The purpose of this chapter is to give an overall view of such happenings, and also to suggest that all of us have a more or less predicted life which is flashed through our psychic sense at some turning points. Whenever there is chance of side-tracking, or living in a different way, as compared to the pattern planned for us by nature, we get a warning through the psychic sense to make the correction and meet the requirements of a destined route. For example, my mother, Laxmi Devi, got repeated hunches and visions to refuse marriage with a man named Goverdhan, who she said was likely to die soon. Her parents had already fixed the marriage and kept on insisting that she accept the proposal. However, she was successful in persuading her parents, and she married my father. Three months later, Goverdhan died in a mysterious way and my mother, saved from being a widow, lived the life she was supposed to lead.

There appears to be a single mysterious force at work in the universe, which is forcing or directing its decisions on human beings, and is beyond the comprehension of the limited human mind. The spontaneous allotment of a name to a person at the time of birth is according to some Divine law and it contains the whole future in it. Each human being appears to be unfolding his or her destiny, event by event, and is in fact a silent observer without having any hold on the happenings. Our future acts seem to be lying at a point to come, but our "conscious self", unaware of them completely, goes on performing them with the assumption that it is exercising its "free will". The above conclusion is based on the fact that two persons unknown to each other, who had identical names and dates of birth, were found to have the same nature, habits and physical appearances. Even similar events took place in their lives at almost the same points of time. Slight variances in nature of events could be attributed to the differences in times of birth on the same date of birth. For example, one became the king of Italy, while the other became the owner of a restaurant at the exact point of time (Kumar, 1).

Some invisible forces are always directing our actions. In fact, we are not totally responsible for any happening, good or bad. The moment one realizes this reality, one is on the path of liberation from falsehood.

The subject of precognition has been in the limelight for more than three decades as far as official investigations are concerned. Parapsychology is one of the modern subjects which has found its place in some of the universities around the world. Nevertheless, it is yet to be accepted as science by the intelligentsia universally. The parapsychologist is trying to find a logical proof of precognition based on experiments in the laboratory. For more than twenty years experiments have been conducted at Duke University in North Carolina, in a quest to find a physical proof of the phenomenon. But so far it has not been possible to conclude any results in the form of a formula. It appears to be an attempt to measure the infinite with the finite scale. Serious investigators like Professor J. B. Rhine, who founded the "Institute of Parapsychology" at Durham, started showing signs of fatigue in the search of a formula, in his lifetime. He expired in 1984. A large number of scientists since then have followed in his work without success. H. L. Edge and R. L. Morris have given a detailed account of such study in *Foundations of Parapsychology* (2).

Since there have been innumerable cases of precognition before the events have taken place, investigations in this direction are natural. Although it has not been possible to fit a physical model to the situation, observations and analysis of cases of precognition will continue. There are two possibilities: either the precognition might be 100 per cent accurate and we need only an eye to see it, or it might never be that accurate and will often be erroneous. In my book *Secrets of Numerology* (1) important illustrative cases are given which suggest that there is a fixed destiny and you need only an eye to see it.

According to Albert Einstein and Costa de Beauregard

(Danah Zohar, 3), the "relativity theory" contains the complete history of the event already, and change is only relative to the perpetual mode of the living being. Humans and the other creatures on earth are compelled to explore little by little the content of the fourth dimension (time), as such a one traverses without stopping and turning back, a time-like trajectory in space-time. This suggests, more or less, that each of us has a fixed destiny. On the other hand, there are thinkers who outrightly reject this ideal in favour of free will. In view of Professor Rhine, if a man knew by precognition that he would be in a train wreck and he could not avoid it, of what avail would precognition be to the man in such a case? Evidence of absolute precognition would imply a fatalism from which no decision could be truly free. Vocational freedom and perfect predictability are thus irreconcilable.

There have been instances in the history of the human race where the future has been predicted with one hundred per cent accuracy. Some five thousand years ago (3000 B.C. approx.) Krishna (the Deity) advised Arjuna (the warrior), who had decided not to fight in the battlefield of Mahabharata because he would have to kill people who were his blood relatives on the opposite side. Krishna told Arjuna that he had looked into the future and had seen that all those people died because of their own fate; Arjuna had only to do his duty as a warrior. Arjuna fought, after getting the wisdom, and the famous people on the opposite side died exactly as predicted by Krishna.

Michael De Nosterdame, better known as "Nostradamus" was a sixteenth century French physician and mystic (Dec. 14, 1503 to July 1566). He wrote his famous book of predictions, *Les Prophesies de M. Michael de Nostradame* in 1568. His quatrains, written some 400 years ago, have come to pass. Most of the details he gave were fascinatingly true, including those about Napoleon Bonaparte, Adolf Hitler, John F. Kennedy, etc. A detailed account of the "Further Prophesies of Nostradamus" can be found in the work of Erika Cheetham (4). The most disturbing prophecy of the former is the end of the world in 1999. According to Cheetham (4, 259), those who demonstrated their ability to make valid predictions or prophesies, whether by inspiration or by rational calculations, such as John Dee, Nostradamus, J. W. Dunne, Jean Dixon, Edgar Cayce and H. G. Wells, have not acted as though they believed in total predestination.

On April 15, 1912, the great ship named "Titanic" sank on her maiden voyage from Southampton to New York. About 1500 of the 2,207 passengers and crew on board lost their lives. The Titanic tragedy was seen by a large number of people in various precognitive insights. These were in the form of dreams, trance-like visions or just plain hunches that something sinister would happen to the ship. The most important case of "psychic intuition" about the disaster was the novel entitled *Futility* written by Morgan Robinson in 1898, some fourteen years before it happened. The details given by Robinson in his novel were remarkably close to the actual figures, as if somebody had told him everything from a remote place and from the future. On April 10, 1912 the day the "Titanic" left Southampton Docks, Mrs. Jack Marshall who was viewing the ship's progress from the roof of her house, suddenly told her family members, who were watching with her, in an agitated state, that the ship was going to sink before it reached America. She could see hundreds of people struggling in icy water five days before it actually happened, through her "psychic sense".

Another instance concerning names occurred just before the allied invasion of Europe in 1944. Every aspect of the huge campaign to drive out the Nazis and end the Second World War was a top secret and referred to only through code words. The operation itself was known as OVERLORD. The naval spearhead was disguised by the name NEPTUNE. The two French beaches where the landing was to take place were coded UTAH and OMAHA. And the artificial harbours to be used to supply the troops at the beach-head were known as 'MULBERRY. Incredibly, on the thirty-third day before D-day, June 6th, each of these secret words appeared as an answer to a clue in the London *Daily Telegraph* crossword. The keyword OVERLORD appeared only four days before the landing. Security men immediately descended on the Fleet Street offices of the *Telegraph* expecting to bag a Nazi spy. Instead, they found schoolmaster Leonard Dawe, who had been harmlessly compiling the paper's crosswords for twenty years. Dawe was flabbergasted. It took a long time to convince Security that he had been totally ignorant of the significance of the words. It was the "psychic sense" of Leonard Dawe which allowed retrieval of the code words from the primal source beyond this world. Or, perhaps the "Super Agency" directed these words to Dawe.

There are many cases of automatic writing or trance-like, pre-vision which have been witnessed and recorded over the years. For example, Dr. John Peters, a young medical student in 1956, described the double labelling experiment in biochemistry showing that acetyl-COA is the starting material. This information flashed into his mind through his "psychic sense", when he was sitting with his eyes closed and concentrating to find the answer. His professor rejected the description given by John Peters in the examination script, saying that there was no proof of such an experiment. The biochemists were still in the dark as to which of the 2-carbon molecules was in fact the starting material for fatty acid synthesis. Eight years later it was proven that acetyl-COA was the starting material in the synthesis process. Details of this account and that of the "Titanic" disaster can be found in the work of Danah Zohar (3) along with a large number of cases of precognition.

Professor Rhine reported the case of a man who wanted to undertake a train journey the next day. That night, he saw in a dream that the same train had crashed and he was injured seriously. Alarmed, the man did not take the train journey the following day. Later, he read in the newspaper that the train he intended to board had actually crashed. There are several instances of this kind in which the precognitive warning was received by the subjects in a dream or intuitively. By adhering to the message, they avoided the disaster, although the calamity took place as predicted. For example, a businessman who cancelled his trip on the "Titanic", Susan B. Anthony's dream of the hotel fire, and Mrs. Warren's dream of the vanguard crash (Zohar, 3).

**2. Precognition and Free Will**

A quantum mechanical model of precognition would describe such a situation very well. Among all the possibilities in any set of given circumstances, the most likely one is suggested by precognition. In compatibility with "free will", the subject can make a decision. This choice alters his most likely course of action and thereby avoids the disaster. If the intending traveller had not heeded the precognitive dream, he would have boarded the train the following day, and would have been involved in the disaster as a requirement of his fate.

Fritjof Capra (5) has drawn a remarkable parallel between Eastern mysticism and modern quantum physics. He has shown that the behaviour of the *Atman* (soul), and the electron are exactly similar. As such, the circumstances of the soul, and hence, of the human being, can be judged through the characteristics of the electron. An electron circling around an atomic nucleus in a stable energy state has its whole future before it. On being disturbed, the electron has an unlimited number of possibilities under which it can settle down in the new energy state... and hence a whole new future. Here the electron has the choice under "free will". But, the fact is, more often than not, the electron chooses its old energy state because it is the easiest and it is accustomed to it. This is exactly what happens to human behaviour. Every human being has his own nature and personal characteristics. As such, out of several possibilities, he knowingly chooses that path which is closest to his personal traits and tendencies and his future is predictable. With rare exceptions a human being does not exercise his right of free will, but out of several possibilities open to him, falls back into his patterned life consciously or subconsciously.

Instances like these fit very well with Einstein's four-dimensional space-time continuum which is also in accord with the views of Minkowski, De Sitter, Luigi, Fantapple, Pascal Jordan (Talamonti, 6). The whole history of an event already exists, and each separate stage in that history is represented as a point on a stationary curve. As Leo Talamonti (6) puts it,

> one controversial question is whether the theory suggested above rules out the possibility of free will. Professor Zora considers that it does, but this is to limit ourselves to Euclidean or Cartesian logic. Others, such as Max Planck, take a different view. Precognition does not imply that the will is bound; the future can be observed from the vantage point of higher dimension, but that does not mean we are not free to shape it by our acts. Paradoxical as it may seem, our future acts exist at some distant point of the space-time continuum although our conscious self has not yet performed them and is not aware of them.

Dr. Paul Kammerer, Director of the Institute of Experimental Biology in Vienna, was the first person to conduct a scientific study of coincidences, which taken together, build up the destiny. He published the results (Kammerer, 7) in the book entitled, *Dass Gasetz der Serue* (The law of seriality). For many years he sat in parks, gardens, public toilets, bus stops, etc., observing people and holding conversations with them. He concluded that the results appeared to be the "clusters of numbers", similar to those dealing with probability and statistics. He finally remarked that, "coincidences were merely the tip of an iceberg in a larger cosmic principle, that mankind, as yet, hardly recognizes." He believed that coincidence is a mystery like gravity, and concluded, "we thus arrived at the image of the word's iceberg or kaleidoscope, which, in spite of constant shuffling and the word, also takes care of bringing the like and like together." The German philosopher Arthur Warriewood (1788-1860) believed that coincidences were a reflection of the wonderful pre-established harmony of the universe, conforming to the idea of predestination.

Two most important scholars of the present century, Wolfgang Pauli (1900-1958), the Nobel Prize winner for physics, and the Swiss psychologist-philosopher, Professor Carl Gustave Jung, collaborated in a search for a theory of coincidences. Finally they published their results which was thought by many to be a paranormal equivalent of a nuclear explosion. The summary of their work points out that, "there is a single mysterious force at work in the universe, which is forcing or directing its decisions on human beings, which is beyond the comprehension of the limited human mind."

Such great thinkers, as cited above, appear to finally believe that there is some superhuman intelligence at work somewhere in the universe. As it tends to suggest, human beings have no control on events and happenings; they keep moving like puppets in the hands of destiny.

However, a particular decision or action may be our own choice—cause and effect—but we do not know it. For example, in the words of Rev. John Cobb, Jr. (The Bhaktivedanta Institute, 8),

> Generally the fall or original sin is understood as a restriction upon free will rather an expression of it. What it means is, we find not just that out there in society where there are all these people who are doing things, but that I myself, am not able to attain purity at will. I know that I should love my neighbour as myself, the first time I actually encounter a neighbour and he says something unpleasant to me, I discover that I do not love my neighbour. So it is my lack of free will rather that my free will that is expressed in original sin. If I had a completely free will then I could decide right now, henceforth, I will love my neighbour as myself. That would be free will. So it is the limitation on the freedom of the will that we call 'original sin.

The formula of cause and effect is what makes our destiny fixed. The superhuman intelligence or the single mysterious force perhaps allots a name and the date to be born to the soul, accordingly. However, the laws of material things apply to human nature as well. For example, "empty vessels make much noise." Hence, my suggestion is that Newton's law of motion, "everybody continues in its state of rest or uniform motion, except in so far as it is compelled by some external force to change that state", does also apply to human nature. The course of destiny can be altered with the application of the external force of free will.

The psychic sense is our inherent quality and it normally gives us the pre-warning of events, especially the fateful ones. For example, Julius Caesar, Abraham Lincoln, John F. Kennedy, and

Indira Gandhi, all received pre-warnings of their assassinations. It then depends on the individual soul to use their free will or not, to change the imminent course of its destiny.

### 3. Conclusion

As it appears, the chain of cause and effect makes the destiny of a person—called *karma*—perhaps under the supervision of a single mysterious force in the universe. The psychic sense foretells in many cases the coming future events. Good future events can be confirmed while the bad ones can be altered through the force of free will, if one can have a strong determination to do so. The "psychic sense" in this manner can avoid the imminent catastrophes and make the world a better place to live in. The "psychic sense" can thus be regarded as the sixth sense beyond the normal five ones, which is slowly developing in more and more people around the world.

### References

1. Kumar, Ravindra; *Secrets of Numerology,* Sterling Publishers (P) Ltd., New Delhi, 1992.
2. Edge, M.L. and Morris, R.L.; *Foundations of Parapsychology,* Routledge and Kegan Paul, plc., Boston, 1986.
3. Zohar, Danah; *Through the Time Barrier,* Granada Publishing Ltd., London, 1983.
4. Cheetham, Erika; *Further Prophecies of Nostradamus,* Bantom Books, USA, 1984.
5. Capra, Fritjof; *The Tao of Physics,* New Science Library, Shambhala, Boston, 1985.
6. Talamonti, Leo; *Forbidden Universe,* The Grandstone Press Ltd., London, 1974.
7. Kammerer, Paul, *Dass Gasetz Der Serue,* 1919
8. Institute, The Bhaktivedanta: *Interviews with Nobel Laureates and other Eminent Scholars,* Bombay, 1986.

# 7

# Posthumous Personality, Reincarnation and Liberation

*Life after death is the continuity of personality with memory, character and individuality remaining intact. There is no better understanding of God than here. The soul repeatedly incarnates to learn in the "school of earth" until there is nothing more to learn, then the liberation from the cycle of death and rebirth takes place. The process to liberation is accelerated through spiritual awakening either accidentally or through sustained efforts of yoga.*

**1. Life After Death**

Considerable research has been done on "apparitions" which are thought to be the vehicles through which the "I - thinking consciousness" takes on a personality, perhaps not fully conscious, as well as in a temporarily visible form (Gurney, Myers and Podmore, (1). The apparitions exhibit one or more of the following properties at a time: visual images, noises and voices, tactile sensations, sensation of a presence and communication with the people—according to the 1980's polls in the United States (McAdams and Bayless, (2). Most of these occurrences take place within twelve hours before or after someone's death. Myers (3) in *Human Personality and Survival of Bodily Death* conceived of a "subliminal consciousness" as the basis from which consciousness springs, and survives the body after death. My hypothesis is that the soul continues with its personality after death. It strives hard to regain its physical body in order to express desires and to finish incomplete work. In this endeavour apparitions are a partial success, while a physical birth through the womb of a mother is a more solid success. This chapter attempts to show that in between two successive incarnations the soul expresses itself through various mediums. A series of incarnations take place until all experiences are undergone and all lessons are learned on earth. Upon completion, liberation from the cycle of death and rebirth takes place for more lessons to be learned on higher realms. Some accidental happenings or yogic practices can expedite the process of learning to achieve fast liberation.

Souls attempt to materialize on earth. This indicates that the worlds on higher realms do not have means of self-expression and personal growth, otherwise they would not try to return to earth. Memory, character and individuality remain intact after death. We simply lose control of our physical senses, which then forces us to use our latent, ordinarily inactive spiritual organisms (*Bhagavad Gita,* Reichenbach 4; Lindgren 5).

The above ideas are reinforced by the following examples: Thoughts, desires and emotions of my grandmother were exactly the same even after several years of her death, when I talked to her through an Ouija board; Patience Worth born in 1649, appeared after nearly three centuries in 1913 through automatic writing to a St. Louis housewife, Pearl Curran, dictating 2,500 poems, plays, short stories, allegories, epigrams and six full-length novels filling twenty-nine volumes (Prince 6, Litvag 7); Saints Michael, Catherine and Margaret from higher realms accompanied "Joan of Arc" in spirit form, and their voices, mostly heard in the waking state, sometimes roused Joan from sleep and gave her instructions and predictions. This included her taking up arms like a man, her breaking up the English siege of Orleans, the crowning of Dauphin Charles as King of France, her being wounded in battle, and ensuring that a great victory would be won over the English within seven years (Myers 3).

The deceased has no more understanding of God than the living (Lindgren 5). The invisibles from beyond said, "Their purpose was to prod humankind into devoting more efforts to spiritual growth on earth" (White 8). According to many occultists, incarnation in the flesh provides certain opportunities for spiritual advancement that are lacking on the other side; the opportunities must be seized for spiritual development and freedom from the cycle of death and rebirth. In the previous chapters it has already been pointed out that the "psychic being", which is responsible for spiritual growth, exists only on earth and on no other plane (Aurobindo and Mother).

The spirit of Seth, a widely known entity through channelling, gave the following message:

> Human beings create their own reality through thoughts, actions and beliefs; in effect they are *co-creators of the universe.* Each individual is a multidimensional being, *existing simultaneously in multiple realities. There are no limits to the growth and development of the self.* Human beings incarnate many times. Lives are not a progression of a single incarnation determined by the karma of the preceding life; in fact, there is no karma that punishes or rewards. Rather, *progress of the soul depends on the psychic and spiritual focus of the lives.* Lives grow out of the inner self. They are forms taken by the consciousness expressing itself. The past, present and future exist in a simultaneous now, and we experience all of our lives simultaneously. God is neither male nor female, but is more than the sum total of all the probable systems of reality he has created, and yet He is within each one of those without exception. Human concepts of personality are too limiting to comprehend God's multidimensional existence...I will undermine all religious organizations and set up a new system of thought that will enable each individual to attain intimate contact with his or her reality, the mediator with All That Is. All of this will be accomplished by the year 2075 (Jane Roberts 9).

The above paragraphs confirm the reality expressed in the *Bhagavad Gita* long ago. Souls after death continue to cherish the same feelings and desires while they were in flesh and are in no way close to the understanding of God. Hence, whatever is to be done for spiritual growth and realization of God, should be done in this physical incarnation only. The position earned here will only determine your place in the higher realms of existence.

**2. The Plight of the Soul**

Some spiritual researchers have proposed that between two earthly incarnations, the soul has the cumulative knowledge of all past lives and experiences. With the direction and advice of the Higher Spirits, the soul decides upon its next incarnation to continue the process of learning. A decision is made about being born as a male or female, sage or simpleton, rich or poor, what country to be born in and even the parents. What is not decided is the "Love of God, recognition of the true home as our origin, and the desire to return." This one has to be earned or learned by oneself. Before birth one forgets everything. A new experience on a clean slate begins as if "living in a life-tight compartment".

In support of the above paragraph I quote Jonas (10):

> At the moment of birth, however, when the soul comes to earth, the angel extinguishes the light of knowledge burning above it, and the soul, enclosed in its earthly envelope, enters this world, having forgotten its lofty wisdom, but always seeks to regain it.

According to Allan Kardec of Brazil (Playfair 11, Rogo 12),

> Each birth, however painful, is necessary to enable the soul to improve and eventually attain a higher plane of existence. It may be true that all souls are created equal, ignorant and untested, and *continue coming back to life until they have nothing to learn*....On physical death the soul reviews its past lives, its progress to enlightenment, and *decides which life path to pursue next.* Each soul has a wide latitude in choosing its next life, and often returns to its earthly family.

Sri Harold Klemp (13, 7), the living Eckmaster of Eckankar has a somewhat different hypothesis:

> The negative power, or Satan, is merely an instructor who is in-charge of God's earthly classroom. It's the place

> where the soul gains purification so it may one day reenter the heavenly states of consciousness and become a Co-worker with God. You and I—Soul—were created in the heart of God and put in the lower worlds because we simply would not serve others. We would not give anything in any way, so we came into the lower worlds.

Joan Grant (14), psychically gifted British writer, tapped into past lives through her technique of past life recall, or "far memories". Even as a toddler, she experienced bits and pieces of past lives, four as a male and three as a female emerged during childhood. Later, six biographies of past lives were published (Kelsey and Grant 15). Grace Cooke (16), having learned meditational techniques from an Eastern adept, could rise through her crown *chakra* and read the Akashik records. In the first case she lived in the Mayan civilization some ten thousand years ago. She married her brother Towaan and was initiated by the Plumed Serpent. In her after life she was born as Ra-min-ati in Egypt and was crowned Pharoah with her husband Ra-hotep. Richard Sutphen through past life regression had the memory of his Mayan life where he was killed by Christian invaders (Dick Sutphen 17).

A large number of cases can be found in the works of Edgar Cayce (Guiley 18) where people remembered their past lives through Cayce's past-life-regression method. A variety of cases are represented where the individual could know the reason for a phobia, a fear or a habit in this life, as an event in a previous life. From then on their lives became peaceful and meaningful. Many people could see a chain of past lives resulting in the present life which saw the spiritual unfoldment. For example, Pythagoras and Jiddu Krishnamurti knew all about their past lives. Eastern mysticism provides for past life recall. Patanjali said that all impressions of *karma* exist in the *chitta*, or subconscious mind, and can be *awakened through yoga and meditation.*

In the *Bhagavad Gita* (Prabhupad 19) Krishna says to Arjuna, "Both I and thou have passed through many births; mine are known to me, but thou knowest not of thine." Lord Krishna repeatedly asked Arjuna to become a yogi and take to meditation which was the only way to break the cycle of death and rebirth. On the arousal of the Kundalini successfully, all past *karma* is burnt and there is no need of further earthly incarnation. One gets the freedom from falsehood and the gateway to heaven is opened.

**3. The Ways of Yoga**

The next step is to find the ways and means by which the process of learning can be expedited and *karma* can be burnt. Saints and yogis after persistent research have laid down the disciplines of Yoga for this purpose. The main streams of yoga are *Hatha Yoga, Bhakti Yoga, Karma Yoga* and *Raja Yoga. Hatha Yoga* endeavours to arouse the sleeping serpent power by the force of yogic exercises or physical pressure using penances. There are stories of many *hatha yogis* in India, for example, someone standing on one leg for twenty years. In *Bhakti Yoga* aspirants use extreme devotional practices to worship God and some examples are Meera, Surdas, Kabir and Nanak. In *Karma Yoga,* individuals devote themselves to tireless and selfless service to mankind, i.e., Mahatma Gandhi, Mother Teresa, Martin Luther King, etc. *Gyan Yoga* and *Raja Yoga* are equally very hard practices of mental perfection leading to wisdom and freedom from falsehood. Some of the practitioners are Ramana Maharshi, Swami Vivekananda, Socrates, Richard Maurice Bucke, etc. Each one of these paths is very difficult and hard to perfect for the modern citizens of the world.

Patanjali advocated the eight fold path with the following steps: (1) *Yama*, meaning moral conduct, e.g., non-violence, non-stealing, truthfulness, continence and non-covetousness; (2) *Niyama*, meaning religious observances, e.g., purity of mind and body, contentment, self-discipline, study of scriptures and devotion to God; (3) *Asana*, meaning yogic postures which keep the spine straight and body fit for meditation; (4) *Pranayama*, meaning control of breath and regulations of "Prana", the subtle life energy; (5) *Pratyahara,* meaning the withdrawal of the senses from external objects; (6) *Dharna*, meaning determination; (7) *Dhyana*, meaning meditation; (8) *Samadhi,* meaning final absorption leading to superconscious experience. These eight steps lead to the realization of the truth beyond all intellectual apprehension. Gautam Buddha, after meditating continuously for seven years, got enlightenment and realized the four Noble Truths: (1) Existence is suffering and suffering is unavoidable; (2) suffering is caused by desire; (3) the elimination of desire will bring suffering to an end; (4) there is a means to eliminate desire and thus suffering. The means consists of the Eightfold Path, called the *middle way* between the extremes of asceticism and worldly life: right speech, right conduct, right livelihood, right effort, right mindfulness, right concentration, right views, and right intentions.

*Patanjali, Buddha and Christ have been the greatest yogis on earth after Lord Shiva.* They had a direct communication with God and showed the way to others for the same achievement. Elizabeth Clare Prophet has written and preached about the hidden years of Jesus before his resurrection, in her book *The Lost Years of Jesus* (Prophet 20). Buddhist manuscripts were discovered in 1987 by Nicholas Notowitch, a Russian journalist, which said that Jesus had spent his missing years in India. Prophet has collected some *eyewitness accounts* of travellers who recreated the alleged trek of Jesus to the Himalayas, where he was popularly known as Saint Issa. Kerston Holger in his book, *Jesus Lived in India*, says that "Jesus travelled through India through the silk route at age thirteen. There he lived until the age of 29 and studied Buddhism. Ahmadia Muslims claimed that Jesus survived the crucifixion and later went to the Near East and then to India where he lived to the age of 120 or so. His tomb allegedly exists in Kashmir" (Holger 21).

By saying that "*One who drinks water of this river, will never thirst again*", *Lord Jesus hinted at the arousal of the sleeping power by direct transmission from him (Shaktipat). He was in touch with the sound current (Word or Holy Ghost) which is the direct way to our true home.* Emperor Babar of India took the disease of his son Humayun (father of Akbar the Great) on himself through intense prayer to God. Humayun recovered and Babar died of the same disease. Jesus Christ took on himself the consequences of others' *karma,* especially his disciples. He surrendered to death by crucifixion, which he perhaps could have avoided through his divine powers, if he had wanted to. He cooperated with the law of cause and effect and died. His disciples, however, were purified and received the *Holy Ghost* (*Sound Current*), opening the gate of heaven for them. I have elaborated on the Sound Current (Aum) in detail in Chapter 2.

Swami Satyananda Saraswati (22) has described the various methods of awakening the spiritual power: awakening by birth, *mantra* (repetition of the names of God), *tapasya* (austerities), awakening through herbs, *Raja Yoga* (development of an equipoised mind), *pranayama* (breath control), *Kriya Yoga* (a set of meditative and yogic exercises), *Tantra Yoga*, *shaktipat* (passing of the power by guru), and self-surrender. And then, there are cases of arousal by accident, for example, fear of death when jumping from a plane and the parachute does not open. This is what happened to a woman diver when she suddenly found herself out-of-body, saw herself falling down in the chute but could immediately realise her mistake of not pressing a particular button. She went back into her body, pressed the button, and landed safely. But then she was not the same person. She had tasted the bliss of higher consciousness, and her whole life changed. She devoted the rest of her life in search of God (Klemp 13, 321-322). As another example, the famous actress, Sarah Miles, passed through an emotional turmoil while rehearsing a scene of masturbation for a film in the presence of several males, and experienced the arousal of the sleeping power after the crisis. Several cases of this kind are well described in the book, *The Glimpses of Reality*, edited by Ronald S. Lello.

All the methods of arousing the sleeping serpent power are divided into three main categories: (1) Slow and steady, comparatively mild methods like, *Karma Yoga* and *Bhakti Yoga*; (2) Accidental happenings, which result from a kind of crisis and turmoil; and (3) Scientific and fast methods, which can give results in a couple of years if every thing goes well. These methods include *Kriya Yoga, shaktipat* and *Tantra Yoga.* Methods of the first category are safer, but slow enough to take several lifetimes unless one is as devoted as Meera, Mother Teresa or Mahatma Gandhi. On the methods of the second category, there is no human control since they happen by themselves. However, an accidental happening takes place successfully only in those individuals who are rightly prepared to receive the power, knowingly or unknowingly. The same is true for the fast method of *shaktipat.* Transmission of power to an unprepared individual can result in disorders like paralysis, brain haemorrhage, etc.

The most suited methods for citizens of the modern world are *Kriya Yoga* and *Tantra Yoga,* since people are enmeshed in the world and at the same time want to know God. *Kriya Yoga* involves yogic practices and movement and actions. There are about 76 exercises to be performed in about 2 to 3 hours everyday, along with other daily disciplines. Hence this method may not suit everyone unless one is physically oriented. Paramahansa Yogananda was a successful *Kriya Yogi* (23). The best method is the "Integrated Path" of Kundalini Yoga which takes a bit from every Yoga (briefly introduced in Chapter 2). Divine laws and knowledge are received intuitively with the transformation of the personality. The individual passes through a set of coherent Exceptional Human Experiences as the spiritual energy passes through the seven *chakras* (see chapter 5 for details). However, the end result of power awakening would be the same, by whatever method one achieves it. Nevertheless, the way of Kundalini is perhaps the *shortest path* to God and it is in line with the necessary aspects of the "short path" elaborated in Chapter 2. According to Agehananda Bharati (24) the *tantrics* agree that their specific method is dangerous, and radical, even though they all claim that it is a short-cut to liberation. However, *Tantra* is included as one of the elements in Kundalini Yoga, and as such is no longer dangerous.

In the opinion of Paramahansa Yogananda (23, 226),

> A true yogi may remain dutiful in the world; there he is like butter on water, and not like unchurned, easily diluted milk of undisciplined humanity. Fulfilling one's earthly responsibilities

need not separate a man from God, providing one maintains mental uninvolvement with egotistical desires and plays his part in life as a willing instrument of the Divine.

## References


1. Gurney, Edmund; Myers, F.W. H. and Podmore, Frank; *Phantasms of the Living,* Kegan Paul, Trench, Trubner & Co., London, 1918 and 1986.
2. McAdams, Elizabeth E. and Bayless, Raymond; *The Case for Life After Death,* Nelson Hall, Chicago,1981.
3. Myers, W.W.Fredric; *Human Personality and It's Survival After Death,* Volumes 1&2, Longmans, Green & Co., New York, New Ed., 1954.
4. Reichenbach, B.A.; Hypnosis: An Empirical Evaluation, *JRPR*, Oct, 1994.
5. Lindgren, C.E., Scientific Investigation and Religious Uncertainty, *JRPR*, April 1994.
6. Prince, Walter Franklin; *The Case of Patience Worth,* Boston Society for Psychical Research, Boston, 1972.
7. Livag, Irving: *Singer in the Shadows: The Strange Story of Patience Worth,* Macmillan, New York, 1972.
8. White, Steward Edward; *The Betty Book: Excursions into the World of Other Consciousness,* Berkley Medallion Books, New York, 1969.
9. Roberts, Jane; *Seth Speaks: The Eternal Validity of the Soul,* Prentice Hall, Englewoods Cliffs, NJ, 1972.
10. Jonas, H.; *The Gnostic Religion,* Beacon Press, Boston, 1958, p. 113.
11. Playfair,Guy Lyon; *The Unknown Powers,* Pocket Books, New York, 1975.
12. Rogo, D. Scott; *The Infinite Boundary,* Dodd, Mead & Co., New York, 1987.
13. Klemp, Harold; *How to Find God,* Eckankar, Minneapolis, MN, 1988, p.7.
14. Grant, Joan: *Far Memory,* Harper & Row, New York,1956.
15. Kelsey, Denys and Grant, Joan; *Many Life Times,* Doubleday & Co., Garden City, New York, 1967.
16. Cooke, Grace; *The Illumined Ones,* White Eagle Trust, New Lands, England, 1966.
17. Sutphen, Dick: *Past Lives, Future Loves,* Pocket Books, New York, 1978.

18. Guiley, Rosemary Ellen; *Tales of Reincarnation,* Pocket Books, New York, 1989.
19. Prabhupad, A.C. Bhaktivedanta, *Bhagavad-Gita As It Is,* Bhaktivedanta Book Trust, New York, 1969, 1972.
20. Prophet, Elizabeth Claire; *The Lost Years of Jesus,* Summit University Press, Livingstone, MT, 1984.
21. Holger, Kersten; *Jesus Lived in India,* Elements Book Ltd., Longmead, Dorset, England, 1986.
22. Saraswati, Swami Satyananda; *Kundalini Tantra,* Bihar School of Yoga, Munger, Bihar, India, 1984.
23. Yogananda, Paramahansa; *Autobiography of a Yogi,* Jaico Publishing House, Bombay, India 1986.
24. Bharti, Agehananda; *The Tantric Tradition,* Doubleday, NY, 1975.

# 8

# Factors that Assist and Catalyse Kundalini

*Factors which assist and act as catalysts in the process of Self/God-realization are: (1) One-pointed concentration on the highest goal, (2) The speeding up of events in everyday life, (3) Loneliness and intense love, (4) Shunning siddhis or miraculous powers, as and when they manifest. Accumulated karma from the past is precipitated to the surface for annihilation by Kundalini, with the advancement on the path.*

**1. Little Goals are Dry Runs**

A single-pointed mind is very necessary to reach the state of Self-realisation. When someone has the highest goal of all in mind—aspiration for the God state—then little goals are dry runs. Unless the whole heart is put into it, the attention may slip at any time and one may lose the goal.

Understand that the Masters have been giving lessons to the disciples in many different ways. The oldest I remember is from the time of the *Mahabharata*. Guru Dronacharya was teaching "Shooting with arrows" to the Pandava and Kaurava brothers. Each time an aspirant wanted to shoot, the Guru asked, "What do you see on the tree?" The aspirant said, "I can see the bird on the tree, the palace behind the tree and tasty food being placed on the table for our breakfast." The Guru replied, "You will not be able to shoot the bird successfully." The aspirant attempted and missed the target. Everyone had his attention somewhere else, and failed to hit the target. When Arjun aimed at the bird, Guru asked the same question. Arjun replied, "I can see only the eye of the bird on the tree, there is nothing else around." Guru said, "You will be successful." In fact, Arjun was the only one who shot the target correctly (*Mahabharat*).

Harold Klemp was about to win the table-tennis tournament, while serving as an airman in Japan. At the last point, the door at the rear of the auditorium banged open, and an airman entered with a huge trophy in his arms. Klemp's eyes opened wide at the huge symbol of triumph. His concentration was broken, his serve missed the table, and he lost the game, which he was about to win. After this lesson, taught to him by his Guru Mahanta, he did not let the God-consciousness slip through his hands when the right moment come. The lesson was: never to give up the precious dream, never to look aside, and always to face God (Klemp 1, 16-17).

Most of the people who achieved success on the path of God outwardly, never cared for a degree, honour, wealth or high official positions in life. Consequently, they remained mediocre individuals in life, since their mind was always towards the highest goal of Self-realization. Jiddu Krishnamurti, although so successfully groomed by Annie Besant and Leadbeater, could not graduate from a college in England. Gopi Krishna never cared to pass his departmental examination, and remained an ordinary clerk in his office throughout his life. Bhaduri Mahasaya had forsaken great family wealth in his early childhood, when single-mindedly he had entered the yogic path (Yogananda 2, 60).

Emmanuel Swedenborg received illumination at the age of 54. Immediately, he resigned from his government job and retired on a half-pension so that he could devote all his waking and sleeping hours to further spiritual explorations (Swedenborg 3). David Spangler was a student at Arizona State University in Tempe, studying for a degree in genetics. He received a strong inner calling to go in a different direction, and he dropped out. He then lectured, gave counselling services and authored several books on spiritual findings (Spangler 4). Dr. B. Goel took voluntary retirement in his early fifties from NCERT, New Delhi, soon after his experience with the Kundalini (Goel 5). He then authored several books on spiritual teachings and established an ashram near Delhi.

Buddha slipped out of his palace, full of riches and comforts, at the age of twenty-nine in search of truth and knowledge. He met many hermits, yogis and Brahmins, but none could provide him the enlightenment he sought. His awakening came when he meditated by himself for seven years. Dr. B. S. Goel also went around in search of yogis for several years without success, until his own meditation led him to the Kundalini awakening and knowledge through intuition. Dr Richard Maurice Bucke, who was always engrossed in thoughts of God, suddenly received enlightenment through an encounter with Light. He received so much knowledge intuitively, in a few seconds, that any amount of books studied for any number of years would not have given him (Bucke 6). The point emerging here is that knowledge and truth come only intuitively and you need one-pointed concentration for the same. Either a person is fully involved in the path of God from the beginning or an "inner calling" comes to him at a certain stage in life; then he must leave every other interest behind and devote himself single-mindedly to God. During meditation, or otherwise, you feel a single big eye is constantly watching you. I have felt it many times during the course of these years. This is the stage in life when you cannot serve two interests at the same time. Living the usual chores of worldly life becomes very difficult, if not impossible. For example, heavy lectures on mathematics which I used to remember by heart and deliver in the classroom, were not the same again. The mind refuses to take heavy calculations. Instead, you have to write them down on paper. The mind also refuses to cooperate in administrative duties because its attention is somewhere else. In fact, a person at this stage is no longer fit to live in the society of this material world. It was at this stage that Swedenborg and Goel took voluntary retirement from government jobs so they could achieve the single-pointed mind to receive the full intuitive knowledge of God. Claire Walker in her article "Long-term Effects of One-time Psychic Experiences" presents the case of Professor Wills Herman and Olympic heavyweight champion, George Foreman, who took immediate retirement from the "worldly life of competition" after their EHE (Walker 7).

Seven out of twelve points emphasised by Pythagoras recommend *silence* for five years from which most of the virtues towards Self-realization emerge. Baba Haridass of Mount Madonna Yoga Center in California has been observing silence for the past several years. Naturally, remaining silent for such a long period of time prevents one from working on a job or participating in social activities during or after the period of silence. However, you might, of course, have significantly advanced on the path of Self/God-realization during silence, and after seeing the bliss of the highest order, you may not care for the social pleasures of the world.

Pythagoras said, "Tread the unfrequented ways." He introduced the symbol -ɡ- which means: "The life of worldly achievements" and the "life of spiritual achievements" do not go together. Priority should be given to one or the other. You may live in the world, without competition and attachment, just to earn your living, without any goal of a material nature. The only goal one should have in mind, day or night, is the goal of God-realization—undeterred by the honours or dishonours in any manner whatsoever. Saint Kabir said that one should listen to the insulting and abusive words of others without being affected and should live in the state of poverty. Most of the poems of Saint Kabir reverberate on one central idea: "God is realized only in the state of poverty." And this is what Jesus Christ meant when he said, *'It is easier for a camel to go through a needle's eye than for a rich man to enter into the Kingdom of God."* Perhaps, when you possess more than what you need, corruption enters your life in some way, on one hand, and the highest goal slips off the mind, on the other.

**2. The Speeding-up of Karma**

When a person is reaching an advancement in spiritual life, two phenomena are clearly noticed: Activities start accelerating, and repeatedly the aspirant comes across the environment and circumstances with ever-new problems to be sorted out. Before the person crosses the line of "no return to the physical world" all one's *karma* stored from the previous lifetimes, start precipitating and coming to the surface for annihilation. Only the pure being, the gold that has passed through the severe fire, gets the permit to go across.

In the words of Harold Klemp,

> Paul Twitchell (the previous leader and founder of Eckankar) said he went to Sudar Singh (the Master from India) because he wanted to learn about Eckankar. He decided to devote his entire life to the teachings of Eckankar and making them available to anybody who wanted to know about them. As soon as he made his commitment, *everything went wrong in his life. He thought he had troubles before--but he had not seen anything yet !* When an individual comes close to the spiritual path or the Master, the spiritual currents are stirred up and the karma that has built up from past centuries begins to work up to the surface in the form of problems. These problems are trying to keep us from the path, but they also serve a useful purpose. By overcoming the blocks, we develop the spiritual strength necessary to take the first step on any path of truth (Klemp 8, 244).

The poet, Saint Surdas of India, after Self-realization, settled in a comfortable accommodation, and was provided with all the necessities along with servants to look after him, by a rich devotee. The very first night Lord Krishna appeared to him in a vision in which He ridiculed him and said, "So your search for the highest position has come to an end?" Surdas understood the warning and left the place the following morning. Once again he was roaming in the streets with the continuous chanting of the names of God. There is "always one more step", as has been rightly said by many realized people, including Gopi Krishna and Harold Klemp.

"God-realization, I found, was simply a gateway to new unfoldment: but beyond that gate, things ran in very high gear" (Klemp 1, 251). "The karmic pattern of life speeds up. All of a sudden your life becomes very active and very interesting and you cannot put your finger on the exact cause of it" (Klemp 8, 159).

This is what has been happening to me for more than two decades. Almost every two years my job has changed from one country to another—India, UK, Iraq, Nigeria, Zimbabwe, Ethiopia, Fiji, Tanzania, USA and now Denmark. Every time a new home is established. Repeatedly the same problems and difficulties occur in a new environment. I wonder, why can't I remain peacefully in one place? None the less, many lessons are learned first-hand—humility, patience, tolerance, forgiveness, and compassion. New relationships are made each time and are easily left behind. The lesson you learn is "non-attachment". You are always alert, waiting for the next experience.

Back at home you may find many emotional problems coming to the surface: division of property, money and other possessions. You are required to show in practice your detachment from material possessions and an equal attitude towards all without exception. You have to tolerate undiplomatic language and show your control of anger. Nature provides you with an accelerated chance of conquering the five enemies—greed, lust, anger, attachment and ego. This is the way to spiritual perfection—but there is always one more step to it.

### 3. Aloneness and Desire for Love

These are two important factors which are generally found in the people following a spiritual path. Aloneness is obvious since such people are normally out of the common masses who waste most of their time in satisfying worldly desires. A spiritually inclined person finds himself alone—even in the most crowded places. If such a person talks about the bliss he has tasted beyond any material pleasure, the result is twofold—a group of individuals believe him and may desire to become his followers so they can experience this bliss; or people are non-believers, and ridicule him on matters of which they know nothing, thereby becoming enemies. Naturally, if the enlightened one has ideas/wisdom/knowledge that contradicts those of the non-believers, their goal will be to get rid of him because their personalities are being down-graded. In fact, if there is a group of overwhelmingly jealous people, they will more than likely remove the spiritual person from the scene. One has greater security, if there is no competition. This is how Buddha was served with poisonous mushrooms when he was eighty. He knew instantly that he was going to die and he conveyed his last message to his disciples. Swami Dayanand Saraswati, founder of the Arya Samaj in India was served with finely-ground powdered glass in milk by a prostitute, and he eventually died.

Pythagoras was assassinated when he was ninety-nine years of age while still in the prime of his life. Socrates was persecuted and condemned to death. Jesus Christ was crucified, as we all know. The great Muslim preacher, Mansur, was put to death by the followers of the king. Personalities like Rama and Krishna always had a group of assassins threatening them but they could not be harmed because they were too strong. In general, you can see that anyone talking about the truth can cultivate believers and associates. By the same token, others may abuse the enlightened one or even perpetrate his demise.

However, aloneness is necessary for spiritual development. The spiritual forces become active inside and outside of you, when you are isolated. Cases of clairvoyance, telepathy, levitation and soul travel or out-of-body experiences are manifested when you are alone. Solitude is the key to spiritual unfoldment, although it may be bitter and difficult to embrace. This is why Pythagoras said, "Tread the unfrequented ways." Another option is *satsang*, associating with God-intoxicated people, where the spiritual development accelerates. Hence, you should be either alone or in the presence of people who are on the path of God.

Desire for love—both giving and taking—is of very high intensity among those on a spiritual path. Saint Tulsidas was madly in love with his wife. When she left for her parents' house located in another town, Tulsidas soon followed. She felt embarrassed and commented, "If you would have loved God with the same intensity, you would have found Him by now." These words shot like an arrow in the heart of Tulsidas. Thereafter he completely forgot about his wife, fell in love with God and eventually found Him.

> Paul Twitchell became a member of the Catholic Church in 1961, several years after his experience with God in 1957, which was recorded in his book, *Tiger's Fang.* This was later attributed to a woman. Love was the motivating force. Paul knew that somewhere there was a female who would help him with his mission. He looked for love and when it came, he loved sincerely. But for one reason or another his relationships always ended with heartaches on both sides. After Paul left Swami Premananda's church in Washington, D.C., he fell in love with a woman named Pat. She soon rejected him and moved to Florida. Paul continued to write her letters from his home in Maryland, trying to keep a hold on her...No matter who you are, you need love. If you cannot love another person or pet, at least you can love yourself. Even the egotist has a place in the world...I do not know how to say it better, but the force of love has to be somewhere in one's life. Love of a human is necessary before one can understand Divine love (Klemp 9, 10).

Love of Meera for Krishna, Tulsidas and Hanuman for Rama, poets Surdas and Rahim for Krishna, Ramakrishna for Mother Goddess, Vivekananda for Guru, Jesus, Socrates and Pythagoras for the Father in Heaven; Mansur, Firdaus and Rumi for Allah are examples of love that crossed all boundaries and eventually united the seekers with God. Countless incidences of this kind can be quoted from East to West, and among all possible cultures from time immemorial.

Thus, "aloneness and love" are two essential factors on the path of God. Currently we even find ourselves repeatedly thrown into circumstances where we have to be alone, yet must find an outlet for love. We sometimes feel surprised and astounded when we look in retrospect at what has been happening to us. The following two paragraphs will illustrate the prominence of solitude and love, respectively, in the life of spiritual seekers.

From ancient Abyssinia, presently Ethiopia, Towart Mangi says,

> To understand being alone in the true sense, is to unlock one of the greatest mysteries of and keys to the heavens...When

> isolation strikes the heart, it is a sign that the soul is being brought to another test and crossroad of life. The question arises: Will the individual drop the state of consciousness that is causing the aloneness, brought on by the Divine Spirit, allowing its loving hand to caress the heart; or will he seek refuge and comfort from the ruthlessness of Spirit through the material worlds. Each time the despair came over me, the Spirit was handing me a choice. I could choose to indulge myself in the loneliness and wallow in it, which would not have done my situation any good, or I could set my pain aside and look to what the Spirit was trying to express to me...all hopes of happiness seemed to be gone for ever. Then I heard its sweet melody--the sound of the flute--sharply singing in my head. Immediately, the pain and despair left me; instantly, I understood loneliness. The dull pain of isolation was caused by the tight grasp with which I held onto the things of my past, which previously provided me happiness. I had lost all material joys of that lifetime. However, by accepting the greater joys of the Spirit, I was able to accept the universal love of life--even for those who were my captors. In doing so, the fist that tightly held at my heart, loosened its grip, enabling me to become one with the Spirit. Ultimately, we face Sugmad (God) alone. It is only while alone that we void ourselves of that which we would grasp and cling to, in hopes of gaining happiness. And it is only when we are empty and alone that we can open ourselves entirely to the outpouring of the Spirit. When loneliness appears in its foreboding, hooded shroud, know that with it will come a new fulfilment of love and light (Morimitsu 10, 14-17).

In the words of Eckmaster,

> There comes a time in the soul's journey through the lower worlds that the instinctive love and desire for home, for Sugmad (God), is incorporated into the lower manifestations, which is to mate with the opposite sex. There is no need to deny or suppress these drives. Recognize with the clear eyes of the Soul what its true wants are. Just remember, the soul's

true quest is to become the lover of God. The love between man and woman is an aspect of this God love. The love of God is the true love from the beginning of time (Morimitsu 10, 145).

**4. Siddhis (Miraculous Powers)**

In the words of Gopi Krishna:

> Siddhis are very rarely met with, in those who practice the system of Yoga advocated by Patanjali or even other systems. Out of millions who practise Raja Yoga, Bhakti Yoga, Karma Yoga, Jnana Yoga, Dhyana Yoga, or Hatha Yoga all over the world, how many are there who can claim to have gained siddhis or miraculous gifts? Out of these who make the claim, how many are prepared to have their claims verified in a laboratory? If there are few it means that the *possession of siddhis is a rare achievement, not possible for millions who practise yoga or other religious disciplines.* In almost all cases of genius and psychic powers, the gift is inborn, being a part of the natural mental endowment of a human being. It is only in extremely few cases, if any at all, that the gifts have been cultivated (Krishna 11).

However, there are certain paranormal powers which manifest themselves temporarily during the process of "Kundalini awakening", for example, clairvoyance, psychic healing, and soul travel or out-of-body experiences. Emannuel Swedenborg saw a house burning 300 miles away from him exactly at the time of incident. Lawrence LeShan developed the power of psychic healing which he uses to heal people at times. Almost everyone on successful meditation has out-of-body experiences as proof of the Self being a soul, provided by nature. Enough has been said about soul-travel in earlier chapters (Kumar 12, 13, 14), where I have also recorded my own out-of-body experiences and other brief encounters with the paranormal during the process of Kundalini awakening. Dr. B. S. Goel once experienced driving for several miles with closed eyes after his Kundalini awakening (Goel 5).

Now there are two approaches—a seeker for the highest goal of God-realization does not pay any attention to the manifestation of these powers, while some people start developing these abilities as a goal. Those who take interest in these capabilities do achieve success in different degrees, but they are arrested at that level. They never come close to God-realization. I can cite examples of two advanced civilizations which were doomed for these reasons—the kingly race of Ravana at the time of Lord Rama, and Atlantis, which was submerged under water before the present civilization of the world came into existence, more than ten thousand years ago.

Ravana was the king of Lanka, at the time of the *Ramayana,* the holy scripture of Hindus. He and his people in the kingdom acquired many miraculous paranormal powers, but they were used for material gains only. The whole race was annihilated in the war by Lord Rama.

As for Atlantis, we have in the words of Master Decates of Eckankar:

> In her greatest times Atlantis knew many airships. Yes, she even colonized many distant planets, including the moon...The priests were highly developed in the art of soul-travel. Then the basic nature of man began to make inroads into their consciousness. At first, they used soul-travel to uncover the useful secrets of the universe for mankind. This was done for fair payment. But with the human consciousness, greed stepped in. The priests slipped from the high form of soul-travel to the lower forms of mental and astral travels. The priests found that for a little more money or other substance, they could perform personal favors. Then the personal favors became corrupt by invading the invisible spaces of others. Payment for these services became more degenerate and vile. The whole planet suffered for these actions. First was the loss of all technology. By using mental and astral travel, the priests found little for going to distant places in the physical for knowledge. They began manifesting materials out of the ethers. This weakened the balance of the material worlds and

> earth's aura weakened. Colonies established on other planets were abandoned or destroyed. Knowledge of the ancient art of soul-travel was turned from its proper purpose. The lower forms of astral and mental travel were used solely for material and selfish gain. The goals of truth and the return to Sugmad (God) were ignored. This brought about the end (Morimitsu 10, 269-271).

Once a yogi boastfully demonstrated his art of levitation, which was the result of his whole life's dedication. He crossed the river by levitating himself in the presence of Buddha. To this Buddha said, "You have wasted this lifetime without any achievement. You could have paid half a rupee to the boatman and he could have taken you across the river."

Some people use their paranormal gift to communicate with the spirits of dead friends and relatives. But this is discouraged by Spiritualists in favour of contact with highly evolved entities and Spiritual Masters (Gauld 15). One step further, Jiddu Krishnamurti dissuaded contact with any entity or Master in favour of a direct relationship with the "Formless Ultimate Reality". Paul Twitchell of Eckankar also advised keeping the attention on the Highest, that is Sugmad (God); the lower contacts and experiences will follow automatically when necessary. So where do you focus your interest? And how do you do it? Krishnamurti reached his state of awareness after the arousal of Kundalini which he experienced in 1922 (Jaykar 16).

The whole Kundalini Yoga never talks about any paranormal powers, and although some of them manifest spontaneously, they go unattended. Soul-travel, for example, takes place at a stage for Self-realization, not for cultivation as an art. Computers are used for the advancement of mathematical theory but a mathematician need not indulge in computer games for fun. One and only one goal of God-realization can bring God-realization, nothing short of it.

## References

1. Klemp, Harold; *Child in the Wilderness,* Eckankar, Minneapolis, MN, 1989.
2. Yogananda, Paramahansa; *The Autobiography of a Yogi,* Jaico Publishing House, Bombay, 1986.
3. Swedenborg, Emmanuel; *Divine Love and Wisdom,* American Swedenborg Printing and Publishing Society, New York, 1894, 1963.
4. Spangler, David; *Emergence: The Rebirth of the Sacred,* Dell, New York, 1984.
5. Goel, Dr.B.; *Third Eye and Kundalini,* Third Eye Foundation of India, New Delhi, 1985.
6. Bucke, Richard Maurice; *Cosmic Consciousness,* Dutton & Co., USA, 1901, 1966.
7. Walker, Claire; *Annual Conference Proceedings,* April, 1992, pp. 127-128.
8. Klemp, Harold; *How to find God,* Eckankar, Minneapolis, MN, 1988.
9. Klemp, Harold; *Cloak of Consciousness,* Eckankar, Minneapolis, MN, 1991.
10. Morimitsu, Phil; *In the Company of Eckmasters,* Eckankar, Minneapolis, MN, 1987.
11. Krishna, Gopi; *Kundalini—The Evolutionary Energy in Man,* Shambhala Publications, Boulder, Colorado, 1967.
12. Kumar, Ravindra; "The Journey Back to our True Home—Part-I", *JRPR,* USA, January 1994.
13. Kumar, Ravindra; "The Journey Back to our True Home—Part-II", *JRPR,* USA, April 1994.
14. Kumar, Ravindra; "The Journey Back to our True Home—Part-III", *JRPR,* USA, July 1994.
15. Gauld, Alan; *The Founders of Psychical Research,* Routledge & Kegan Paul, London, 1968.
16. Jaykar, Pupul; *Krishnamurti: A Biography,* Harper & Row, San Francisco, 1986.

# 9

# Self-realization and the Direct Feeling of God

*The following questions are the concern of this chapter: What do we understand from self-realization? What is the cosmic empire of endless bliss? What is the direct feeling of God? It seems to me that the universe is divided into various planes/heavens with increasing degrees of refinement and subtlety. The highest plane is the "nameless plane" where the Ultimate Reality--God - resides. At the end of evolution the Soul sees itself as a formless, and infinite being full of bliss and knowledge. God is omnipresent as Light and Sound, which is the direct feeling of It.*

### 1. Evolution and Self-Realization

What is the cause of cosmic illusion in which the soul finds itself? How did the formless, infinite, eternal Soul come to experience itself as having shape and being finite? Saints have endeavoured to answer these queries in the following manner.

The soul must assume some vehicle (as its medium) for experiencing the world. The degree and kind of consciousness are determined by the nature of the form which it used as a medium (Meher Baba 1, Vol. II, 140; Holcombe, *JRPR*, Oct. 1994, 227). Beginning with the most partial, rudimentary and most undeveloped form (e.g., that of a stone), the evolution began. The soul assumed higher and higher forms according to the momentum which consciousness received owing to the conservation of the impressions (*sanskars*) left by diverse desires and conditions. Thus it appears that the soul moved from stone to more evolved structural elements like metal, vegetable, worm, fish, bird, animal, until eventually it assumed a human form, in which it has developed full consciousness (in all the aspects of knowing, feeling and willingness) of the gross world. The evolution of configurations, therefore, comes to an end with the attainment of the human form.

> If a man desires to become a king, for example, he can only experience this by actually donning kingly garbs and going to the stage. This is true of aspirations and desires, which can only be worked out and fulfilled by bringing about an actual change in the entire situation, as well as the medium, through which the event may be adequately experienced. To experience the sanskars cultivated in the human form, the soul has to *incarnate* again and again in physical bodies. The innumerable human vehicles, through which the soul has to pass, are determined by the laws of karma, or the nature of previous sanskars (i.e., whether of virtue or vice, happiness or misery etc.). During these lives, the soul, which is eternal, *identifies itself with the gross body*, which is destructible (Meher Baba 1, Vol. II, 142).

Ultimately,

> each spirit soul graduates from the path and does not need to reincarnate anymore (Rev. 3; 10-12), it is permanentized, having demonstrated that it is able to live in three dimensional planes without giving up its spirituality, the required character. Thus one's objective is to seek permanence with the ability to move into whatever material planes are available in the entire universe. Returning here at the will of the Lord, or even at one's own desire, providing it is known to be permissible, or even mandated, to help others along the way (Holcombe, *JRPR*, Oct. 1994, 228).

According to many saints, the soul simultaneously develops the subtle and mental bodies, while developing full consciousness of the gross world. It becomes conscious of these bodies and the corresponding worlds only when its full consciousness turns inwards, i.e., towards itself. When the soul is conscious of the subtle world through the subtle body, it identifies itself with this body. When it is conscious of the mental world through the mental body, it identifies itself with the latter, just as it identifies itself with the gross body when it is conscious of the gross world through the gross body.

In summary, the homeward journey of the soul consists in freeing itself from the illusion of being identical with its bodies—gross, subtle, and mental. With attention turning inward for self-realization, the *sanskars* and desires disappear and the veil of cosmic illusion is pierced. In the words of Meher Baba (1, Vol. II, 144):

> The soul ceases to identify its self with any of the three bodies which it had to develop for evolving full consciousness. Now it not only knows itself to be formless and beyond all the bodies of the world, but also realizes with full consciousness its own unity with the Oversoul, which is One, Indivisible, Real and Infinite. In this knowingness it enjoys infinite bliss, peace, power and knowledge, which are characteristics of the Oversoul. At this stage, the soul completely transcends the phenomenal world and becomes Self-Conscious and Self-Realized.

To reiterate the words of Saint Asaramji, (2, 5):

> Paramatma is the source of cosmic energy which activates our consciousness. That consciousness sees the world through our senses. That consciousness makes the world of dreams in Hita nerve. That consciousness in paralytic state is converted into deep sleep. Attainment of Atma-Paramatma or awareness or knowledge of It for even three minutes by someone will not let one suffer the agony of being in the womb of a mother again. One becomes a liberated soul.

The witnessing of Its formless state, by the soul, is termed the state of Self-realization or attainment of the God-state. Before achieving this goal, the soul has to pass through the gross, subtle and mental planes, which may be collectively called the Cosmic empire.

**2. The Cosmic Empire**

Bhaduri Mahasaya was a levitating saint of India who had forsaken great family wealth in his early childhood, when he had single-mindedly entered the yogic path. When a student commented on his renouncing riches and comforts to seek God and to teach them wisdom, the saint said with a mild rebuke on his face:

> You are reversing the case. I have left a few paltry rupees, a few petty pleasures, for a cosmic empire of endless bliss. How then have I denied myself anything? I know the joy of sharing the treasure. Is that a sacrifice? The short-sighted worldly folk are verily the renunciates! They relinquish an unparalleled divine possession for a poor handful of earthly toys (Yogananda 3, 62).

He further said, "The divine order arranges our future more wisely than any insurance company." Now let us explore the depth of his statements.

As several saints, for example, Kabir, Muktananda, Nanak and Harold Klemp have verbalized, the cosmic empire of endless bliss is divided into various planes. Beyond the physical plane of this world we come across the astral plane, causal plane, mental plane, etheric plane and finally the soul plane. The soul plane is the dividing plane between the lower planes and the real spiritual planes, where for the first time the soul sees itself as the dimensionless point of existence. The spiritual realms have several divisions, gradually increasing in order of refinement, until we arrive at the plane of "Ultimate Reality". The hierarchy of planes can be found in many texts, for example, in the works of Dr. Chaturbhuj Sahai (4), Thurman (5), Stephen O'Brien (6), and Prabhupad (7).

The various planes in the *Bible* have been referred to as heavens. The book of Enoch lists heavenly levels above the earth plane, with Michael the Archangel as Prince of the seventh and highest plane (Holcombe, *JRPR*, April 1994, 96). Thus, St. Paul stated that he had been stuck in the third heaven, that is, the mental plane. Saint Kabir of India travelled far beyond the soul plane and divided the whole cosmos into more that twelve divisions. Mohammad had an encounter with a subtle being, perhaps in the etheric plane. Lord Jesus clearly said, "There are many mansions in my Father's house," meaning thereby, various heavens or planes. Swami Muktananda (8) has described his journeys to various planes in the book, *The Play of Consciousness.* Sri Harold Klemp and successful followers of Eckankar perform soul journeys to various heavens in the dream state. Yogis and adepts in meditation travel to numerous planes in the state of trance. Emannuel Swedenborg got an abrupt illumination at the age of 54, when he travelled to several spiritual planes and talked with Jesus and God (Swedenborg 9). I have described my journeys to these planes in Chapter 5.

Our immediate neighbour of the physical plane we live on, is the astral plane, which appears to have extremely large dimensions. People after death from physical planes like ours, reside in the *Astral Plane* in astral bodies which are similar to our current bodies. They build houses, make colonies, and create things with the power of thoughts, their eating/drinking habits continue from the physical life and ideas/interests remain the same. Slowly they realize it is not necessary to eat and drink for their sustenance. This is the upper part of astral plane or heaven where people live happily. In the lower sector of the astral plane, people remain dissatisfied. For gratification they continue to visit and interact with people who have physical bodies until they realize the futility of it. Conditions of hell constitute many discontented and unhappy people who live in groups with the same mindset.

A large number of books are available providing descriptions of the astral planes, good or bad. These publications are written by saints, yogis, mediums and NDE-researchers, as an authentic account of their findings. I can validate their stories through my personal experiences of visiting several astral colonies in my astral body. I could fly over them, descend down on land and talk to someone, interact with them and take off again to the sky. Some good books I can recommend are the works of Muktananda (8), Yogananda (3), Swain (10), Prabhupad (7), Twitchell (11), O'Brien (12), Moody (13), Garrett (14), Roberts (15), Klemp (16), and Morimitsu (17). Of course, an earlier and more authentic account had been given by C. W. Leadbeater in one of his books, entitled, *The Astral Plane* (18).

The next plane on the ladder is the *Mental Plane* which is more refined and subtle. It contains all the ideas/forms that have ever existed or will ever come to exist on any of the physical worlds like ours. Masterpieces of every prose piece or poetry by William Wordsworth, Tennyson or Rabindranath Tagore have come from this plane. Many times in a trance or during meditation or in the twilight period before or after sleep, I have had glimpses of rows of beautiful flowers in magnificent colours which you never see on earth. I have also seen elaborate gardens, unusual buildings and fairy-like people which have been described in prize-winning verses and poems all over the world.

Next to the mental plane in the hierarchy is the *Causal Plane,* where the causes to all effects are found in storage. You can call it the library of Akashic-records. When Pythagoras saw his ninety-nine thousand incarnations in a row, he was in connection with the cosmic library at the causal plane. All saints and mediums are in touch with this library whenever they want to know about the past. One can acquire skills to allow a connection with this library. Similarly, you find museums full of future scientific researches and inventions yet to be made. When a scientist, a poet, a writer, etc., pauses for a moment to get ideas, one is in touch with this museum in a trance-like state for a few moments. The intuitive ideas flow into the mind, creating an invention on the physical plane of a model which already exists on the causal plane. That is why we do not really invent new creations on earth. All spiritual Masters have repeatedly advised us to transcend this world of scientific toys.

Going further we find the *Etheric Plane* which has very fine vibrations. This is the home of etheric bodies which we all possess. It is from this realm that the Holy Sound/Word/*Aum*/

*Kalma-i-Ilahi* or *Shabad* originates and is heard through one's inner ears on successful meditation (refer to Chapter 2). The emanating sound can be like the "buzzing of bees".

The Etheric Plane and the next, the *Soul Plane* are the residences of the lower world's creators. The Masters on these realms, who are the co-workers with God, have been described in the form of the Holy Trinity by most religions. For example, Hindus call them Brahma-Vishnu-Mahesh, while the Christians call them, Father-Son-Holy Ghost (Holcombe, *JRPR*, April 1994, 94). Perhaps, similar names can be found in other religions. The Trinity is Creator-Sustainer-Destroyer. The Sound which emanates from this heaven is a sharp and piercing single note, like that of a flute. We hear it through inner ears in conjunction with the blue light or pearl seen through inner eyes. This Light and Sound are the twin pillars of God which are experienced and described by all saints and prophets. Most of the references cited in this chapter talk about this twin aspect of God. This subject will be covered in the next section of this chapter.

From the soul plane upwards are the Spiritual Planes. They belong to the state of Seeing-Knowing-Being, and are hard to describe. Most of the successful people on a spiritual path with an awakened Kundalini or who are under the guidance of a living Master or Guru, arrive straight on the Soul Plane from the physical plane. They have qualified to bypass the intermediate planes. At this stage the aspirant is halfway home to God (Klemp 19, 165).

### 3. The Direct Feeling of God

Jiddu Krishnamurti gave vitality to words like lucid, undermine, vulnerable, stillness, not by using this vocabulary, but in effect, by reawakening the significance of such words. "Can thought find its source?..." "The photograph of my mother—accurate though it may be, is not my mother." "If I spend my whole life indoors reading about rain, will that make it happen?" Just as you cannot feel your mother by seeing her picture, you cannot feel rain by reading about it. People today cannot feel God. They cover God with the language of belief, of atheism, of existentialism. We worship language. Suppose there were no books, no gurus, no teachers, what would you do? "Can the consciousness empty itself of all contents?" That is the essence of the mysticism of Jiddu Krishnamurti. But how do I do it? How do I get there? (Nicoletti, *JRPR* Jan. 1994, 24-25; Rohit Mehta in *The Nameless Experience,* 1976, Delhi, Motilal Banarsidass).

This is the gist of every religion which Krishnamurti has been talking about. He condemned every organized religion and laid emphasis on feeling God by clearing the mind of all its contents. I fully endorse his views. Even the German mystic, Johannes Eckhart (Bancroft 20) said, "You must know that to be empty of all created things is to be full of God. To be full of created things is to be empty of God." Recently Rhea A. White stated, "I feel that parapsychology should seek the kingdom of God first, and funding and other forms of support will follow" (ARPR 1992, Annual Conference Proceedings, 4). Now, three things arise: (1) What is the direct feeling of God? (2) How do we do it? (3) How do we get there? This is the main concern of Geoff Louis Nicoletti, because Krishnamurti simply said that everyone has to find one's own way, independent of every organized religion.

Accordingly, I am going to elaborate on "what we understand from the direct feeling of God". An "exceptional human experience" has to contain "something more" which is not to be found in the meaningful object or situation itself but always beyond it (Robinson 21).

According to numerous saints, as discussed earlier, the Ultimate Reality resides in the Nameless Plane. It is the highest of the Spiritual Planes which lie beyond the Soul Plane. It is an uncountable large number of light-years away from earth. Yet it is present in every part of the Universe (Omnipresent) in the form of Light and Sound—the twin-pillars of God—the Ultimate Reality. In the beginning was the Word, and the Word was with God, and the Word was God. The "Truth" is rightly expressed in the *Bible.* In Hinduism the Word is called *Aum* or *Shabd;* in Sufism it is called *Kalma-i-Ilahi* which is God in first hand.

The Word was made flesh and there was nothing which was not made by the Word. There are two representations found in Hinduism—*Varnatmak* and *Dhunatmak*. *Varnatmak* is the descriptive form of God which changes with the time and place, for example, Rama, Krishna, Buddha, Jesus, Allah, or Word. On the arousal of Kundalini or otherwise, by the direct grace of the Guru or Master, you come in the direct touch/connection with the Sound Current—*Aum*—or Word. You hear it intermittently through inner ears, which is the witness of the Divine Presence (Yogananda 3).

*Aum* of the *Vedas* became *Hum* of the Tibetans, *Amin* of Moslems, and *Amen* of Egyptians, Greeks, Romans, Jews, and Christians. Its meaning in Hebrew is sure, faithful (Yogananda 3, 237). Spirit can come to us as unexpected, sparkling pinpoints of Light, or often unnoticed inner sounds—like the hum of high tension wires, the whisper of a sweeping wind, or the mellow sound of a flute. Sometimes it nudges us through dreams, a strange coincidence, or an intuitive hunch. This is the first-hand experience of God (Klemp 19, back cover).

However, in the successful state of meditation or otherwise, the Spirit forms a matrix—which appears in the form of Devi, Krishna, Christ or any other form of *Varnatmak* which the aspirant has been cherishing. Thus, I saw It in the form of Devi (Mother Goddess); Swami Yogananda and Sri Aurobindo saw It as Lord Krishna; Dr. B. S. Goel saw it as Sai Baba (Goel 22), St. Teresa of Avila saw It as Lord Jesus Christ (Paul 23). There are several other real life examples that can be quoted here.

The important thing to be noted is that it is not necessary to see Spirit in the *Varnatmak* form. It happens for the personal satisfaction and assurance of the aspirant. And then It is only the *Dhunatmak* form of Sound which remains permanently heard through the inner ears. Many great people realized God directly in the formless state. For example, St. Hildegard of Bingen saw It as the Living Light (Hozeski 24). Moses, Mohammed and St. Paul saw It as Light. Socrates and Nanak realized It as direct knowledge and understanding, without any form. Nanak on emergence from enlightenment said only two words 'Eck Onkar', meaning "God is One". Harold Klemp realized It as Light and Sound (Klemp 25). Buddha called God the "Light of the Void" How childish it looks at this stage—man fighting man in the name of religion— none of them knowing in reality what God is.

"All that is really needed is a link up, or connection, with the Light and Sound of God. Simply that and nothing more. Anything else is merely form, including even the outer appearance of the Master" (Klemp 26, 122). "As soul gets a little of this Light and Sound of Spirit, it is drawn on just like the honeybee to the flower or moth to the ligh" (Klemp 19, 122-123).

> A God-aware person has simply caught a recognition of his true identity: He knows his relationship with God. It is a "realization"—not a belief, nor a feeling, nor an understanding. He just knows. He gathered this certainty through the high experience of God, which has transformed him into a perfect carrier of Light and Sound. From that day on he is agent for God, delivering the message of spiritual freedom to all who will hear (Klemp 25, 225-226).

Observations made in the above paragraph are in conformation with the Hindu Scriptures written some four to five thousand years ago, or perhaps they are "timeless writings, from everlasting to everlasting" (Huxley 27). These are very significant conclusions, especially useful for the advanced seekers. I further corroborate them through my personal experiences over the years. In variations, these statements have also been given by saints and realized persons from other faiths. These are the landmarks of Self/God—realization. In the words of the great psychologist, Carl Gustav Jung:

> (This kind of experience) cannot be disputed. You can only say that you have never had such an experience, where upon your opponent will reply: 'Sorry, I have'. And there your discussion will come to an end. No matter what the world thinks about (this kind of experience), the one who has it possesses a great treasure, a thing that has become for him a source of life, meaning and beauty, and

has given a new splendour to the world and to mankind. He has *pistils* and peace. Where is the criterion by which you could say that such a life is not legitimate, that such *pistils* is mere illusion? Is there, as a matter of fact, any better truth about the ultimate things than the one that helps you to live? That is the reason why I take careful account...of the symbols produced by the consciousness (Hoeller 28, 156).

**4. Conclusion**

When the evolution of a man is completed, either in the natural way or through induced methods, such as meditation, yoga, or metaphysical pursuits, the mind is left behind and the Soul sees itself as a formless, infinite being who is full of bliss and knowledge. In the process, the Soul crosses several intermediate planes wherein its physicality goes on reducing while its subtlety, power and knowledge goes on increasing. In states of realization God appears before the aspirant in his/her most cherished form. God is felt from time to time as sparkles of Light, inner Sounds, nudging through dreams, strange coincidences, a touch by an invisible Being, intuitive hunches, etc.

However, there are different degrees of God-realization, as Meher Baba (1, Vol. III, 28) puts it: "Thus, it is better to feel God than to study Him, it is better to experience God than to feel Him; and it is better to become God than to experience Him."

**References**

1. Baba, Meher; *Discourses of Meher Baba,* Vol. I, II, III, Sufism Reoriented Inc. San Francisco, 1967.
2. Asaramji, Swami; *Sacha Sukh,* Yoga Vedanta Samiti, Ahmedabad, India, 1994.
3. Yogananda, Paramahansa; *Autobiography of a Yogi,* Jaico Publishing House, Bombay, India 1986.
4. Sahai, Dr. Chaturbhuj; *Sadhana Ke Anubhava,* Ramashraya Satsang, Mathura, India, 1987.

5. Thurman, Robert, A.F; *The Tibetan Book of the Dead,* Bantom Books, 1984.
6. O'Brien, Stephen; *Visions of Another World,* The Acquarian Press, London, 1989.
7. Prabhupad, Swami; *An Easy Journey to Other Planets,* International Society for Krishna Consciousness, West Virginia, 1980.
8. Muktananda, Swami; *The Play of Consciousness,* Gurudev Siddhapeeth, Maharashtra, India,1972.
9. Swedenborg, Emmanuel; *Divine Providence,* The Swedenborg Foundation, New York, 1972.
10. Swain, Jasper; *On the Death of My Son,* Turnstone Books, London, 1982.
11. Twitchell, Paul; *The Tiger's Fang,* Lancet Books, New York, 1967.
12. O'Brien, Stephen; *In Touch With Eternity,* A Bantom Book, UK, 1992.
13. Moody, Dr. Raymond; *Life After Life,* Bantom Books, NY, 1986.
14. Garret, Eileen J; *Many Voices: Autobiography of a Medium,* G.P. Putman's Sons, NY 1968.
15. Roberts, Jane; *Seth Speaks: The Eternal Validity of the Soul,* Prentice Hall, Englewood Cliffs, NJ, 1972.
16. Klemp, Harold; *Soul Travellers of the Far Country,* Eckankar Minneapolis, MN, 1987.
17. Morimitsu, Phil, *In the Company of Eckmasters,* Eckankar, Minneapolis, MN,1987.
18. Leadbeater, C.W. *The Astral Plane,* The Theosophical Publishing House, Adyar, Madras, India; Wheaton, III., USA; London, 1993.
19. Klemp, Harold; *How to Find God,* Eckankar, Minneapolis, MN, 1988.
20. Bancroft, Anne; *The Luminous Vision: Six Mediaeval Mystics and Their Teachings,* George Allen and Unwin, London, 1982.
21. Robinson, Edward; *The Original Vision: A Study of the Religious Experience of Childhood,* Religious Experience Unit, Oxford, 1977, pp. 146-147.
22. Goel, Dr.B.S.; *Third Eye and Kundalini,* Third Eye Foundation of India, New Delhi, 1985.
23. Paul, Irwin; "Santa Teresa de Jesus de Avila", *JRPR,* Oct. 1981, pp.179-181.
24. Hozeski, Bruce, *Hildegard of Bingen's Scivias,* Bear & Co., Santa Fe, N.M., 1986.

25. Klemp, Harold; *Child in the Wilderness,* Eckankar, Minneapolis, Mn, 1989.
26. Klemp, Harold; *Cloak of Consciousness,* Eckankar, Minneapolis, MN. 1991.
27. Huxvy, Aldous; *The Perennial Philosophy,* Harper & Row, Publishers, New York, 1994.
28. Hoeller, S.A.; *The Gnostic Jung,* The Theosophical Publishing House, Wheaton, III, USA, 1982

# 10

# Life after Awakening

*Reaching halfway to God is marked by listening to the inner Sound and seeing the inner Light—the twin-aspects of God. Kundalini at this stage is at the fourth centre of energy, called the heart centre. This is the stage where the aspirant must relinquish active participation in the affairs of the world, for furthering the journey towards God. Knowledge continues to be received intuitively as the Kundalini proceeds to higher centres of energy. There is a marked difference in the degree of realization at each stage. There are facts which are known in person and they are never written down or spoken of.*

### 1. Halfway to God

It was pointed out earlier that the inner Light and Sound are the twin-pillars of God—the form in which God appears to the aspirant anywhere in the universe. The end result of all pursuits in any religion is to get connected with this Light and Sound, and once it is done, you are halfway through towards God. At this point the Guru or Master leaves you alone. Henceforth, you are the master of your own experiences. In the words of the Master (Klemp 1, 157):

> My purpose is to link the Soul with the Sound and Light of God. As you get this link up, you become your own authority about what is truth and what is not. No longer do you have to listen to a man in a pulpit or even to myself standing on a stage and telling you about truth. *Truth is not the same for any two people. No two individuals have exactly the same outlook on life. Each one of your experiences is unique; the Soul is unique.*

The Light of God, as it appears clearly in the inner vision without a mistake left for the imagination, is of the blue colour—a star or a globe. Its appearance indicates that the consciousness of the aspirant is raised above the cosmic consciousness and it is of a very high degree. Furthermore, the Spirit has taken over the soul in tow. The experiences of life at this stage are for the enrichment of the person, showing one the direct path back home towards God. The other and more important aspect of the Spirit is Sound, which is the voice of God, the creative current which has created the lower worlds. It emanates from the centre of God, spreading like radio waves into the whole universe, and then returning to the centre of God. The returning aspect of the Sound wave, which is for bringing the soul back home towards God, is called God-realization.

Dr. Ramesh Paramahansa (2, 150) has said in clear words that one should leave all controversies whatsoever and sink into the Sound Current so that one can be brought back home. Saint Kabir in his beautiful poetry conveys the idea that we should not be paying attention to the sound of the morning bird on a tree but concentrating on the inner Sound and finding out where it comes from. This is "homecoming". Dr. Chaturbhuj Sahai and Harold Klemp have talked about riding the Sound current and travelling to the heart of the universe and finally to the centre of God.

The Sound aspect of God is more important than the Light. Sound is soothing, comforting and protecting. Light, if encountered by the aspirant, can be uncontrollable and damaging. Mohammed and Saint Paul both encountered an enormous Light which blinded them for several days. Many saints could not proceed further on the spiritual path due to the damage caused by excessive Light without the protection of Sound. Recently, Dr. B. S. Goel (3) encountered lights of different colours in his visions whenever he closed his eyes. For several years he could not sleep properly. He was afraid of closing his eyes. Only when the Sound aspect of God manifested Itself in him did he find soothing protection which provided some relief. A limited amount of Light, which is necessary for progress, now appears. As I can say with my own experience, I encountered Sound in 1987, and after a few months I saw the manifestation of Light; perhaps this was the reason why the disturbing experiences did not take place with me, by the will/grace of God.

The higher you transcend, the more narrow becomes the path—some call it the "razor's edge" (Klemp 1, 158). Some of the five enemies—greed, lust, anger, attachment, and ego—may still be persisting with the aspirant. The most powerful is the ego. Closely attached to intellect, travelling with it up to the end, may be the cause of one's downfall or stumbling block. The aspirant may find himself at the "end of the road", not finding the way to proceed further. However, the stage has to be crossed some way or the other. "Swallowing insults and still smiling is a characteristic expressed by the laughing Buddha with the enormous belly. This tells us the necessity of going beyond praise and blame (Radha 4, 96)."

At this middle stage, the aspirant may still be oscillating between the material life (though in a limited way) and the spiritual life. Once one crosses the "razor's edge", complete annihilation may take place. This is the stage of *Nirvikalpa Samadhi* or complete absorption. Paul Twitchell called it "Consciousness Five", perhaps relating it to the consciousness beyond to the fifth plane— the Soul Plane. It is something like trying to climb a wall and telling others, "Wait, let me look at the other side and then I will tell you what is there." When he is successful in climbing the wall and looks to the other side, he is completely absorbed and annihilated. He jumps to the other side, and now there is no one left behind to tell us. Whenever Ramakrishna used to describe the other side to his disciples, he could only talk up to a certain stage. Beyond a certain point his tongue would falter and refuse to speak because of two reasons: first, there are no words that can describe the spiritual experience; second, the consciousness is absorbed into God-consciousness —becoming one with it—so the person who would talk is not there anymore. According to Whitman: "When I undertake to tell the best, I find I cannot, my tongue is ineffectual on its pivots; my breath will not be obedient to its organs; I become a dumb man" (Bucke 5, 115).

*He who knows, speaks not, and he who speaks, knows not.*

However, there is a stage up to which the saints have been telling others what they have come to know about God. After a certain point they get clear instructions from the other side not to reveal the secrets which they are now going to know. Swami Muktananda (6) was told by the "Blue Personality" never to write in black and white what It was going to tell him then. Yogananda (7, 425) says, "Sri Yukteswar gave me light on certain matters which I cannot reveal here." Harold Klemp (8, 143) said, "When you learn the wisdom and knowledge that comes at each level, to reveal the secrets of your circle of initiation is a violation of the spiritual law." Hence, the higher knowledge and truth about God will never appear in black and white on paper. Of course, guidance and help will always be available to get there, but you can never tell others what is there.

**2. The Revelation**

The most profound teachings come to the aspirant intuitively — thoughts entering the mind in a state of quiet and stillness, when one is qualified to receive them. According to Shankar (the great guru of the Advaita tradition of the eighth century A. D.), "The conviction of the truth is seen to proceed from the reasoning upon the salutary council of the wise, and not by bathing in sacred waters, nor by gifts, nor by a hundred *pranayams* (control of breath)" (Chatterji 9).

> Ramana Maharshi attained self-realization without controlling his body in any way and without involving himself in the complexities of pranayama. Ramana's yoga consisted in asking the thought-provoking existential question 'Who am I?' Then he meditated and contemplated on this, until he gained a particular insight through his person which he generalized for all humanity (Billimoria 10, 54)".

According to sri Aurobindo, all life is yoga, and that yoga consists more in one's *philosophical outlook and attitude* than in the planthora of physical exercises, only a modicum of which he considered to be necessary. He recommended contemplation on the teachings of the *Upanishads* and *Bhagavad Gita*, with an understandable bias towards a mystical interpretation of *Vedic tracks.* The common awareness shared by present-day Indian masters, such as those emphasized in the teachings of Shankaracharya, Sathya Sai Baba and Swami Sivananda among others, is that without ethical consciousness harnessed through yoga, the triumphs of materialism and technology may well bring greater psychological stresses, anxieties and frustrations than we have yet seen in a rapidly modernizing world. Such critiques of modern technology have, of course, come from Western thinkers as well, from Heidegger and Erza Pound, to Marcuse and Norman O'Brown, as well as from global thinkers of whom Gandhi would be one good example.

> International research has shown that yogic training and disciplines in the right context lead to reduction in mean cholesterol, fats and acid levels in the body, followed by neurological regulation and improvement in concentration, retentive power and reasoning. Cardiac and brain-wave stabilization also has been recorded. Dr. Ainslie Meares, an Australian psychiatrist who had studied in India, claimed in a number of his published articles and books that relaxation and meditational techniques help retard formation of cancer cells (Billimoria 10, 54-56)".

The gist of the above paragraphs is that although "knowledge and truth" are perceived intuitively, yogic disciplines and the study of scriptures and biographies of saints are necessary to prepare the required mental platform in the aspirant. This shows that the "Integral Path" proposed in Chapter 2, and consolidated in further writings, is the right approach that takes care of all aspects. The opening of the *chakras* one-by-one, through the *ascension of Kundalini*, brings the *intuitive knowledge and truth* in the following steps:

1. Freedom from all sin by recognizing mistakes and controlling impulses. Sin in the yogic terms is the intentional repetition of well-known mistakes. Freedom from selfishness and greed gives the state of "always living in gladness", creativity, power of speech and intuitive learning of past mistakes.

2. Conquest of self-will, self-importance and ego removes the clouds which were obscuring the Light. Mind dwells in the beauty of the Most High, the ability of well-reasoned discourse is acquired and high levels of speech, writing of prose or verse result.
3. Further conquest of the five passions—lust, greed, anger, attachment and ego—is achieved. This leads to inner harmony. Ideas expressed and the intonation of the voice create an environment of blissful happiness which can bring quietness in a tumultuous group of people and can open a sense of higher perception in them. Higher awareness gives discrimination as applied to the events in daily life. *Jewels of intuition may glitter as flashes at times.*
4. Having learned from past mistakes, better understanding and discrimination is developed and fewer mistakes are made in the present. *Sincerity, honesty and humility, now possessed, ensure a future of harmony and happiness. Increased awareness at this stage is an "advance glimpse" of the slowly building illumination.* Having stopped all internal noises of the mind, the unstruck sound of Cosmic Aum or Word is now heard through inner ears. Keeping the senses under control, living wisely, doing noble deeds, having conquered self-will and having attained an extraordinary power of concentration, one can put oneself in another's shoes and understand the person. This is the philosophical side of invisibility. *Through devotion, the aspirant becomes receptive to Divine knowledge and lives like a bee collecting honey from the flowers.*
5. Freedom from worldly desires unlocks and redirects the energy from the pursuits of worldly goals to the pursuits of Divine satisfactions—the person is raised to a higher plane —called the "gateway of liberation". Increased concentration unites the subjective and objective, leading to "complete knowledge" and understanding the real union called "Yoga". *'Peace of mind" is attained through an understanding of a level higher than intellectual.* With a greater clarity one can look back into the past, understand the present and anticipate the future. Taking more care in all actions, impulsive decisions are

avoided and one knows "what to do" and "what not to do". We now begin to understand we are a product of "environment and ignorance". *We are now ready to take greater responsibilities, show mercy to all and render selfless service—getting close to Divinity.*

6. Compassion, which at first was for friends and close ones, at the second stage is moved to those who were brought to your attention and were worthy of help, while at the third and final stage you are all out to help everyone—good or bad; it has touched Divinity. *You feel grateful to even those who were your critics and made you miserable.* You know now that you were the creator of your own difficulties, pain and problems. You know now what to preserve and what to destroy. You know now to control the powers and not to be consumed by them. *A perfect balance between the male and female aspects—intellect and intuition—represented by the "ardhanaarishwara" form of Lord Shiva, who is half-male and half-female, brings you close to the Divine Union of the "Self" with the Ultimate Reality.*
7. *The perfect state of pure intellect, wisdom and power is further transcended to plunge into the merging with the Supreme. The yogi is now in a position to choose his mode and time of death. The body drops like a ripe fruit from the tree.*

The soul having learned all that was necessary on the physical plane has now qualified to live on higher realms to learn more and to be a co-worker with God. It is not obliged to return to earth again, unless by its own choice for love of mankind. It may come back to tell the truth to its brothers and sisters.

### 3. Journey beyond Halfway

It is normally a period of *twelve years* which the physiology and chemistry of the body takes to adapt itself to the newly awakened and more powerful energy flowing into the nerves after the awakening of the Kundalini. The Kundalini unlocks the doors of the prison and unwinds the obstructing sheaths that had caused the Soul to forget its identity. *Accumulated karmic harvest of the past determines the time of illumination. "The yogi, labouring with assiduity, purified from sin, fully perfected through manifold births, he reacheth the supreme goal"* (*Bhagavad Gita,* VI, 45).

According to Shankaracharya,

> That kind of mental function— which recognizes only the identity of the Self and Brahma, purified of all adjuncts, which is free from duality, and which concerns itself only with pure intelligence— is called *illumination.* He whose illumination is steady, who has constant bliss and who has almost forgotten the phenomenal universe, is accepted as a man liberated in this very life (Vivekchudamani).

Now there are various factors which will assist and catalyse the progress to this state of perfection. After the awakening of Kundalini, one has to take care that it neither slips back, nor overshoots the crown *chakra* prematurely. Its reversal is checked if it has crossed the third *chakra* called the *manipura.* Having reached that far it does not fall back. Whenever it is overactive, we have to use sedative methods to keep it under control. Cessation of yogic and meditational practices, intake of heavy food and limited intake of alcohol (if the aspirant has been taking it), keeps the Kundalini under control. However, at the right time, it has to reach and establish itself in the crown *chakra* to produce the permanent state of illumination.

As Shankaracharya has said, one has to forget the phenomenal world. That is why, retirement from active participation in the affairs of the world is recommended at this stage, which in most cases takes place by itself. And then, most of the time the aspirant should be involved in the thoughts of God, for which religious songs—called *bhajan* and *kirtan* in India—are very helpful. With these two factors the process of spiritual perfection is expedited.

The remaining time should be devoted to spiritual talks and guidance to interested people; as well as lectures and writing of spiritual knowledge received intuitively from time to time. Silence must be observed most of the other times. All this requires living in an ashram— a secluded place, away from the hustle and bustle of the busy world, free from materialism and a fully spiritual environment.

Nisargadatta Maharaj (11), a realized saint from Maharashtra, India, has authored a couple of books on spiritual development and illumination. He has answered some very pertinent questions in his book, *I Am That.* He says that you must give up all anchors and become vulnerable to make a way for God. A person living a worldly life and also completing the requirements of spiritual life receives knowledge, no doubt, but it is like the wisdom of one trapped in a "cocoon". Living with ideas of the world and ideas of God at the same time, does not go hand in hand. One chain of thoughts has to be broken for the other. Many times you are in touch with God for several days. For example, for five days Meher Baba did not know what he was eating, drinking, wearing or doing under a spell of God-intoxication. If an aspirant is not prepared to undergo such periods in which he is totally cut-off from the world, why should one choose to go on the path of God? If one is ready to get involved in such experiences, how can they keep pace with the daily chores of life, i.e., going to an office from 8 to 5, or other routines.

One can go up to the stage of "halfway to God", maintaining full relations with the material world although with a difference. After that, it may not be possible to keep pace with both ways of living, if the aspirant really wants to go the way of God. I have met some people who are in a state of unhappiness because they find their development has stopped at some point. The reason is because to be full of material things is to be empty of God, and to be full of God is to be empty of material things. A clear choice has to be made mainly at this stage, if not earlier, and that is called *"sanyas"*.

I do not know how to say it. If you pursue God as a part-timer, the results will also be in parts, never in full. We may remain a parapsychologist like a person in any other profession, we may do research on the awakening of Kundalini and its effects, gather a team of participants with various specialities, but we remain far from the actual experience of God. A science is a science; an experience is an experience. This will continue for several lifetimes until we take a clear decision, here and now, at a certain point, in a particular lifetime. Professor J. B. Rhine set up a laboratory at Duke University in 1920 and a team of researchers have seriously engaged themselves in fitting a "physical or mathematical formula" to the paranormal, such as telepathy, telekinesis, levitation, precognition, clairvoyance and so on. They could witness the phenomena but they could not find any formula for any one of them so far. Can you contain the "infinite" in a "finite" frame? The defeat is obvious and clearly admitted by Professor Rhine (see for example, *The Fundamentals of Parapsychology* by Morris and Edge etc.) Someone has rightly said, *"You may become God but you may not know God."*

Many times you feel that something wants to open up to you—but it does not. You clearly feel that there is *some sheath yet undropped, some barrier yet uncrossed.* Swami Sivananda Radha says the following:

> To strive for the Most High and yet have a family and all the responsibilities that go with it is, for the average person, almost impossible. Even in other aspects of life, in careers of men and women, it has been shown that it is barely possible to handle both jobs with equal attention and quality. If in a marriage one partner is wholly dedicated to a career and does not pay attention to the family, the marriage suffers from the neglect of that partner. If there are children, they also suffer. The marriage may even break up. However, some great yogis are known to have been married. In such cases, the partner gladly becomes the "servant" of the other, considering it a blessing to have a companion who pursues the spiritual path (4, 55).

And again:

> Another secret power is withdrawing the life force. I have met the son of a yogi who, although at first was angry and disappointed that his father had deserted the family for the yogic path, was himself in the process of doing the same thing when I knew him. His father had allowed him to observe the procedure when he withdrew the life force, consciously and at will, after explaining in detail what he was going to do and how long it would take. Although this young man had decided

to also follow the yogic path, he was making preparations to ensure that his family would not suffer from his actions (4, 334).

Thus it is quite plain to see that the latest stage at which time the aspirant should turn towards God fully, is after reaching the halfway point. A good compromise would be to spend half the year in an ashram and half the year in conveying intuitive knowledge to the world for the benefit of mankind. This is what many famous yogis have done. *One should not leave the world with the feeling that one could not convey the Truth to others. Because this would be the "seed" for "returning to physical world" once again.* I personally do not relish that idea. Whatever is to be done must be done now. You should still be serving others in the higher worlds with your own ongoing evolution. There would be many others to take care of the tasks in the physical world.

**References**

1. Klemp, Harold; *How to Find God,* Eckankar, Minneapolis, MN, 1988.
2. Paramhansa, Dr. Ramesh; *Shabda Brahama,* Shanti Prakashan, Kanpur, India, 1990.
3. Goel, Dr. B.S.; *Third Eye and Kundalini,* Third Eye Foundation of India, New Delhi, 1985.
4. Radha, Swami Shivananda; *Kundalini Yoga,* Motilal Banarsidass Publishers, Delhi, India, 1992.
5. Bucke, Richard Maurice, *Cosmic Consciousness,* The Citadel Press, New Jersey, 1961.
6. Muktananda, Swami; *Chitshaki Vilas,* Gurudev Siddhapeeth, Maharashtra, India, 1972.
7. Yogananda, Paramahansa; *Autobiography of a Yogi,* Jaico Publishing House, Bombay, India, 1986.
8. Klemp, Harold; *Cloak of Consciousness,* Eckankar, Minneapolis, MN, 1991.
9. Chatterji, Mohini M.; *Viveka-Chudamani or the Crest-Jewel of Wisdom,* The Theosophical Publishing House, Adyar, India, 1932.
10. Billimoria, P., *Yoga, Meditation and the Guru,* Sterling Publishers Pvt. Ltd., Delhi 1993.
11. Maharaj, Sri Nisargadatta; *I Am That,* The Acorn Press, Durham, N.C., USA, 1973.

# 11

# Psychic Individuation and Self-realization

*There are five stages of soul-development which may span many lifetimes. At the final stage of inner turmoil the person takes to either of the two courses: meditation or intellectual metaphysics. When the male and female principles, that is, intellectual and intuitive aspects in a person, get balanced, the process of individuation begins and it leads to Self-Realization. This process, normally supported by symbols in dreams, runs parallel to the development of the personality. The three-self (low, middle, high) man becomes the new High-Self, representing the united pair on blending with the soul-mate. High-Self or the Psychic Being, discussed earlier, provides direction and guidance from time to time. Self-realization is a repeatable and ongoing process both on earth and the unseen realms beyond physical reality.*

**1. Search for the Self**

A time comes in a person's life, in a particular incarnation, when he begins to lose interest in the affairs of the world, knowingly or unknowingly. He may feel that he does not belong to the world, and the objects of the world no longer give him satisfaction. Though not clearly perceived, somehow intuitively he senses that the objects of sense gratification which he has sought over and over again, perhaps in several incarnations, have brought him nowhere. A faint idea starts to haunt his thoughts that he belongs to some other reality of existence and that his home is somewhere else. This is the beginning of the search for that permanent element which now we call "soul".

A person experiences *five different stages* of development in the search for lasting happiness and the true home. In the *first stage*, the person has no consideration for the feelings of others, he lives entirely for sense gratification through the objects of the world at the cost of others, and this appears to him as the highest good on earth. He does not have any idea that there could be some power above the human being.

In the *second stage*, the feeling enters the person that there is perhaps some higher power, but he continues to live his old life of sense gratification in the fully material way. He is doubtful about the concept of the higher power; although he may from time to time think about it, he does nothing to try to recognize this power in some way. In the *third stage*, the concept of higher power becomes more firmly grounded in his consciousness, and he begins to take an interest in prayers and rituals to please that higher power for personal gains.

He may call this higher power God, but he will disregard the beliefs and faiths of others of different religions. The state of irresponsibility continues. In the *fourth stage*, he starts to respect the beliefs of others, and he assumes self-responsibility as a result of the long experience. He realizes that he must be involved in something more concrete in order to find the truth. Simple reliance on the dogma no longer satisfies him. Gradually the inner turmoil starts becoming more intense. In the *fifth* and *final stage*, the meaninglessness of life becomes paramount in his consciousness. Inner turmoil comes to the surface and forces the person to look for the meaning of life and to find the answers to the questions which have been vexing his inner self. This leads him to associate with various societies which are involved in the fields of philosophy, parapsychology, occultism, mysticism or spirituality. He takes to extensive studies of scriptures and literature connected with the life of the people who had been in search for God. His activities include reading, writing and speaking about the paranormal or the life beyond, and nothing else interests him anymore. Being set on the path of evolution, the person takes to either of the two courses: meditation or intellectual metaphysics. Often it is a combination of both, to varying degrees. This is the stage which Lord Krishna spoke of in the *Bhagavad Gita* and Lord Jesus Christ referred to when he said, "Blessed are the persecuted because they will see the Kingdom of God." These five stages of development may span many lifetimes. They have been given the following names by Dr. Joel L. Whitton and Joe Fisher (1):

Stage 1: Materialism
Stage 2: Superstition
Stage 3: Fundamentalism
Stage 4: Philosophy
Stage 5: Persecution

However, I have already elaborated the fact that most religions have a similar classification of the various stages of inner development leading to persecution/inner turmoil (Kumar 2). Aldous Huxley (3) has pointed out that the study of perennial philosophy can begin through three different gates:

Gate 1: The lower gate is that preferred by strictly practical teachers, men like Gautam Buddha who have no use for speculation and whose primary concern is to put out the hideous fires of greed, resentment and infatuation in men's hearts.

Gate 2: Through the upper gate go those whose vocation is to think and speculate: the born philosophers and theologians.

Gate 3: The middle gate gives entrance to the exponents of what has been called "spiritual religion": the devout contemplatives of India, the Sufis of Islam, the Catholic mystics of the later Middle Ages, and, in the Protestant tradition, such men as Denk and Castellio, as Everard and John Smith and the first Quakers and William Law.

According to Huxley, it is easy for the mind to move in either direction if the start is made through the middle gate. This has been my approach over the years to my own spiritual development. It is the method of reading, writing and speaking according to one's own stage of development, so that one continually checks one's own personal experiences with what is written by or in the scriptures. This is corroborating with the Truth because the writer is writing what he has himself seen and gone through.

Robert Assagioli (4) has drawn a general outline of the disturbances which can arise at the various stages of spiritual development and has offered some indications about how best to deal with them. He recognizes four critical stages in this process:

Phase 1: Crisis preceding the spiritual awakening.
Phase 2: Crisis caused by the spiritual awakening.
Phase 3: Reactions following the spiritual awakening.
Phase 4. Phase of the process of transmutation.

"Awakening" refers to a new awareness, the opening of the hitherto closed eyes to an inner reality previously unknown. Freud's successors, such as Dr. C. G. Jung (5) and Esther Harding (6), believed in a "Higher Unifying Centre" for the superconscious and for the life of the individual as a whole. This centre can be called the Transpersonal or Higher Self. Spiritual unfoldment may give experiences of the superconscious realms and/or the awareness of the Self. The process known as Self-Realization leads to the identification of "I" with the Higher Self.

"Crisis before the awakening" normally includes a series of disappointments, a growing sense of dissatisfaction, an awareness that something is missing in life, a shift in personal interests, a moral crisis and a feeling of guilt, a sense of self-responsibility—all of them bringing those elements of personality to the surface which need revision in the wake of spiritual tendencies. These symptoms appear in variations in different individuals, depending on the preparations by the individuals.

When awakening is rightly understood, there seems to be a real solution of the internal crisis, and positive effects are noticed in the person. In such cases, conflicts and suffering vanish; a feeling of joy, happiness, and participation in some way in the divine nature results. Some seekers have visions, hear voices, and begin to write a prose or poetry coloured with the ideas of God. The quality of writing varies from person to person. Some writings are very fine teachings for which the person may become famous. In cases in which the process is not rightly understood, the individuals may not be able to assimilate the new light and energy. They may confuse a relative with an absolute truth, and the personal ego may be wrongly inflated. In some cases, people have declared themselves God or have formed a new sect or religion. Self-deception may occur, and qualities of the lower personality may be attributed to the Higher Self. Sudden contact with truths too incomprehensible or energies too powerful to assimilate may result in psychic disorders.

Reactions of awakening are the peak experiences of joy, ecstasy and mental illumination. Three different cases arise at this level: permanent integration leading to permanent uplifting and transformation of an individual's life; partial transformation, which can be completed through a sense of direction and purposeful methods; insufficient flow of energy from the Higher Self, which goes unrecognized and leads to a painful experience. However, there is a recognition of obstacles to be overcome in the future, in the last case, and a taste of the after-life sets a model to be navigated. In any case, there is a marked change in everyday life and the haunting of a divine homesickness.

The process of transmutation has three phases—removal of the obstacles from the path of inflow of superconscious energy from the High Self to the personal Self; the development of higher functions which have been dormant so far; and recognition of the periods in which the Higher Self is active. Diverse elements of the personality are gradually harmonized in the wake of the higher unifying centre, leading towards completeness. Living in the family and performing daily personal and social duties, has to advance to the path leading to Self-realization. It is advisable to recall the vision vividly and as frequently as possible and to keep it even before one as a goal. The goal is to achieve the state of consciousness characterized by joy, serenity, inner security, a sense of calm power, clear understanding and radiant love. In its highest aspects it is the realization of the essential Being, of communion and identification with the Universal life (Assagioli 4).

**2. The Inner Process of Balancing**

Inner turmoil leading to Self-realization is preceded by a long and arduous process of balancing the male and female elements in every individual, whether man or woman. These elements are intellectuality, representing the masculine principle, and emotionality, representing the feminine principle of nature. Understanding of this aspect is quite necessary, for both advanced people and beginners on the path. To the advanced persons this would be to maintain their position of realisation without falling back, and to the beginners it would be a "way shower".

According to Dr. C. G. Jung,

> In the Middle ages, long before the psychologists demonstrated that by reason of our glandular structure there are both male and female elements in all of us, it was said that every man carries a woman within himself. It is this female element in every male that I have called 'anima'. This feminine aspect is essentially a certain inferior kind of *relatedness to the surroundings*, and *particularly to women*, which is kept carefully concealed from others as well as from oneself. In other words, though an individual's visible personality may seem quite normal, he may well be concealing from others—or even from himself—the deplorable condition of 'the woman within' (Jung 5).

Thus it is the "inner woman" governing the unconscious of the man, who should be blamed for mistakes and not the woman in flesh-and-blood, who is his partner. If the "old woman" within or anima is permitted to take charge of the affairs of the man, he may acquire a womanish character and lose his manhood. So, care must be taken that the anima does not gain an upper hand in his psyche.

However, the woman within is neither good nor bad. It is an energy which can be used to serve the ends of human love and cultural developments, rather than allowed to become destructive. Men are more prone to touch the warmth in an erotic situation and fall a victim of the trick. Women are in general cool and calculative even when under erotic influences. He erroneously thinks this animal-like instinct to be his inevitable mate and falls prey to it. He can avoid this vulnerability by developing a creative relation with the feminine principle and learn to discriminate between the false and true in a woman's attitude to him. If the danger is not recognised, he may get so severely burnt that he may become embittered against the whole sex.

We now get a very clear picture of the whole matter. Every man has an "inner woman" which is related to the surroundings, especially to the women, but he is not consciously aware of this fact. This inner woman or anima has a very important impression on his psyche, unconsciously. The anima wants a manifestation in the form of an outer woman in flesh-and-blood, a girlfriend, wife or significant other. Consequently, the man goes on matching this requirement of his psyche with the women whom he meets in life. The best suited one, at the time of need, is adopted by him. He is initially satisfied that he has found his soul mate, and he begins his life with her. Not understanding the trick of the anima, he slowly discovers that she no longer matches his inner requirement, and he looks for a change. In the course of time he finds another woman, and the same pattern is repeated once again. This explains why men get separated and divorced and remarried many times in life and still remain unsatisfied. They develop a persistent disliking for the opposite sex, which can cause certain psychic disorders. On the other hand, there are men who live with the same woman throughout, even though they are not satisfied with sex, due to the trick of the anima. Similar situations prevail in the case of women. The "inner man" in every woman is called "animus", and a woman runs through a similar course of events in which she matches the "outer man" with the "inner man" and often remains unsatisfied until the end.

However, men and women, because of their complementary natures, have an inescapable need for each other and are compelled to make an attempt for a mutual relationship. But the divergence of their aims is so great that, sooner or later, they fall apart. The external conflict between men and women is, in fact, a picture of the inner subjective conflict within each individual. No individual is entirely male or female, but a composite of both elements, which are in perpetual conflict with each other within the psyche. Unless this conflict is resolved, and unless the man has come to terms with the inner woman, no genuine relation can be formed with a physical woman. He has to face squarely his "lack of wholeness" and find a relation between the male and female aspects of his psyche in order to become "whole". The same is true for women. A woman has to make herself whole initially if she has to have a fruitful relation with a man.

Let us look at the "inner balance" versus "outer relationship". The need of a man and a woman being together physically is a requirement of their complementary nature. If the functions of the domestic and official life are carefully divided between the man and woman, a harmony is established and life runs smoothly in a balanced way. If a man follows blindly one anima projection after another so as to have an immediate satisfaction of the desire, he can conveniently be said to be living in a "childish phase" of emotional development. This childish phase extends indefinitely, not only in a single lifetime, but from one life to another, and the desired satisfaction never comes. The moment a man recognizes this fact and stops identifying his anima projection from one woman to another, he is close to the "point of graduation" on earth and can be said to have a kind of *initiation*. When he learns to sacrifice his sexual instinct and withdraw from the woman who attracts him in a compulsive way, he has come to know the main reason or cause of repeated incarnations. This *initiation* comes only after thorough experience of life and understanding of one's own nature. This is the *conquest of sex* which is an essential step towards the *liberation from falsehood* and Self-realization. Once the "inner balance" is achieved, there is, in fact, no need of an "outer relationship". The man or the woman is happy and satisfied, with or without a physical spouse. Marriage becomes a matter of convenience and personal choice, without any compulsiveness. This explains the attitude of a *yogi roaming alone* round the world, full of happiness and bliss with almost no physical wants.

In the words of Harold Coward (7):

> When a whole is divided into parts, such as male and female, says Jung, this causes the polarization which results in energy or libido tension between the opposites. Even though everyone is physically separated out from the unit, or whole, in this way from the beginning of life, psychological individuation only occurs when one becomes conscious of one's separate existence. As young children or primitive people we identify strongly with the whole, in what Young refers to as *participation mystique*, but maturity and psychic integration is realized only when our balanced unity in the center of the pairs of opposites is achieved. All of this Jung found well illustrated and supported in both the Brahmanical teachings of Hinduism and the practices of Tantric yoga.

The merging of the opposites is a very important and far-reaching change in the psyche of an individual. The person becomes androgynous, having the intelligence associated with masculinity and emotional sensitivity associated with femininity. The unification of the opposites is like an *inner marriage* which is so profoundly depicted in the half-male-half-female form of Lord Shiva in the Hindu temples. The alchemical androgyne, shows the active and passive principles of nature depicted by male and female figures. When these two principles were harmoniously conjoined in any one nature or body, it was customary to symbolize this state of perfect equilibrium by the composite figure of an androgyne. This inner marriage gives birth to the *inner child* which is brought to birth through inner experiences. This child is not a carnal one but a psychic (spiritual) one, representing the new individuality. Chinese teachings have also elaborated this birth of the *Holy Child*, as for example in *The Secrets of the Golden Flower* (Wilhelm 9) on which C. G. Jung has given an illuminating psychological commentary. If the energy flows outward, it creates in the outer world, while if it is checked and flows inward, it creates within the individual. The inner creation is the *psychic child* which corresponds to Jung's concept of the individuality.

In "Gospel of the Egyptians" a conversation between Jesus Christ and a woman disciple named Salome is reported. Christ advises her that immortality will be achieved when females will stop producing children. When asked to clarify, the Lord said: "When ye trample upon the garment of shame; when the Two become one, and male with female neither male nor female". According to M. Esther Harding:

> The saying 'When the two become one, and male with female neither male nor female' suggests an inner marriage of the male and female parts of the psyche, through which the individual will become whole. If I am right in this reading of the text, the Lord's reply would mean that an inner marriage will give rise to that inner child whose birth brings release from the power of death. This rendering accords with the Hindu saying 'What need we have of children, we who have this self?'...The Eros of the feminine principles is here united to the Logos of masculine principle and the fruit of the union, represented by the moon man, the Hero Child is the foreshadowing of the Self of which the Hindus speak with such certainty.

We are created by God as the Soul akin to Him, perfect in all aspects and details. At some point of time our psyche was separated into male and female forms. Since then, each one of us has been looking for our soul mate from time immemorial. We have been searching for this soul mate in a person of the opposite sex, while in fact it is the "other side" of our own psyche. Whenever this fact is discovered and we are united with our own "other side", we become whole, and this union produces the "inner child" as the birth of a new individuality. As a ***complete unit*** in ourselves, we are now qualified to return to our *True Home* as a co-worker with God. All hankerings come to an end, and the chain of death and rebirth is broken. We have graduated from the "school of world/earth", and there is no return as a new incarnation unless we want it of our own, mainly to help our fellow beings.

The supervising nature of the High Self and the birth of the "inner child" can be corroborated through personal experiences of several seekers including myself. You may constantly feel that a *big single eye* is watching you from a distance. According to Hindu belief this is the "hint" that the aspirant should now give up the worldly life completely and should pursue the spiritual path for a fuller development. An unusually beautiful child may appear in your vision at the "twilight period", that is, when you are half-asleep-half-awake, before falling asleep in the night or before leaving the bed in the morning. Hindus call it *Child Brahma* or *Bal Shiva* or the child form of Lord Krishna. This indicates the actual beginning of the spiritual path. It was on one of these days that I dreamed of crossing a wide ocean of clear blue water in my soul form, as if moving swiftly on a very narrow hair-line bridge. According to Jungian philosophy this indicated the clear change in the attitude towards life.

### 3. Process of Individuation and Guidance through Dreams and Visions

The inner process of individuation, normally supported by the symbols in dreams, runs parallel to the development of the personality. Not only Freud and Jung have laid full emphasis on dreams, but the Indian yogis have always advised the disciples to take a careful note of their dreams and take guidance from them. We find a similar direction from Egyptian and Chinese Masters. Dreams have been a commonly accepted factor in spiritual growth in most of the religions of the world. Let us see how dreams and visions constantly keep telling us about our development and give warnings from time to time.

Reiterating Swami Satyananda Saraswati (10), energy at different levels is known by different names:

Level 1: At the lowest level it is known as *Ignorance*
Level 2: On the physical level it is known as *Sex*
Level 3: On the emotional level it is known as *Love*
Level 4: At the highest level it is called *Spiritual Experience*

The anima and animus also have the four stages of development as they appear in dreams, in accordance with the levels defined above. M. L. Von Franz (Jung 5, 158-229) has given a very detailed development of the inner woman/ man through the successive stages of growth in personality. As the man matures in his relationship with the woman, the anima also matures, and the female figures appearing in dreams change from the lowest to the highest levels:

Level 1: Primitive woman, symbolizing ignorance: for example, Eve

Level 2: Romanticized beauty, such as Cleopatra, Helen of Troy or Faust's Helen; symbolizing sex

Level 3: Virgin Mary, feeding milk to the Christ child through her breásts, symbolizing love. A red robe symbolizes the feeling of love

Level 4: The Greek goddess of wisdom—Athena, the Mona Lisa— wearing her mysterious smile, Sapienta, or Shulamite in the song of Solomon, Devi Durga or Shakti, all pointing towards spiritual experience

The fourth stage is rarely achieved by the modern man in the process of psychic development. Similarly, the animus appears in male form in women's dreams in four distinctive levels of development:

Level 1: The wholly physical man, the fictional jungle man, Tarzan

Level 2: The "romantic man", ranging from the 19th century British poet Shelley or "the man of action" to America's Ernest Hemingway, war hero, hunter, etc.

Level 3: The bearer of the "word"—Lloyd George, the great political orator

Level 4: The wise guide to spiritual truth—often projected on Mahatma Gandhi, Jesus Christ or Buddha

The dreams are found to follow an arrangement or pattern, which Jung called the *process of individuation.* There is a sort of hidden regulating or directing tendency at work, creating a slow, imperceptible process of psychic growth. Gradually, a wider and more mature personality emerges, and by degrees becomes effective and even visible to others. The centre of the psyche from which the regulatory effect stems is called the *Self*, which is the totality of the whole psyche, distinguished from *Ego* which is only a small part of the total psyche. Old civilizations have been aware of this centre intuitively. Thus, Greeks called it "inner demon", Egyptians called it "Ba-Soul" and Romans worshipped it as the "genius" of the individual. East Indians call it "Atman" which is always guiding the individual in various ways. The Naskapi Indians have addressed it as the "inner companion". The Self, which is working in accordance with some secret design, is sometimes felt as an unseen supervisor or onlooker. The Self becomes active only after the ego gets rid of the selfish and wishful aims and tries to understand the deeper meaning of life. One must surrender consciously to the power of the unconscious.

The first encounter with the Self is usually an awakening through a shock or initial crisis. In the words of Franz (Jung 5, 166-167):

> The actual process of individuation—the conscious coming-to-terms with one's own inner centre (psychic nucleus) or Self—generally begins with a wounding of the personality and the suffering that accompanies it. This initial shock amounts to a sort of 'call', although it is not often recognized as such. On the contrary, the ego feels hampered in its will or desire and usually projects the obstruction onto something external. That is, the ego accuses God or the economic situation or the boss or the marriage partner of being responsible for whatever is obstructing it. Or perhaps everything seems outwardly right, but beneath the surface a person is suffering from a deadly boredom that makes everything seem meaningless and empty...Thus it seems as if the initial encounter with the Self casts a dark 'shadow' ahead of him, or as if the

'inner friend' comes at first like a trapper to catch the helplessly struggling ego in his snare.

The shadow representing the unconscious part of the personality appears in dreams in a personified form. Thus one can get acquainted with aspects of one's own personality through dreams. The shadow appears as a person of the same sex as that of the dreamer. It contains values that are required by consciousness, although the form of representation is difficult to understand and integrate in one's life. This is the problem encountered when one meets one's "other side". The unconscious appears in many different forms, for example, an unconscious ambition may be represented by a successful character in dreams. The shadow normally represents the opposite side of the ego and embodies just those qualities that one dislikes most in other people. Using one's insight and by being honest, one can integrate the shadow in the conscious personality. To make the shadow a friend or an enemy depends on ourselves.

Personification of the Self and the secret creative action of God can be understood through a tale in the *Quran.* Moses meets the first angel of god, named Khidr, in the desert. Before wandering in the desert, Khidr warns Moses not to become indignant by his actions, or otherwise he will go away. They see some poor villagers on a fishing boat. Khidr scuttles the boat and kills one of the young men. Moses expresses his indignation and Khidr leaves. However, before leaving, Khidr explains that he scuttled the boat so that it would be saved from the pirates who were going to steal it. Also, he killed the handsome young man in order to stop him from committing a crime which would have led his pious parents to infamy. Thus the acts of Khidr which seemed evil were, in fact, not so.

Normally, it is very difficult in a dream to discern whether we are encountering our own shadow or the Self or perhaps both at the same time. If it is a shadow, some shortcoming may be symbolized by the character in the dreams. If it is the Self, some guidance may be on the way. However, there is always an inner voice which tells us what we should do and what we should not do. But the ego may not allow the inner voice to be heard. The only way is to have an honest self-examination and reorganization of one's life.

The anima is a personification of all feminine psychological tendencies in a man's psyche and his relation to the unconscious. Basically, it is shaped by his relation with his mother. If the mother's influence has been negative, the anima figure creates negative feelings in a man, and he tends to become fearful, weak and impotent. In some extreme cases of this kind, the personified inner woman even makes the man commit suicide. Erotic fantasies are a common feature in man, drawing him from woman to woman without satisfaction. This happens when he has not cultivated the desired balance and has not outgrown the desire for sex, as discussed in the previous section. If the mother's influence has been overstrong, this can also lead to making the man effeminate or easily preyed upon by women, making him incapable of facing the difficulties of life. The solution lies in recognising the anima as an "inner power" of the unconscious whose aim is to develop a man to maturity by integrating his unconscious personality and bringing it to the surface consciously.

When such an integration has been achieved, the anima helps in very positive ways, such as choosing the right partners for marriage, digging hidden facts from the unconscious, and, most importantly, leading the man to the inner depth of the psyche. A beautiful relationship is set up with the Self, with the anima acting as guide to the inner realms and the Self.

During my spiritual journey over the years, I remember going through various stages of anima representations. However, the second and fourth stages have been more prominent. In the second stage, for several years, I used to see female characters who were the source of attraction for physical love and began to change. Female figures in dreams became less disturbing. Gradually, stability was reached. It was the month of July, 1987, when I first saw the Mother Goddess with an exceptionally beautiful face and mysterious smile like that of Mona Lisa. She was wearing a red sari and bangles on her wrist. I saw myself in a pure white dress bowing down before her with my folded hands. Her right hand was on my head with the gesture of blessings. This was not a dream but a vision during the hours of meditation. Bliss and happiness followed, and I was in a state of intoxication for many days. This was perhaps an initiation into a high and more spiritual form of life. The scene was repeated three to four times in visions and dreams in a period of about two months. At this time I experienced the awakening of Kundalini, the spiritual energy sleeping at the base of the spine. My whole life and interests drastically changed after this experience. My focus shifted from mathematics to religion and psychology. I have been reading, writing and speaking only on these subjects since that time.

The animus, which is the male personification of the unconscious of a woman, can be both good or bad, depending on the development of the woman's psyche. Just as the mother influences the anima in man, it is the father who influences the animus in a woman. Normally the "inner man" in a woman's psyche is negative and can make her project one image from another, thus creating marital troubles similar to those experienced by men. In the words of Franz (Jung 5, 191):

> The woman may be possessed by the figure from the unconscious, which lures women away from all human relationships and especially from all contacts from real men. He personifies a cocoon of dreamy thoughts, filled with desire and judgements about how things ought to be, which cut a woman off from the reality of life...By nursing secret destructive attitudes, a wife can drive her husband, and a mother her children, into illness, accidents, or even death. Or she may decide to keep the children from marrying—a deeply hidden form of evil that rarely comes to the surface of the mother's conscious mind...In the depths of woman's being, the animus whispers: 'You are hopeless. What's the use of trying? There is no point in doing anything. Life will never change for the better.

However, the main purpose of the animus, like the anima, is to develop the woman's psyche so that she can outgrow the negative influences, integrate her unconscious personality, and bring it to the surface of conscious life. It could be rightly said that the anima/animus are the personifications of the *Kaal* of Hindus and *Satan* of Christians. It cannot be bad since it is also created by God. Its purpose is to prepare the man and woman for a higher and more spiritual form of life. It has a very positive and valuable side; it can build the bridge to the Self through its creative nature.

The animus also passes through four stages as indicated in the beginning of this section:

Stage 1. Personification of mere power—an athlete or champion

Stage 2: Purposeful application of initiative and capacity for planned work

Stage 3: A teacher/preacher or clergyman

Stage 4: The meaningful existence through courage, truthfulness and religious/spiritual profundity

It takes the woman towards spiritual evolution. When she has found courage and inner broad-mindedness towards the sacredness of her own convictions, the manifestations of the Self will get through to her. For example, my mother invariably sees the image of Lord Krishna in her vision whenever she sits for meditation. The image moves, smiles and shows gestures of blessings to her. The Self is personified in dreams and visions sometimes as a superior human figure, such as a Master or Saint, and sometimes as a wise and powerful god or goddess: Krishna, Jesus, Sophia, Kwan-Yin, Athena, Isis, Fatima, Shakti, Durga, Saraswati, Shekinah, Mary, and Kwanoon.

**4. The Ego and the Self**

Every individual has an ego or personal self which deals with the phenomenal world and a Self or Atman which is our oversoul and is akin to God. According to Franz (Jung 5, 208):

> In our civilized world, most dreams have to do with the development (by the ego) of the 'right' inner attitude towards Self, for this relationship is far more disturbed in us by modern ways of thinking than in the case with primitive people. They generally live directly from inner centre, but we, with our uprooted consciousness, are so entangled with our external, completely foreign matters that it is very difficult for the messages of the Self to get through to us. Our conscious mind continually creates the illusion of a clearly shaped 'real' outer world that blocks off many other perceptions. Yet through our unconscious nature we are inexplicably connected to our psychic and physical environment.

Two important observations are made in the above paragraph. First, there is an "inner attitude", an ego and then Self. According to Huna, teachings from very old times:

> Three separate selves or spirits make up the man—subconscious, conscious and superconscious. The superconscious self may be compared to the 'Guardian Angel' of some religions. For convenience sake the three selves of Huna are called, the low self, the middle self and the High Self. The low and the middle selves live in the physical body, which is controlled in large part by the low self. The High Self lives in a 'halo' type of body which is invisible and which remains outside and above the physical body, but which is connected to it by an invisible cord made of the same thin substance as the 'shadow' bodies about to be listed. Second, it is the ego which, by learning the ways of the world, has created obstructions on the way to the Self.

Perhaps it was much easier and straightforward for the herdsman at the time of Krishna, shepherds of Jesus' day and simple businessmen of Mohammed to understand spiritual teachings than for the educated men of today. Consequently, we have to uneducate ourselves to understand God.

The Self appears in the dreams of a man as an outstanding young man providing initiation, a guardian, an Indian guru, a wise old man, even a spirit of nature. In the case of women the Self may appear as a superior female, such as a priestess, sorceress, goddess of love, mother earth goddess. The purpose of the personification of the Self in dreams or visions is to provide guidance and help at the crucial moments or turning points in life. The individual is initiated into the new form of life which is often symbolized by crossing a river or an ocean. If there is a problem in crossing the water the personification of the Self comes to help. The Self may appear at various times during the life, which shows that it takes care of us throughout our existence on earth. With the initiation or crossing of the water, there is a fundamental change in the attitude. This is the beginning of the spiritual journey.

The more important description of the Self is that it is akin to God; it lives in the heart of every individual and yet at the same time it is omnipresent in the entire universe. This means that understanding the Self leads to the understanding of God. In its omnipresence the Self has been called a Cosmic Man by most religions on earth. In India it is called *Purusha*, and it is described as the *Virat Swarup* in the *Bhagavad Gita*. In Hindu traditions the Cosmic Man is called the *Atman*. The individual who has seen his *Atman Swarup* is liberated from the cycle of death and rebirth. He is called *Jeevan Mukta*, that is "liberated while still living on earth". The Chinese in the ancient times called this Cosmic Man by the name of P'an Ku, who was the creator of the earth, heaven, sky, sun, moon, river and mountains. In ancient Persia, the Great Man was known as Gayomart who was shown as a huge figure emitting light. In the Jewish tradition he is known as Adam, Son of Man, or more widely as Adam Kadmon. The Cosmic Man is identified with Christ in the West and with Krishna or Buddha in the East. Meditation on one of these great personalities leads to the realization of the Self.

The purpose of human existence is not the satisfaction of hunger, power, sex or procreation but to be human. The ego's extraverted orientation towards the outer world disappears, desires cease, and the ego merges into the Self when the *inner man* is encountered. An encounter with the inner man takes place when the male and female aspects within the individual are balanced. This balance is depicted by the half-male half-female form of Shiva-Parvati in India, the hermaphroditic statue of the Greek goddess and the androgynous figure of the alchemists. It is the symbol of psychic totality. Only by accepting the earthly contact and suffering and by living and outgrowing the friction of marriage can this be achieved as it is shown in the previous section. Passion going beyond the limits in order to fuse into the other person is a desire for achieving wholeness. From ancient times, a round stone has symbolized wholeness and hence the Self. Elements in a crystal are rightly arranged and so it is considered to be the symbol of the union of the extreme opposites, matter and spirit. For this reason the presence of a crystal is known to evoke intuition. Stone images are worshipped in India as God. Moslems make their pilgrimage to Ka'aba, the black stone in Mecca. Ancient Germans believed that the spirits of their ancestors lived in their tombstones. Placing of a stone on the grave is perhaps done because it symbolizes eternity and it reminds us of immortality. Christ has been called "the stone which the builders rejected", which became " the head of the corner". He is also known as the spiritual rock from with the water of life springs.

Before the development of science, the alchemists searched for God in their famous philosopher's stone. An old Arabian alchemist Morienus, said: "This thing (the philosopher's stone) is extracted from *you: you* are its mineral and one can find it in you: or, to put it more clearly, they (Alchemists) take it from you. If you recognise this, the love and approbation of the stone will grow within you. Know that this is true without doubt." The stone symbolizes eternal mystical experience of God within the soul. When the superfluous matter burns through sufferings, the stone within shines. When the inner experience is recognized and permanentized as a stone "the Self becomes the inner partner toward whom one's attention is continually turned."

There has been much misunderstanding about the theory of "soul mates" in the past. According to the creation legend in the Huna system, Adam was divided in two parts, male and female

(Long 11, 21). The two sexes were separated early in the evolutionary climb, and only when the self has risen high enough to become the High Self, the two halves of the symbolic Adam are united to become the *whole*. The High Self was known to be the "utterly Trustworthy Parental Pair" and was called *Aumakua*. Thus the union with the soul mate, the union of *Atman* with *Paramatman* in yoga and the union of opposites Yin and Yang in China, symbolize the High Self as composed of the male and female principles in balance. The three-self (low, middle and High) man normally passes through a dozen incarnations at each stage of self before becoming the new High Self, representing the united pair on blending with the soul mate. This agrees very well with the half-male-half-female form of Shiva and Shakti, symbolising the *united whole* in Hinduism. The team is never broken and the High Self steps up to the level above it, called *Akua Aumakuas* or "High Self Gods". There are levels and more levels above this, which cannot be grasped mentally by the middle self man. The Ultimate or Final God is something which is beyond imagination.

In the three-self team, when the low self graduates to the middle self, a vacancy is created at the low self level. This vacancy is filled with a new low self, called 'Totem' which is well known in India through *kahuna* teachings at a very early date. However, the secrets have been forgotten by the priests. That one of Maori tribes which settled in New Zealand had been in contact for a time with India seems certain because its members had some of the legends of that land well preserved enough to be identified (Long 11, 35).

A comparison between the beliefs of Huna, India and Egypt is drawn in tabular form by Long. The three lower worlds are—Physical, Astral and Mental—the three forms in which the soul manifests itself. Higher than the three worlds, existence is *Arupa* or formless, and the "principles" are Divine rather than human. The Table has been adopted from the Powis Hoult's *Dictionary of Theosophical Terms*.

The final formation of the High Self comes in two stages: first the male and female principles are to be untied in a single middle self: and then the three selves—low, middle and High—are to be united in the High Self. This theory is in agreement with the doctrine of Dr. Jung, on one hand, and with other religions on the other. Facts for comparison are presented in Tables 1 and 2.

Teachings of Jesus Christ recorded in the Gnostic are in accord with the idea above. In the Gospel of Thomas we read: "When the Lord was asked by a certain man, when should his kingdom come, He saith to him: When two shall be one, and the without be as within and the male with the female neither male nor female; for every woman who has become male will enter the kingdom of heaven'.

**Table 1**

**Union of the Male and Female Principles**

| *S.No.* | *Religion* | *Belief* |
|---|---|---|
| 1. | Huna | Union of the two halves of the symbolic Adam. |
| 2. | China | Balancing of Yin and Yang. |
| 3. | Hinduism | Union of Shiva and Shakti. The half-male-half-female form of Shiva-Ardhanaarishwara. |
| 4. | Christianity | Jesus (Gospel of Thomas): When two shall be one, and the without be as within, and the male with the female, neither male nor female. |
| 5. | Greece | The hermaphroditic Greek head, having all the grace and charm of either sex. |
| 6. | Alchemy | Androgyne, showing the active and passive principles of Nature depicted by male and female figures. |
| 7. | Jungian Psychology | Balancing the man within (animus) or the woman within (anima). |

**Table 2**
**The Three Selves KA (Soul) HUNA (Secret) POLYNESIA**

| *SELF* | *Physical (Body)* | *LOW (Soul)* | *MIDDLE (Mind)* | *HIGH (Spiritual)* |
|---|---|---|---|---|
| Form (body) | *Kino* | *Aka* (shadow, cord) *Unihipili* (sticky) | *Uhane* (Maya) | *Aum-akua* (Cosmic) |
| Force (power) | Health | *Mana* (vital, etheric), | *Mana Mana* | *Mana Loa* |
| Director (mind) | Animal electro-chemical | Instincts, energy, memory, emotion | Logic-reason | Self-realisation |
| State | LOOKS (illusion) | LIFE (energy) | LIVING (action) | ENLIGHTENMENT |
| Analogy | Corpse | Heart-water (grasshopper) HA (breath) | Head (Will-imagination) LA (Light) | Parents-guide Bird-angel |
| **Comparative Terms-Religions-Mythology** | | | | |
| Freud | Personality | Libido-id | Consciousness | Super ego |
| Jung | Persona (mask) | Psyche, personal unconscious | Consciousness (I) | Union of opposites Collective uncs ego |
| Christian | Man untrained | Soul - Holy Spirit | Son of Man | Glorified Christ, Son of God |
| *Bible* | Jar of clay | Silver cord, spring - cistern | Golden bowl | God |

*(Contd.)*

*(Contd.)*

| Function | Animal | Emotes - Memory | Reasons - logic Awareness | Self-Realisation |
|---|---|---|---|---|
| Hebrew | Children of Israel | Shakina | Òld Adam | New-Adam Kadmon |
| *Ka-ba-la* | *Malkuth* | *Yesod* (foundation) | *Hod* (knowledge) | *Tipareth* (true self) |
| | *Assiah* | *Nephesh* (soul) | *Hod* | *Rua ch* |
| China | Earth | *Chi* (darkness) | Will-mind-director | Tao-light-way, golden |
| Greek | *Hiero* (pilgrim) | *Psyche animal* (breath) | *Nous* | Christos Deus-Zeus |
| Buddhist Monad | *Soma* | *Prana-Kundalini* | *Manus* | *Atma-nirvana,* Buddha |
| Egypt | *Khat* | *Ab* (heart) *KA-Khaibit* | *Khu-khoo* | *Sahu-Ba* |
| Alchemy | *Earth* (solid) | Water (moon) | Air (wind) | Fire (sun) |
| Hindu | *Soma-sharira* | Shiva-Shakti, *Kama-Akasha* | Vishnu-Shakti | *Atman*-Union |
| | *Chila-Sthola* | *Manas* | *Chitta*/Buddhi | |
| *Chakra* | Kundalini | *Muladhara* (root) | *Hridaya*-Heart | *Sahasrar*-Crown |
| *Upanishads* | Gross physical | *Naga-chandra, Varuna-subtle* | Surya-Radha *Arunja*-Causal. | Arhant Khristina |
| Japan | *Ryobu* (world) | *Neno Kuni* (male) *Sumo* (Arena of life). | Unpolished Mirror *Sokono kuni* (female) | *Amaterasu,* Sun Rising |

Many stand outside the door, but it is only the solitaries who enter into the chamber." The passages clearly indicate that balancing of the male and female principles is the requirement for entry into the kingdom of heaven.

The High Self is symbolized by the Light and by the Holy Spirit, Sound or Word. Speaking of Jesus, John the Baptist promised : "He who shall come after me, will baptize me, will baptize you with the Holy Spirit and fire. The fire creates light, and the Holy Spirit is represented by the Holy Sound. Thus Light and Sound are the twin pillars of God, and of the High Self. The Light and Holy Spirit/Sound are involved in the superior baptism or high initiation or final cleansing. An individual living with the lower selves ordinarily, is cleansed by the endless kind and loving High Self as the "Mother" shows love and pardons her children for whatever faults they may have. Jesus made contact with the High Self in his baptism. John the Baptist claimed: "I have beheld the Spirit descending as a dove out of heaven, and it is a dove in me.

To become a "Son of God" is "to become one with one's own High Self." The phrase, "Son of man" applies to Jesus as an ordinary man. The phrase, "Son of God", applies to Jesus as the initiated one who was conscious of his union with the High Self (Long 11, 107).

The words of Jesus saying that he is "one with the father" meant that he is one with his High Self. This statement has been misunderstood by most people. However, it is clarified in the words. "Believest thou not that I am in the Father, and the Father in me? The words I speak not of myself—but the Father that dwelleth in me, he doeth the works (John 14: 7-11)." One of the most important secrets is revealed here. Whenever a "self-realised man", a saint or a prophet is speaking the words from the High Self, the High Self is speaking through him. One can understand clearly now what Lord Krishna meant when He said: "I am God, I am the creator, I am the Ultimate" and He asked Arjuna to surrender to Him and to meditate on Him. The message is: Through meditation on Krishna or Jesus, who were

Self/God-realized Beings, the lesser man can become one with his own High Self.

According to the Huna code, the female of the male on graduation gives up bearing children and leaves the material world. The man changes to something non-material, a ghost. This is the High Self, which does not incarnate in flesh. It has a shadowy body and one cannot lay hold of it. The symbol of the High Self is "light" and it is sometimes seen in the physical sense as an intense white light which comes from no known source and which has no heat in it (Long 11, 228-229). The transformation appears to be a change in more than "appearance" or "form"; into something which shines with the *amazingly white light*, the High Self, housed in its robe or "aka" body.

I consider the above paragraph to be quite important for it says that the invisible High Self can sometimes manifest in the form of an "intense white light" which has no source and no heat. I would like to corroborate it by my own experience which I had in the year 1984 while I was teaching at the University of Port Harcourt, Nigeria; the details have been given in earlier chapters. Similar experiences have been reported by Swami Muktananda (12), and Eckankar leader Sri Harold Klemp (13) and several others. I would think that there are other ways, too, through which the High Self manifests, perhaps according to the requirement of the individual. If you are feeling lonely, someone may come and kiss you from beyond and the bliss may last for the whole day. You may feel the presence of a Being around you which is so pleasing and soothing that you cannot exactly describe it. Who can this Being be? Your High Self? Your female half from the spirit world or God Himself?

However, the "comforter" should perhaps be the High Self (John 14:16-19): "And I will pray the Father, and He shall give you another Comforter, whom the world cannot receive, because it seeth him not, neither knoweth him; but you know him; for he dwelleth with you and shall be in you. I will not leave you comfortless—I will come to you." Here Jesus is praying as an ordinary man and giving advice as the High Self.

**5. Salvation and Self-realization**

According to mainstream Christianity, salvation is crucifixion, death and resurrection—an unrepeatable event. Gnostics hold the view that salvation or liberation is a repeatable ongoing process both on earth and the unseen realms beyond physical reality, which is in line with Huna belief. Both Corpocrates and Paul postulated that this process continues through a number of lifetimes; as the Hindus say. Paul used to say that "he dies everyday." In spiritual terms he used to "strain forward" to "what lies ahead" and "press on towards the goal". Similarly, in the Johannie literature there are numerous hints indicating that salvation is a process of revelation of Truth in the life of the individual (Hoeller 12, 89-90).

The whole gamut is about achieving salvation/liberation or Self-realization. The above passage is a good summary of the fact that orthodox religions have a fixed ancient view of salvation. The modern approach shows that this "fixed old view" is obsolete and non-practical. Paul had indicated repeatedly in his letters the modern approach which is shared fully by the Gnostics and all open-minded seekers from different faiths and religions. Self-realization or salvation is indeed a repeatable event and a continual process of spiritual growth both on earth and on higher realms beyond this world. Paul said that he dies everyday which means that he goes out-of-body in astral forms to higher realms for further spiritual knowledge and personal growth. The process is unending. There is always one more step. The only difference is that the spiritual seeker is on the path of liberation while the others are not. The whole world can be divided into these two categories. Those who are on the path continue to evolve endlessly on higher realms, even after breaking the cycle of reincarnations on earth. This is what the Huna code means by saying that the lower self and middle self graduate to the Higher Self which in turn graduates to the further Higher self and the process continues getting closer to Absolute God. A similar view is shared by Hindus, Buddhists, Sufis and other seekers who have a scientifically open mind in search of truth. I would further corroborate it with my own experiences in which I have been travelling into higher realms in an astral or soul body for approximately the last two decades. Similar are the experiences of many yogis in India and other parts of the world for several millenniums.

The Yoga practice of Hindus, Buddhists and Chinese have a similar approach. Jung's suggested way of getting to one's inner centre and making contact with the living mystery of the unconscious, alone and unaided, is what Jiddu Krishnamurti had repeatedly said. Everyone has to find one's own way. Yet the well-known paths are always a help in giving some direction; the experiences, although seemingly different in many details are basically the same. One's mind may be attending to the outer duties but at the same time one remains alert for hints and signs, both in dreams and daily outward happenings, which the Self symbolizes from time to time.

According to Franz (Jung 5, 212):

> One's attention should not be too sharp— nor should it be too dull. There is always a right level of perception. If the training is undergone in this manner... it will be effective as time goes on, and when the cause comes to fruition, like a ripe melon that automatically falls, anything may happen to touch or make contact with, will suddenly cause the individual's supreme awakening. This is the moment when the practitioner will be like one who drinks water and alone knows whether it is cold or warm. He becomes free of all doubts about himself and experiences a great happiness similar to what one feels in meeting one's own father at the cross-roads.

This is the state of salvation or Self-realization. Liberation from falsehood is achieved and one lives in a perpetual state of happiness which does not depend on any external factor.

Several examples can be quoted from the lives of those seekers who experienced these stages of development. Through "inner ears" you may begin hearing the "Unstruck Sound" called *Om* or Logos or Word and you may begin seeing the "blue light" through "inner eyes". The medical doctors may have nothing to say about it. You may have continual visits to higher realms in the astral soul body. Your attitude concerning worldly matters may completely change. No desire for power or position or material acquisition may be left in you. There is a constant inner happiness and peace of mind. Neither honours nor insults may affect you. The world, its objects, and relations with people appear to be insignificant compared with turning inward and living with inner happiness instantly. I lost my interest in mathematics and I am reading, writing and speaking only on spiritual subjects since that experience. Eventually I resigned from my position as a professor of mathematics, so as to live fully with the process going inside me. Perhaps this is what Emannuel Swedenborg did when he resigned from his job on half pension at the age of 54 after his first spiritual experience. That is why Dr. B.S. Geol resigned from his job at age 52 and is now living in his ashram.

There is much to be said about the goal of humanity. A comparative study of the different methods of reaching that goal will show an individual the path that suits him best. And above all, we have to realize that there is a common denominator which is the foundation of all religions, and that differences lie only on the external surface. I will explore these points in further writings.

**References**

1. Whitton, Joel L. and Fisher, Joe; *Life Between Life,* Grafton, London, 1986.
2. Kumar, R; *The Journey Back to Our True Home-I, JRPR.* Jan. 1994.
3. Huxley, Aldous; *The Perennial Philosophy,* Harper & Row, 1995, p.l.
4. Assagioli, R; "Self-Realization and Psychological Disturbances", *The Quest*, Winter/Spring.1986, p.21.
5. Jung, C. J; *Man and His Symbols,* Doubleday & Co, Inc., Garden City, New York, 1964, p.31.
6. Harding, M.E; *Woman's Mysteries,* P. Putman's Sons, New York, 1971.

7. Coward, H.; *Jung and Eastern Thought,* State University of New York Press, 1985.
8. Hall, Manly P., *An Encyclopaedic Outline of Masonic, Hermetic, Qabbalistic and Rosicrucian Symbolical Philosophy,* H.S.Crocker Company, San Francisco, 1928.
9. Wilhelm, Richard; *The Secrets of the Golden Flower,* Harcourt Brace Jovanovich, Publishers, New York, 1931.
10. Saraswati, Swami Satyananda; *Kundalini Tantra,* Bihar School of Yoga, Munger, India, 1984, p.161.
11. Long, Max Freedom; *The Huna Code in Religions,* Huna Research Publications, California, 1965.
12. Muktananda, Swami; *The Play of Consciousness,* Gurudev Siddhapeeth, Maharashtra, India, 1972.
13. Klemp, Harold; *How to find God,* Eckankar Minneapolis, MN, 1988.
14. Hoeller, Stephen A.; *The Gnostic Jung and the Seven Sermons to the Dead,* The Theosophical Publishing House, Wheaton, Illinois, 1982.

# 12

# Healing through Psychic Intervention

*Awakening of Kundalini takes place at the quantum level, and hence, the energy automatically heals the practitioner; and then, the person can heal others with that power in himself. Healers are only an agent: the real work is done by the energy from a Higher Source. They meditate or pray to God or a deity/spirit to invoke that power or energy. Consequently, if the healer cannot get into the mediative level, the healing may not take place. It is at the quantum level that energy and matter are interchangeable. Prana, the unit of cosmic energy at that level, is responsible for life and healing. The integral path of yoga can lead to two-prong results: healing for the Self and others, and salvation—as compared to other methods which may lead to healing alone.*

**1. Introduction**

Yogis and saints have always been known to possess very good health and powers for healing the sick. Innumerable persons have been cured of their incurable diseases by the "children of God" from the time of Buddha and Christ to the present time of Sri Sathya Sai Baba. However, saints are the means while the actual healing is done by the Energy of Absolute God. The same Energy is invoked by the healers which works through them. The difference between the saints and the healers is that, although both are healers, the saints are liberated from falsehood and are God-realised individuals. The Integral Path of Yoga proposed by me and reiterated later in this chapter, therefore, can lead to the dual achievements: Self/God-realisation and "powers of healing".

Based on his own experiences and those of many others, Dr. B.S. Goel in his book *Third Eye and Kundalini* states the following (p.288):

> *Kundalini* can cure any disease like cancer, heart trouble, asthma, provided one is able to attract the mercy of the Guru through whom God is operating. In fact, *Kundalini* is the Shakti of the Lord and anything can be accomplished through it. Indeed, 'things that are impossible for man are possible for the Lord'.

Let us look into the phenomenon of healing as such.

**2. Healing through Faith and Spirit**

Healing a person through a Higher Source Energy, which is not a known physical faculty, is prevalent from the ancient times. Various names associated with this kind of treatment are faith healing, paranormal healing, spiritual healing, psychic healing, absent healing, magnetic healing, mental healing, and New Thought Healing. Procedures involved under the different terms are not necessarily the same, yet the common factor is that the healing energy belongs to the non-physical Higher Realm of existence.

Thus there are two different approaches in healing: a holistic foundation which takes into account the interrelations between mind, body and spirit and also between the human organism and environment; the other one is Western medicine which is based on the Cartesian philosophy of dualism, that is, the separation of mind and body. Although there have been attempts during the last three decades to integrate the two approaches, our concern in this chapter is to elaborate the first approach.

The common denominator in all such techniques is to invoke a Higher Power for help—be it God, deities of various faiths, or the spirit of a dead ancestor. Even when the hands are laid on the patient's body or the will is projected towards a patient at a long distance, assistance is invariably sought from a Higher Source. Hence, the healing is done by the "Higher Energy" through the agency of the healer, as is honestly admitted by most healers. It is not necessary for the patient to be religious to receive the healing. Hence, one can be cured regardless of whatever religion one belongs to. However, it is desirable to have faith in the power of the healer for the treatment to be effective. The healers, of course, have their own spiritual convictions or strong personal faiths through which they draw the power.

I had the opportunity to stay and work with William Henry Belk at the Belk Research Foundation in Charlotte, North Carolina, for a period of six months in 1995. Henry Belk and Harold Sherman investigated the Philippine healers in Manila during the 1960's. Later Herald Sherman wrote the book *Wonder Healers of the Philippines.* I thus had a chance of knowing the first-hand experiences of Henry Belk through his talks and video-recordings. Two senior citizens, Veronica Peace and Jacques Brack, used to visit Henry Belk. Both of them were operated upon psychically, infected portions were removed from their bodies, and both were completely cured of the diseases from which they were suffering. The surgery left no mark, and no pain was felt by either of them. Naturally, I am convinced of the genuineness of the psychic surgery. During the same time, a camp was organized in Columbia for two Philippine healers, who treated about 250 patients in three days, charging 40 dollars from each patient. Most patients were satisfied but some were not, and I was one of them. For a recurring pain in my left arm, the healer showed me a three-inch long piece of material removed from my body, but my pain did not subside thereafter. I am quite sure that nothing was removed from my body. I was later cured by Dr. Sandy Moon, an acupuncture specialist. Hence, my conclusion is that although psychic surgery is genuine, some of the healers do not hesitate to fake the event for money or reputation, but, of course this happens in all walks of life.

Perhaps the most important name in psychic surgery is that of Antonio Agpaoa of the Philippines, nicknamed as Tony. He was interviewed by Sherman and Belk in Manila. Some of the reports by patients run as follows (Sherman 1, 10):

"Tony?...Antonio Agpaoa? He is a man of God—the wonder healer of the age!"

"See my nose? He opened it up. Took out polyps! Now I can breathe freely. You cannot see where he operated. No?"

"I was almost blind and he removed cataracts from my eyes—just with his hands. Now I can read without glasses!"

"A tumour he took from my intestines. In less than five minutes! I felt no pain—nothing—and I am well now. Went back to work right away."

"My heart! It was a block clot. He opened up my chest—cut through the ribs with his bare hands and removed the clot with his fingers! All the time I was conscious, feeling no pain, and my heart beating in his hand! Oh, I tell you, it's the healing power of God in him. It was to be. For me to be alive and well is a miracle—the greatest!"

Tony makes no distinction whatsoever, and there is never any charge. He will accept what they offer, whether it be a few centavos or pesos. It's all the same for him because Tony's "protector", as he calls him, this God-like power that is operating through him, is apparently "running the show". Thus, healing help is freely given to all, regardless of economic status, colour, religion, or station in life. Dr. Hiroshi Motoyama (2), Japanese scientist, who made a study of the "bare hand psychic surgery" of Tony Agpaoa and others proclaimed them "Wonder Healers".

Tony used to meditate before he operated. He has had his power from the age of 9, which he received after fasting and meditating on the mountains after being invited by some Higher Beings, invisible to others. Drinking, smoking, sex, all in moderation, do not interfere with his healing power. The power is not to be used for selfish ends. Tony could treat patients just by looking at them, while he was operating on others with hands. He believed that a beam of power emanated from his eyes. His hands would change colours when he laid them on patients, and the colour would tell about the sickness and its location. Tony believes that this power of God can be transferred to others if they would fast and meditate and work with him. He feels that his life was always protected by an invisible power whenever somebody wanted to harm or kill him.

Psychic surgery falls in two categories. In the first category the body is opened with bare hands and the diseased tissue is visibly removed from the body. After the tissue is removed, the opening is closed without a scar. In addition to Tony Agpaoa, the other important names are Rev. Alex Orbito of Philippine (Martin 3) and Ze Arigo of Brazil (Fuller 4) who were reputed to perform nearly 300 operations a day. In the second category, physical hands are not the instruments; rather it is the mental-spiritual energy which radiates from the fingers, specially the middle one, and the palm, which penetrates the body and reaches the diseased part. The diseased part is first removed from the body in astral dimension and then it is rematerialized in the physical dimension, which is visible to the physical eyes. The dematerialized diseased part is converted into bioplasm, after externalization through a psychic *chakra;* the materialization is through the formation of ectoplasm. The process of restructuring continues further, and only in ideal cases does it take the form of actual bodily tissues. In the process of dematerialization, the organic matter is dissolved and turned into a new state of energy which is not known to the material world. This happens due to intense concentration of the healer. The subtle etheric energy is directed either by the healer's mind or by some entity on the Higher Realm which is using the healer as a channel. According to my proposition, it is the same energy which is known to be activated by a yogi around his body through which he can walk on fire or perform similar feats. Through this energy only a karate expert breaks the block of concrete through his bare bands. The partition of the block is affected by the spiritual energy, while the acting is done by his hand. In psychic healing the cellular tissues are simply separated without being damaged and are quickly rejoined together through fusion by the electromagnetic energy of the terrestrial energy field. These are the views of several healers/

researchers (Licauco 5). Shirley Maclaine has written about the psychic surgeon Rev. Alex Orbito in her book, *Going Within.*

Another form of psychic healing is faith/spiritual healing in which the *divine energy* is transferred through touch or passes of the hand. The transfer will generally take place with sensations of heat, tingling, changing colours or electric shocks. The healer may feel that some sort of air is leaving his body, perhaps through the hands. Ambrose and Olga Worral (6) have been two renowned healers of this kind. In long-distance healing Worral felt energy leaving through his solar plexus. The Worrals believed it to be the power of God which they invoked through prayer or meditation.

Lawrence Leshan (7), in his work with psychic healers, came to the conclusion that the healing takes place in an altered state of consciousness which is called "calirvoyant reality". He used various meditation techniques for about a year and a half before attaining a shift of consciousness. Those working with him experienced physical or psychological changes which were beneficial to them. However, Leshan concluded that this clairvoyant reality was unreliable and unpredictable. He claimed that he could teach others about how to awaken their healing powers through meditation. Leshan worked with Irish clairvoyant Eileen J. Garrett on the subject of healing and postulated that: time existed in an eternal now; there existed a central unity to all things, which are a part of a larger pattern; the harmonic whole of the cosmic is above good and evil which are just illusions and that there existed a better way to get information other than the five senses. Garret worked with Prof. Rhine at the Duke University, and she wrote about psychic healing in some of her books (Garrett 8).

Benjamin O. Bibb, D.D. and Joseph J. Weed have been other renowned healers who stressed the importance of quieting the outer or conscious mind and slowing it down to the meditative level where the inner mind can be contacted. *Meditation* is certainly an excellent way to achieve this. They talk about developing a "mental telephone" and outline the following method: (i) contact the inner mind of the subject and observe the true nature of the injury or malfunction, (ii) use mental pictures to show the subject's inner mind and how to correct this, (iii) supply healing energy and instruct the subject's inner mind on how to obtain the energy necessary for it to perform and sustain the healing, (iv) see the subject perfectly healed, then break contact gently and give it no further thought at that time, although the treatment may be repeated later. They suggest the use of simple pictures for the inner mind: "If a muscle is torn, tie it together. If a subject's lungs are filled with mucus, use a vacuum cleaner. If there is a growth to be removed, pluck it out with your fingers. Never, never visualize the use of a knife; there should be no cutting. You are to heal tissues, not destroy them. If a tooth is loose, take it out with your fingers mentally, clean it thoroughly and return it after first packing the cavity with glue (mentally, of course) (Bibb and Weed 9, 35)."

One very wonderful healer says that she employs the "shutting out the world" method recommended by Hindu teachers. Joyce Dix of West Palm Beach, Florida treats headaches by placing her hands on the patient's head as her own mind instructs her, and then pours *white healing energy* into the area indicated. France M. Eyberse of Lisbon, Ct. would pour white healing energy into the area affected. In her words, "On two occasions I stopped earaches in my son by merely placing my hands over the boy's ears and pouring white energy down through my arms and into his ears." In relieving a severe hacking cough, Eyberse says, "I turned her onto her stomach in her bed and placed my right hand on the back of her neck with my fingers touching the skull area; then I poured powerful blue-white light down my arms and into the area covered by my hands. She slept throughout the rest of the night and awoke feeling bright, fresh and very much relieved (Bibb and Weed 9, 39-40)." A large variety of cases are cited in which the healing takes place through the pouring of white/blue light energy mentally, even in the orthopedic cases of joining broken bones.

### 3. The Hidden Physiology and the Quantum Leap

Ayurveda from ancient India has the reputation of curing disease at the incurable stages through yoga exercises, meditation and a strictly low cholesterol diet. Latest examples include the curing of forty advanced heart patients by shrinking the fatty plaque deposits which were blocking their coronary arteries. Dr. Dean Ornish, a San Francisco cardiologist, brought these miraculous healings through yoga and meditation rather than by the conventional drugs or surgery in 1988 (Chopra 10, 8). According to Ornish's study, what we build in our bodies can also be unbuilt. And thus heart disease can be reversed once it has started.

Andreas Schmidt, a well-educated Swiss man in his early fifties, developed melanoma, the fastest spreading and most virulent form of skin cancer. After initial surgery, through which the melanoma cells were removed, Andreas refused to undergo further surgical treatment. His oncologist said that if the treatment were discontinued, the disease may return in six months. If treated, the patient may live for a few years but only ten per cent would live for more than five years. At this stage Andreas used Ayurvedic mental techniques together with purification treatments. After four months he reported that his swollen lymph node had subsided. According to X-rays and blood tests no trace of melanoma was found in his body. He would not have survived more than three months after the recurrence of the cancer, as the Swiss oncologist said, but now he is leading a normal life for about the last two years (Chopra 10, 18-19). Gerald Rice, himself a medical doctor from Boston, was diagnosed at age 50 with chronic myelogenous leukaemia. People with such a disease may live for about three years after the initial diagnosis. His blood count had soared to 52,000; after the Ayurvedic treatment, it dramatically dropped to 28,000, over 40 per cent. If he had turned to conventional chemotherapy, a reduction of 10,000 in his blood counts would have been considered a success. But then he had to go through nausea, hair loss, physical debilitation, depression and other side effects. Dr. Gerald was amazed by the results and commented that "nothing medical had happened to him". He continues to benefit from the approach, although he finds it hard to break out of his old patterns completely. Laura Simons is another case of remarkable performance after being treated for her advanced breast cancer by Dr. Deepak Chopra through the Ayurvedic bliss technique.

Anecdotal reports have convinced Chopra (10, 136) that hundreds of patients suffering from heart diseases, cancer, multiple sclerosis and even AIDS have reported alleviation of pain, anxiety and various other troubling systems through different Ayurvedic treatments which are completely non-surgical. We have now to see what lies at the bottom of the Ayurvedic approaches which baffles the orthodox medical practitioners as mysteries.

There is a quantum body, known as the astral body in parapsychology, paralleling the physical one. Such a body has long been known as *Sukshma Sharira* in Hinduism. A quantum is between 10,000,000 and 100,000,000 times smaller than the smallest possible atom. It is the basic fibre through which nature first builds the quantum body and then the physical body comes into being. The quantum, known as *prana* in Kundalini Yoga, is the invisible vibration awaiting physical manifestation. At this level matter and energy are interchangeable. The *pranic* vibrations first transform into impulses of energy and then into particles of matters (Chopra 10).

The conventional medicine is confined to the gross level of physiology. It cannot penetrate deeper to the level of the quantum body, where the power is available at the infinitely greater level, such as the explosion of the atom bomb and the laser beam which cuts through the steel. These are the examples of the tremendous power at the quantum level. At the subtlest level of nature, energy has the greatest potential, and it can take the *quantum leap* like that of an atom bomb or a laser beam. That is the level at which Ayurveda works and on which *yoga philosophy and meditation* are based. That is why the results of Ayurvedic treatment or yoga and meditation, which is a still higher level of quantum mechanism, are of such a nature that orthodox medicine cannot comprehend it. Living examples are the yogis of India and in other parts of the world, who defied old age and maintained perfect health, looking almost half their actual age.

Holistic medicine has taken its names from the Greek *holos*, meaning "whole". Maslow (11) and others developed the psychology of health and transcendence that treat the human beings as a whole organism and not as a collection of parts. Psychologists Robert Ader and Nicholas Cohen found that rats could be conditioned to depress their immune system, and they coined the term PNI (psycho-neuroimmunology). Further research showed that the immune system produces chemicals that feed information back to the brain. This was the result of the work of neuroscientist Karen Bulloch in the 1970's. Norman Cousins suffering from "ankylosing spondilytis" concerned with the distintegration of the spine made a full recovery through vitamin C and "humour therapy", although doctors put his chances of recovery at 1 in 500. This was an example of the role played by emotions on health, showing, in a way, that the body is a mirror of the mind (Locke and Colligan 12). Relaxation, change of attitude and imagery can increase the number of white blood cells and also the level of thymosinalpha-1, a hormone known to produce the feelings of well-being, resulting in dramatic improvements in catastrophic illness such as cancer (Rossman 13, Meek 14). Surgeon Bernie S. Siegel (15) hypothesizes that conditional love or lack of love is at the root of all diseases. Siegel was renowned for his alternative therapy for the patients of cancer. Cardiologist Herbert Benson believed that the "faith factor", religious or psychological, plays an important role in health (Wechseler 16).

The quantum fibre *prana* pervading the whole universe is a vital force or energy transcending time and space and is responsible for life and health. The Hindu word *prana* has been known by different names in different faiths: *qi* in china, *ki* in Japan, *telesma* in the writings of Hermes Trismegistus, *astral light* in Kabbala and *mana* in Polynesia (Hoffman 17). Alchemist Robert Fludd called it *spiritus,* Hippocrates called it *Vis Medicatrix Nature* and hypnotist Franz Anton Mesmer called it *Pneuma.* Thus the knowledge of the quantum unit *prana* has been with mankind from ancient times. Although it permeates all things in the universe, it is highly concentrated on mountain-tops and near running water, corresponding with the concentration of the negative ions. Furthermore, its circulation is highest in the morning, around noon and in the evening around sunset (Friedman, Milton 18).

A German chemist Baron Karl Von Reichenbach (19) called *prana* by the name *Od* and said that it can be seen by clairvoyants as luminous radiations and felt as hot or cold. His theory was agreed with by psychiatrist Wilhelm Reich (20, 21) of Austria who called it *orgone* as the universal biological force with blue colour, as the basis of sex and psychosomatic neuroses. He developed a device called "orgone accumulator" and used it on cancer patients, reporting positive results. The latest term coined for *prana* is "bio-energy". Researchers in Czechoslovakia and Soviet Union have claimed to store this bio-energy in generators and use it in healing. Several books offer detailed study of *prana:* Leadbeater (22), Krishna (23), Kieffer (24), Lemaitre (25), McGill (26), and Mookerjee and Khanna (27). A body filled with *prana* is strong and resistant to disease and illness, and is likely to live a long life.

Ayurveda and yoga/meditation are in fact technologies for contacting the quantum/*pranic* level inside ourselves. Anything in the body can be changed with the flick of an intention. As an example, consider people with multiple personalities. They may appear to be psychological cases, but as one personality is dropped and another is put on, the body may undergo remarkable changes. Thus, one personality may be afflicted with diabetes and the person will be insulin-deficient as long as the personality is in force. However, the other personality may be diabetes free and may be testing for insulin levels. The same thing applies to a patient of blood pressure; even scars, warts, sores, and other skin blemishes have been seen to appear and disappear with the changing personalities. Even the colour of their eyes can change from blue to brown. One woman had three separate menstrual periods each month, corresponding to her three separate personalities (Chopra 10, 11).

Signals from the quantum mechanical body can bring instantaneous changes in the physical body. Thus, the white cells of the immune system, coated with antibodies that cause the allergic reaction wait patiently for the contact of the antigen. When contact occurs, a series of chemical reactions are triggered automatically. As such, a patient may choose to be allergic at a time and not so at another. It is just like saying that the sugar may choose to be sweet at a time and not so at another. That is, the molecules have the power of decision-making. Thus we confront the possibility that we are choosing our own diseases, too (Chopra 10, 11). Having understood this, one can make use of the inner technologies which operate at the quantum/*pranic* level and cause the eradication of diseases. Awareness has a healing capacity, and this seems to explain the sudden cures even in the most advanced cases of incurable diseases.

People with a strong "faith factor", religious or psychological, who regularly and persistently practise yoga and meditation, may not only achieve immunity to diseases for themselves, but also may acquire an inner power to heal others, even those suffering with chronic/incurable diseases. I believe that such people become storehouses of *prana,* which perhaps passes into the patients they touch consciously or unconsciously, causing the start of the healing process, terminating the disease sooner or later. It would be appropriate to quote an instance or two from India at this juncture.

A sweeper by the name of Jhabban lived in a poor community of the town Ranikhet in the northern part of India. He got married but was ill-treated by his wife and also by some relatives and friends at times. He never reacted to any insult, kept calm and withdrew from the scene. He moved to another town, Bareilly where he was appointed as a nurse to help Dr. Hey at the new Christian mission under the new name, Peter.

Some people have some kind of healing power in their hands. Peter (Jhabban) had the same power. His touch was so gentle that it would delight the patients. There were several trained nurses and interns, but patients would prefer Peter to give them medicine or shots. Slowly he became known as Dr. Peter, although he was illiterate. If he cleaned a wound, it started healing immediately. If he gave medicine, the fever would subside immediately. Although Dr. Hey called it superstition, Peter became famous, and his experience was greater than that of any doctor who had studied in a medical school. He did not know how to read or write, but the name of every instrument in the hospital or any kind of medicine and its use was imprinted in his mind. To Peter, Hindu, Muslim, Christian, all believers were the same. He was very polite, kind, and ready to serve people day and night. The patients would say, "Peter has magic in his hands. If he touches a patient, he starts getting cured."

The landlord of the village of Ratlam had a skin disease which affected his arm. Several doctors had given him medicine, but it was never cured. Peter had never seen such a disease. He patiently said, "Sir, I can make a medicine. It will probably work, but I am not sure." He gave an ointment to the landlord who was cured in less than a week. The landlord gave a huge amount of money to Peter which he refused to accept in his name. However, a hospital was built and doctors and other staff were appointed. Peter had no desire to get a salary. He wanted to serve the poor. For some reason he believed that if he accepted a salary, he could not cure people. However, dirty politics developed in the hospital, and Peter was forced to leave the hospital quietly one evening.

Wearing dirty clothes and with no money in his pocket he went to the railway station. The driver of the engine gave him a lift, asking him to cure his arm of a disease which was not healed by several medicines. Needless to say, the driver was cured overnight and was highly amazed to see the miracle.

Peter settled in the town of Mussoorie, cleaning temples, churches, mosques and streets. He became known by the name of Bhagatji (devoted person). Bhagatji's healing power was now greater than before. His mind was not at all in worldly things. He was not aware of his powers.

One day he was sweeping a street. A woman came running towards him with her dead child in her arms, crying bitterly. Bhagatji took the child to his room and closed the door. After some time when he opened the door, the child was crying in his arms. The public was amazed to see that the dead child was revived by Bhagatji.

Bhagatji closed the door, and the people slowly left. He sat down on his bed and began to think, 'Oh, even compassion, kindness and helping others is a desire. That desire is also a trap. Imprisonment in a house or in a palace is the same because in both places the desire of getting free is the same. To find complete freedom I have to go beyond desires. I have nothing left in the world. I want to dive and dissolve in the ocean of peace'. His mind began to turn inward and he lost consciousness of the body and world. He was in a state of deep trance. When he came to his senses he found that he had no desire to communicate to the outer world in any way. From that day no one saw Bhagatji—neither in the church, nor in the temple. He stopped going out of his room. The sweepers would bring him food, and he wanted nothing else.

One day he was found dead in his room with the following note in his pocket: "This body will die in Mussoorie by burial under the snow on Christmas day. This is the will of God—Jhabban, Ratlam Hospital, Bareilly District." He foresaw his death long before it took place.

What class of spiritual person did Jhabban belong to? Perhaps a *karmayogi*, but quite different from even Mahatma Gandhi and Mother Teresa, who did not have those miraculous healing powers, nor did they achieve salvation in their lifetimes. Jhabban had the state of complete desirelessness coupled with intense love for God which spontaneously triggered paranormal powers, including healing. Yet the seeker is not interested in them. The goal is nothing short of merging with Brahman. The full account of Jhabban's true life story can be found in the book, *Sweeper to Saint* by Baba Haridass (28). The book has other true life stories showing miraculous healing powers of the Inner Sound Currents.

**4. Conclusion**

Almost all the methods of psychic healing have the following features in common:

i) The healer is only an agent; the real work is done by the energy from a Higher Source.

ii) The healer meditates or prays to God or a deity/spirit

of a dead ancestor to invoke that energy or power. Consequently, if the healer cannot get into the meditative level, the healing may not take place.

iii) It is at the quantum level that energy and matter are interchangeable. *Prana* is the unit of cosmic energy at that level, which, therefore, is responsible for life and healing.

iv) The best or perhaps the unanimous way of attracting and/or directing *prana* is through meditation, in which the conscious mind becomes quiet and the inner or subtle mind takes over.

Yoga is the preparation for meditation. Each of the different paths of yoga, such as *Hatha Yoga, Bhakti Yoga, Karma Yoga, Tantra Yoga,* or *Raja Yoga* can lead to the end result. However, the best way would be the Integral Path which combines elements from each one of them. The Integral Path, which is similar to the one proposed by Sri Aurobindo, was proposed by me (Kumar 29) in a manner more suitable to the modern householder, as follows: (i) Yogic exercises for about 45 minutes, (ii) Meditation for 1 to 3 hours, preferably with the chanting of a *mantra,* (iii) Reading case histories of spiritually realized persons and scriptures for 2 to 4 hours, (iv) Regulated sex life between married partners, depending on personal factors and variations.

A successful practice leads to the awakening of the spiritual energy, Kundalini, which rises through seven centres of energy, called *chakras.* At the third centre the seeker is in touch with the paranormal and gets the first-hand knowledge of higher realms through out-of-body experiences or through nightly dream sequences. This confirms the scriptures in various religions. When the sub-centre called *Bindu,* between the sixth and seventh centres, is awakened, a nectar flows from there which drenches the whole body, giving it "perfect health" and making it immune to diseases and accidents (Saraswati 30). Others who remain in contact with such a person also achieve perfect health and immunity to diseases and accidents.

Thus the following double purpose is served:

i) Acquiring perfect health with a self-healing internal system and to provide the same to others.

ii) Attain salvation in one lifetime.

However, the choice rests with the practitioner, whether to remain at the level of healer or to go beyond it. There are unimaginable activities on the Higher Planes. One who gets the taste of it, by accident or by preparation, does one's best to break ties with the material world so as to be absorbed in inner realms as much as possible and thus finally achieve Self-realization and the intuitive knowledge of God.

**References**

1. Sherman, Herald; *Wonder Healers of the Philippines,* De Vorss & Co, Los Angeles, CA, 1967.
2. Motoyama, Hiroshi, *Tony Agpaoa's Psychic Surgery and its Mechanism,* Institute for Religious Psychology, Tokyo, 1978.
3. Martin, Harvey; "Psychic Surgery", *The Journal of Border Line Research,* March-April. 1991, p.17.
4. Fuller, John G.; *Arigo: Surgeon of the Rusty Knife,* Thomas Y. Crowell Co., 1974.
5. Licauco Jaine T.; *The Truth Behind Faith Healing in the Philippines,* National Book Store, Metro, Manila, Philippines, 1982.
6. Worrall, Ambrose A, and Worrall, Olga N., *The Gift of Healing: A Personal Story of Spiritual Therapy,* Harper & Row, New York, 1965.
7. Leshan, Lawrence; *The Medium, the Mystic and the Physicist: Toward the General Theory of the Paranormal,* Viking Press, New York, 1974.
8. Garrett, Eileen; *Adventures in the Supernormal: A Personal Memoir,* Garrett Publications, New York, 1949.
9. Bibb, Benjamin O. and Weed, Joseph J.; *Amazing Secrets of Psychic Healing,* Parker Publishing Co., Inc., NY, 1976.
10. Chopra, Deepak; *Perfect Health,* Harmony Books, New York, 1990.
11. Maslow, Abraham H.; *Toward a Psychology of Being,* Van Nostrand, Princeton, 1962.
12. Locke, Steven E. and Colligan, Douglas; *The Healer Within,* E.P. Dutton, New York, 1986.

13. Rossman, Martin L.; *Healing Yourself: A Step-by-Step Program for Better Health through Imagery,* Pocket Books, New York, 1987.
14. Meek, George W. Ed, *Healing Process,* The Theosophical Publishing House, Wheaton, III., 1997.
15. Siegel, Bernie S.; *Love, Medicine and Miracles,* Harper & Row, New York, 1986.
16. Wechseler, Rob; A New Prescription: Mind Over Melody, *Discover,* Feb. 1987, pp.51-61.
17. Hoffman, Enid; *Huna: A Beginner's Guide,* Para Research, Rockpocket, MA, 1976.
18. Friedman, Milton; *From Poland with Prana, New Realities,* 1984, no.6, pp. 10-15.
19. Reichenbach, Kari Von: *The Odic Force: Letters on Od and Magnetism,* University Books, Secaucus, NJ, 1968 (Originally published in Germany in 1926).
20. Reich, Wilhelm; *The Discovery of the Orgone: The Function of the Orgasm; Sex—Economical Problems of Biological Energy,* 1942.
21. Reich, Wilhelm; *The Cancer Biopathy,* 1948.
22. Leadbeater, C.W.; *The Chakras,* Theosophical Publishing House, Wheaton, ILL, 1994.
23. Krishna, Gopi; *Kundalini - the Evolutionary Energy in Man,* Shambhala Publications, Boulder, Colorado, 1967.
24. Kieffer, Gene; *Kundalini for the New Age: Selected Writings of Gopi Krishna,* Bantom Books, New York, 1988.
25. Lemaitre, Solange, *Ramakrishna and the Vitality of Hinduism,* The Overlook Press, Woodstock, New York, 1984.
26. McGill, Ormond; *The Mysticism and Magic of India,* A.S. Barness & Co., Cranbury, NJ, 1977.
27. Mookerjee, Ajit and Khanna, Madhu; *The Tantric Way: Art, Science and Ritual,* New York Graphic Society, Boston, 1977.
28. Haridass, Baba; *From Sweeper to Saint,* Sri Rama Publishing, Santa Cruz, California, 1980.
29. Kumar, Ravindra; "The Journey Back to our True Home—Part-I", *JRPR,* Jan. 1994.
30. Saraswati. Swami Satyananda, *Kundalini Tantra,* Bihar School of Yoga, Munger, Bihar, India, 1984.

# Last Words

Believing that all religions have a common source, it has been my earnest desire to prove and present the common denominator at the base of most cases of enlightenment. Awakening of the Kundalini coupled with sincere devotion towards the search for Self or God, is the surest and shortest way to God-realization. Following the Integral Path, elaborated in Chapter 2, one can know the Self, and hence God, in this lifetime. And that is the end of the cycle of death and rebirth. A new life awaits the aspirant in a higher realm, where one came from, the "True Home".

However, there is always one more step in the spiritual journey. We keep on evolving even on higher planes, but with the satisfaction that we are now the co-workers with God.

The human psyche is found to have two divisions: a conscious self, associated with the phenomenal worlds; and a greater unconscious Self, which is our source and which keeps us in contact with God through guidance, dreams, visions and the like. The spiritual quest culminates in bringing the unconscious Self to the level of waking consciousness. Since the Soul or Self is akin to God, this means God-realization, when inferred intuitively.

Accounts of Self or God-realization from a large number of saints, prophets, and other modern seekers who were successful, have the common feature of a blissful rapture accompanied with knowing and witnessing the Self by the Self without any intermediary medium, whatsoever. At this point of time one sees the Self as a formless, infinite entity full of knowledge and bliss. From then on the aspirant has inner peace, tranquillity, affectionate detachment and a complete faith and surrender to the will of God.

It signifies the death of the old personality and *rebirth* in the form of the new personality. I propose the following model:

Stage 1: Persecution/inner turmoil/helplessness and surrender.

State 2: The experience of death (of ego).

Stage 3: Resurrection, opening of the third eye and experience of bliss, higher realms of existence and/or deity.

Some report more than one experience of death and the total pattern may unfold gradually in a series of related experiences. Elements may emerge piecemeal, depending on the training and circumstances.

Anyone passing through these stages can understand that the awakening has taken place in him/her, and then one would need to manage:

1) The tongue and the reproductive organ, both of which are highly energized, and any misuse can burn them.
2) Withdrawal from power, position, materialism and worldly relations.
3) Immersion into devotional songs of God, which is now the means to achieve the final goal.

Emmanuel Swedenborg, Dr.B.S. Goel and others took immediate retirement from active worldly life in order to allow the process to fully grow in them. Those who continue with the affairs of the world will have the Kundalini residing in the *manipura chakra* (navel centre) only. Liberation is not achieved. You can analyze a *Sadhu* but you cannot become a *Sadhu*.

Kundalini awakening is like getting a visitor's visa for higher realms. To become a permanent citizen, you must co-operate with the process in a complete way.

I suggest a ***six-hour daily programme*** under the "Integral Path" as follows:

(1) Two-hour workshop early in the morning, comprising-

i) Yogic exercises for about 45 minutes.

ii) *Pranayama* (deep breathing) with the three locks: root lock, naval lock and throat lock, known as ***mool-bandha, uddayan-bandha*** and *jalandhar-bandha* in Kundalini Yoga, for a period of 20 minutes.

iii) Chanting of OM (AUM) with concentration on the position of the third eye between the eyebrows, for a period of 20 minutes.

iv) Closing all the doors of the physical senses, invite white Light as the personification of God and feel it entering your body through the crown centre. In this way, practise *samadhi* for about half an hour.

2) Two-hour reading of scriptures and case histories of realised persons.

3) Two-hour chanting of a *mantra* given by the Guru or selected by oneself.

4) Married practitioners should learn the way of regulated sex life. This is an additional factor which expedites the whole process as a catalytic agent.

Lastly, I would like to comment on the inability of people to devote 6 hours a day for God. To obtain a degree in engineering, medicine, accounting etc., one has to devote one's whole day for about 5 to 6 years. God is not cheaper than a degree. If you remember God on a part-time basis, He will also reveal Himself to you on a part-time basis, which might take several lifetimes. Those who cannot devote 6 hours to God due to their involvement in the affairs of the world, have not actually earned this privilege through their *karmas* in the past lives. They have yet to learn many lessons in the school of earth before they can devote necessary time in search of Self or God. However, there is always a way out if the determination is strong.

# Appendix I

# Why Everyone is Not Attracted to the Path of God

*Since time immemorial Saints and Prophets like Buddha, Jesus, Mohammed and Nanak have been preaching Godliness, yet only a selected few have taken to the search of Ultimate Reality. The gap could not be bridged between different religions on one hand and between science and religion on the other. The reason is that each one of us incarnates in a particular lifetime to learn a particular lesson. It is only when all the lessons have been learnt that the individual takes to the religious path in a particular lifetime. The fact is explained through the science of numbers. Suggestions are given to open-minded non-believers to try and see this fact for themselves.*

**1. Introduction**

Born in Greece, Pythagoras was an extraordinary man of the sixth century B.C. He had a three-sided personality—a mathematician, a numerologist, and a spiritualist. He is known to the world only as a mathematician, giving a theorem in geometry which states that the square on a hypotenuse is equal to the sum of the squares on the other two sides of a right-angled triangle. It is unfortunate that the material world did not pay attention to his findings in numerology and spiritualism which are closely related to each other as a rule of mathematics. A dynamic, handsome sportsman, he married one of his disciples in his early sixties, got initiations from many masters, realized Self/God and set up the Centre of Pythagorean thoughts as a "school of initiation". He was still in his prime when he was assassinated at the age of 99 years by his non-believers.

Pythagoras introduced the symbol - --- meaning that the paths of worldliness and Godliness are in opposition to each other. An individual can travel on one path or the other, but not on both. A person has to "tread the unfrequented ways" to find peace and God. Pythagoras lived a full, worldly life, but in his later days his interest started changing. Gradually he became a man of God. He is a very good example for the Westerners and people of modern thoughts round the world. With a sustained practice and an open mind, any person living a material life can redirect one's energies towards spiritual goals and thereby attain peace and God.

Pythagoras believed that each attribution of life is related to a specific number...thus, the whole universe is numerical. A person is born in a particular incarnation at a very specific, unique time in accordance with his destiny, based on one's next incarnation with the help of Astral Masters on higher planes. One enters the womb of one's mother when the Divine forces of nature are in concurrence with one's requirements and the birth takes place. (See for example Lynn Elwell Sparrow 1.) And then a name is given to him/her by a priest or relative in accordance with the Divine command. This name and date of birth can now be interpreted to know the character and events in the life of a person.

Some people are born with emphasis on physical activities, some on mental activities, some on emotional activities and some on spiritual activities. Thus a person with maximum points and a particular number on the spiritual plane treads the path of God. Seemingly, the destiny of a person is fixed, yet it can be changed through efforts. According to an Indian proverb, "A yogi makes his own destiny".

There are seven *chakras* or centres of energy in the human body; *mooladhara, swadhishthan, manipura, anahata, vishuddhi, ajna* and *sahasrara.* In the words of Swami Satyananda Saraswati (2), "In *anahata chakra*, the freedom to escape from a preordained fate and to determine one's own destiny becomes a reality." Once the consciousness ascends through the *manipura chakra*, you become master over some of the situations of life, but you are still influenced and bound by your *Prarabdha Karma.* You know that you can ascend it, but you do not know how. People who accept their fate as inevitable have not yet transcended *mooladhara* and *swadhishthan chakras. Manipura* is still considered earthly, although it lies at the boundary between mortal and immortal planes. Those who actively shape their destiny through strength of will channelled in a positive direction, which leads to realization and achievements, are in the realm of *manipura.*

In *anahata chakra* one realizes that fate is of course real, but still one can go totally beyond its dictates. It is like throwing something in the sky beyond the gravitational field. Consciousness is accelerated in *anahata chakra* to the speed of free-will in order to transcend the pull of latent *sanskaras.* Only in *anahata* do you become a yogi, who can shape your own destiny. You depend solely upon the power of your own consciousness rather that on anything that is external or concerning faith.

**2. The Science of Numbers**

Following Pythagoras, several researchers have worked in the field and consolidated the theory of numbers. See for example my book *Secrets of Numerology* (3).

Each letter of the alphabet has a numerical value and its meaning according to the following table:

A, J, S - 1 - Courage, Initiative, Individuality, Leadership, Attainment.

B, K, T - 2 - Peace, Partnership, Cooperation, Diplomacy, Spirituality.

C, L, U - 3 - Imagination, Self-expression, Joy of Living, Creativity, Good Luck, Satisfaction of Desires.

D, M, V- 4 - Construction, Order, Service, Limitation, Application, Builder.

E, N, W- 5 - Sexuality, Constructive Freedom, Progress, Knowledge, Fluctuations in Fortune.

F, O, X - 6 - Artist, Balance, Responsibility, Love, Domesticity, Humanitarian Service and its Rewards.

G, P, Y - 7 - Analysis, Understanding, Investigation, Specialization, Meditation.

H, Q, Z - 8 - Judgement, Material Satisfaction, Power, Organization, Philosophy, Ambition, Authority.

I, R - 9 - Forgiveness, Selflessness, Tolerance, Artistic and Dramatic Talents, Charitable, Philanthropic, Religionist.

Avoiding details in other directions, one can see that the main numbers of spiritual interest are 7 and 9 and to some extent 2 (made by 11, in particular). In fact, the compound numbers 11 and 16 represent spiritual illumination. It will be shown that most yogis, prophets, saints and philanthropists and those working for the cause of humanity had these numbers prominent in their names. The total of the numerical values of letters in a name represents the *Destiny Number,* the total of the numerical values of all vowels in a name represents the *Heart Number,* and the total of the date of birth represents the *Talent Number* of the person. These numbers are known as the Major Numbers or numbers on the major positions. A detailed discussion of major and minor number is presented in my book, *Secrets of Numerology.* Numbers 4 and 5 represent the Physical Plane; 1 and 8 represent the Mental Plane; 2,3, and 6 represent the Emotional Plane; and 7 and 9 represent the Intuitional Plane.

Thus, numbers of 4's and 5's in a name account for the value at P; numbers of 1's and 8's for the value M; numbers of 2's, 3's and 6's for the value E; and numbers of 7's and 9's for the value at I.

Although 7, 9, 2, 11, and 16 are main spiritual numbers, a Karmic Number represents loss in the material world but achievement in spiritual direction. The Karmic Numbers are 11/2, 13/4, 14/5, 16/7, 19/1, 22/4 and 26/8.

D = Destiny Number, representing events, circumstances and achievements in life.

T = Talent Number, representing personality traits/characteristics/abilities and tools in hand.

H = Heart Number, representing the desire of the heart.

P = Physical Plane

M = Mental Plane

E = Emotional Plane

I = Intuitional Plane

ü ý þ : Temperament, according to which the energy flows.

**3. *Illustrative Examples***

Let us look at the names and dates of birth of the famous spiritual giants and understand the mystery behind their success.

*Name* *Date of Birth*

$\frac{12/3}{1\,1\,9\,1} + \frac{4}{1\,1\,1\,1}$ = 7 - H

Ramakrishna Paramhansa

$\frac{914\ 12991851}{50/5} + \frac{71914\ 81511}{38/11/2}$ = 7 - D

P - 4 1-2-3-4-5-6-7-8-9
M-11/2 9 1 0 2 2 0 1 2 4
E - 1
I - 5

$\frac{12/3}{9\text{·}3} + \frac{22/4}{9\ 1\,3\,9}$ = 7 - H

Jiddu Krishnamurti

$\frac{19443}{21/3} + \frac{299185143929}{62/8}$ = 11/ 2 - D

P - 4 1-2-3-4-5-6-7-8-9
M - 4 3 2 2 3 1 0 0 1 5
E - 4
I - 5

$\frac{8}{5\ 3} + \frac{9}{9}$ = 17/ 8 - H

Jesus Christ — August 21, 7 B.C.

15131 / 11/2 + 389912 / 32/5 = 7 - D — 8 + 3 + 7 = 18/9 - T

11/2 / 9 1 1 + 5 / 1 3 1 = 7 - H

Siddhartha / 47/11/2 + Gautam (Buddha) / 18/9 = 11/2 - D

11/2 / 1 19 + 2 / 1 1 = 4 ——— - H

Dalai / 41319 / 18/9 + Lama / 3141 / 9 = 18 / 9 - D

10/1 / 1 9 + 11/2 / 6 5 = 3 ——— - H

Franklin Jones (Da-Free John of U.S. settled in Fiji)

69152395 / 40/4 + 16551 / 18/9 = 13/4 - D — November 3, 1939: 11/2 +3+22/4 = 9—T

4 / 13 + 14/5 / 9 5 = 9 ———H

Paul Twitchell (The late Eckankar leader)

7133 / 14/5 + 259238533 / 40/4 = 9 ----------- H

7 / 1 6 + 5 / 5 = 12/ 3 - H

Harold Klemp (present Eckankar leader)

819634 / 31/4 + 23547 / 21/3 = 7 ———D

15/6 / 96 + 14/5 / 6 3 5 = 11/2 - H

Dion Fortune

$$\frac{4965}{24/6} + \frac{6692355}{36/9} = 15/6 - D$$

**December 6, 1890**

12/3+6+18/9 = 18/ 9 - T

$$\frac{4}{1\ 3} + \frac{10/1}{1\ 3\ 3\ 3} + \frac{6}{6} = 11/2 - H$$

Arthur Augustus Ford

$$\frac{192839}{32/5} + \frac{1\ 3\ 731231}{21\ 7\ 3} + \frac{6694}{25/7} = 15/6 - D$$

**January 8, 1897**

1 + 8+ 25/7 = 16/7 - T

$$\frac{12/3}{3\ 9} + \frac{10/1}{5\ 5} = 4 - H$$

Uri Geller

$$\frac{399}{21/3} + \frac{753359}{32/5} = 8 — D$$

**December 20, 1946**

12/3 + 2 + 20/2 = 7 - T

P - 2 1-2-3-4-5-6-7-8-9
M - 0 0 0 3 0 2 0 1 0 3
E - 3
I - 4

$$\frac{1}{1} + \frac{4}{3\ \ 1} + \frac{3}{3} = 8 —— H$$

Carl Gustav Jung

$$\frac{3193}{16/7} + \frac{731214}{18/9} + \frac{1357}{16/7} = 23/5 - D$$

July 26, 1875

7 + 8 + 21/3 = 18/9 - T

$$\frac{25/7}{1\ 3\ 6\ 9\ 6} + \frac{11/2}{6\ 5} = 9 — H$$

Aurobindo Ghose

$$\frac{139629546}{45/9} + \frac{78615}{27/9} = 18/9 - D$$

$$\frac{6}{5\ 1} + \frac{6}{1\ 5} = 12/3 - H$$

Edgar Cayce

$$\frac{54719}{26/8} + \frac{31735}{19/1} = 8 — D$$

$$\frac{1}{1} + \frac{17/8}{6\ 6\ 5} + \frac{12/3}{5\ 6\ 1} = 12/\ 3 - H$$

Gladys + Osborne + Leonard

$$\frac{731471}{23/5} + \frac{6126955}{4/7} + \frac{3565194}{31/4} = 16/7 - D$$

P - 5 1-2-3-4-5-6-7-8-9
M-4 2 0 2 2 4 3 3 2 6
E - 5
I - 9

$$\frac{6}{6} + \frac{38/2}{9\ 6\ 95\ 9} + \frac{14/5}{5\ 9} = 13/4 - H$$

Wolf + Grigorievich + Messing

$$\frac{5636}{20/2} + \frac{799769954938}{85/13/4} + \frac{4511957}{32/5} = 11/2 - D$$

September 10, 1899
9 + 1 + 9 = 19/1 - T

P - 6 1-2-3-4-5-6-7-8-9
M - 3 2 0 2 2 4 3 3 1 6
E - 5
I - 9

$$\frac{10/1}{9\ 1} + \frac{6}{1\ 5} = 7 \text{ ——— } H$$

Richard + Alpert (Ram Dass)

$$\frac{9938194}{43/7} + \frac{137592}{27/9} = 16\ /\ 7 - D$$

P - 2 1-2-3-4-5-6-7-8-9
M - 3 2 1 2 1 1 0 1 1 4
E - 3
I - 5

$$\frac{15/6}{9\ 6} + \frac{29/2}{5\ 9\ 6\ 9} + \frac{13/4}{1\ 3\ 9} = 12/3 - H$$

Grigory + Yefimorich + Rasputin

$$\frac{7997697}{54/9} + \frac{7569469938}{61/7} + \frac{91173295}{37/1} = 17/8 - D$$

P - 4 1-2-3-4-5-6-7-8-9
M - 3 2 1 2 1 2 3 5 1 8
E - 6
I - 12/3

$$\frac{10/1}{1\ 9} + \frac{6}{1\ 5} = 7 \text{ — H}$$

David Spangler

$$\frac{41494}{22/4} + \frac{17157359}{38/11/2} = 6 \text{ —— D}$$

January 7, 1945

1+7+19/1 = 9 - T

P - 5 1-2-3-4-5-6-7-8-9
M - 3 3 0 1 3 2 0 2 0 2
E - 1
I - 4

$$\frac{9}{3\ 6} + \frac{19/1}{59\ 5} = 10/1 \text{ - H}$$

Rudolf Steiner

$$\frac{934636}{31/4} + \frac{1259559}{36/9} = 13/4 \text{ - D}$$

February 27, 1861

2+9+16/7 = 18/9 - T

$$\frac{10/1}{9\ 1} + \frac{8}{3\ 5} = 9 \text{ — H}$$

Richard Sutphen

$$\frac{9938194}{43/7} + \frac{1\ 327855}{31/4} = 11/2 \text{ - D}$$

P - 3 1-2-3-4-5-6-7-8-9
M - 4 2 1 2 1 2 0 1 2 3
E - 3
I - 4

$$\frac{19/1}{95\ 5} + \frac{15/6}{59\ 1} + \frac{5}{5} + \frac{10/1}{1\ 9} = 13/4 \text{ - H}$$

Pierre Teilhard De Chardin

$$\frac{795995}{44/8} + \frac{25938194}{41/5} + \frac{45}{13/4} + \frac{3819495}{39/3} = 20/2 \text{ - D}$$

P - 8 1-2-3-4-5-6-7-8-9
M - 4 2 1 2 3 5 0 1 2 7
E - 3
I - 8

St. Teresa of Avila

March 28, 1515
3 + 10/1+12/3 = 7 - T

11/2 / 6 5 + 6 / 1 5 = 8 - H

Joseph + Campbell
161578 + 31472533
28/1 + 28/1 = 2 - D

March 26, 1904
3 + 8 +14/5 = 16/7 - T

7 / 6 1 + 4 / 3 1 = 11 / 2 - D

Chogyam + Trungpa
3867714 + 2935771
36/9 + 34/7 = 16 / 7 - D

P - 2 1-2-3-4-5-6-7-8-9
M - 3 2 1 2 1 1 1 4 1 1
E - 4
I - 5

6 / 5 1 + 6 / 5 1 + 14/5 / 9 5 = 17/8 - H

Stewart + Edward + White
1255192 + 545194 + 58925
25/7 + 28/1 + 29/2 = 10/1 - D

March 12, 1873
3 + 3 + 19/1 = 7 - T

Paracelsus
7191353131
34/7 = 7 — D

November 10, 1493
11/2 +1+17/8 =11/2 - T

Muhammad
4 3 8 14 4 14
29/11/2 = 11/2 - D

OR

Mohammed
4 68 14 4 58
36/9 = 9 - D

Plotinus
73629531
36/9 = 9 — D

**4. Analysis**

Most of the spiritual leaders have had two or more major numbers out of: 7, 9, 11, 16 or 2. Some of them had the additional force of the practical numbers 4 or 5 on their intuitive plane. Some of them had one or more Karmic numbers making their worldly life difficult, but inclined to spiritual pursuits.

Having a big total on the intuitive plane shows that the person received higher ideas from astral planes intuitively, without effort. But a 9 on I - plane made Wolf G. Messing a famous psychic and clairvoyant who met Einstein, Freud and Stalin and impressed them. An 8 on I - plane made P. Teilhard De Chardin a theologian, philosopher and deeply interested in meditation and religion. A 12/3, being too high a number on I - plane made Rasputin use his psychic powers for self-gratification as a requirement of number 3. For some people complete details not being available, their names at least had the total being a "spiritual number", especially the first name. For example, Jesus, Siddhartha, Dalai, Carl, Wolf, Richard, Grigory, Chogyam, Muhammad, Paracelsus, and Plotinus have a total of 2, 7 or 9.

Some people are born with number 3 on I - plane which gives them "sensitivity to ideas from beyond" and "psychic inclination". Cases of this category are Sir Arthur Conan Doyle, Aurobindo Ghose, Edgar Cayce, Siddharta Gautam (Buddha), Sigmund Freud, Carl Gustav Jung and Rudolf Steiner.

A rare example of displaying yogic powers was found in the following case:

$$\frac{15/6}{1\ 95} + \frac{4}{31} + \frac{11/2}{6\ 5} = 12/3 \text{ - H}$$

Daniel Dunglas Home — March 20, 1833

$$\frac{415953}{27/9} + \frac{4357311}{24/6} + \frac{8\ 64\ 5}{23/5} = 20/2 \text{ - D}$$

3+2+15/6 = 11/2 - T

**Home was a Scottish physical medium who could stretch his body upto 11 inches and contract by a similar measurement. He had direct communication with spirits. Look at his 2 Destiny and 2 Talent enhanced by a 3 at Heart, making him psychic and** sensitive to ideas from beyond.

**5. Conclusion**

The date of birth and the name given at the time of birth by a priest or relative clearly indicate the mode of life a person is going to live. Hence those who achieved spiritual perfection in a particular incarnation were destined to do so as a result of *sat karma* (good actions) accumulated in previous lives. A person with spiritual numbers is naturally attracted to talk about God, has faith in the Ultimate Reality and does everything possible to perfect the spiritual path. It then goes without saying that persons with physical, mental or emotional numbers at major positions do not pay heed to the messages of God. They will be fussy and argumentative about the whole idea. They will criticize any talk of God, leave alone having faith in Him. This is the reason why only a very few people listen to the discourses of saints, prophets or to spiritually inclined conversation.

Thus one can verify that the mental giants like Jawaharlal Nehru, Chandrashekhar Venkatraman (Nobel Laureate Physicist), Margaret Thatcher and Mohandas Karamchand Gandhi had maximum points on the mental plane. Martin Luther King, Elizabeth Taylor and John Llewellyn Lewis all had their maximum points on the emotional plane, showing their achievements in the field of emotions. However, King became a leader of human rights, Taylor became a film actress and Lewis became a mass murderer due to repressed emotions. They all made history in the United States in the field of emotions. Most of the businessmen and those involved deeply in the activities of the world have their maximum points on the physical plane. The famous spiritual giant of Russia, George Ivanovitch Gurdjieff, had the most powerful intuitive number 9 on the I - plane. Uri Geller with 7 Talent and a 4 on I - plane is an Israeli psychic born in Tel Aviv. Extra-terrestrial aliens have been telling him of the imminent destruction of the world. Edgar Cayce was born on March 18, 1877 which gives his Talent number as 8 which stands for power, materialism or philosophy. Because of his 9 Destiny and 3 on I - plane he drew only the philosophy part from 8, ignoring power and materialism. The same happened with Madam Helena Petrovna Blavatsky, founder of the Theosophical Society. (For more details see my book *Secrets of Numerology (3).)*

It is perfectly clear that everyone cannot be induced into the search for God. People like Jesus Christ and his killers existed simultaneously. An individual has to learn several lessons in the field of physical, mental and emotional activities over the period of many lifetimes before one is born with spiritual numbers at the major positions.

Individuals with an open mind, no matter what kind of numbers they are born with, have an opportunity to experiment through yoga and meditation. Both can provide a pathway allowing one to get closer to the Truth as a scientific fact. In the course of seven *chakras* through which the Kundalini passes, a person becomes the designer of his own fate once the fourth *chakra*, called *Anahata*, is evoked. On the awakening of the sixth *chakra,* called *ajna*, one sits under the wish-fulfilment tree where anything one wishes for comes true, under the limitations of the ways of the world. I have come across a couple of people in the world whose events and circumstances are different from what their numbers tell. These persons are the makers of their own fate through karma. When the higher *chakras* are awakened, the individual has already transcended desires of physical, mental and emotional planes after having seen the fate of the material world. The only desires left at this stage are in the field of intuition, spiritualism and in the search for God.

One can also make alterations in one's name so as to force one's destiny in the spiritual direction. Of course, this is the method of trial and error and in no way comparable to those who are born naturally with spiritual numbers. Yet, one can always experiment. The new numbers start showing their effect after a period of approximately six months. However, the Talent number cannot be changed since the date of birth is fixed once for all.

### References

1. Sparrow, Lynn Elwell; *Edgar Cayce's Wisdom for the New Age-Reincarnation,* Harper & Row, Publishers, San Francisco, 1988.
2. Saraswati, Swami Satyananda, *Kundalini Tantra,* Bihar School of Yoga, Munger, India, 1984, pp. 174-175.
3. Kumar, Ravindra; *Secrets of Numerology,* Sterling Publishers Pvt. Ltd., New Delhi, India, 1992.

# Appendix II

# Letters to *JRPR* Editor

*Letters written to friends from time to time throw some light on the "ways of nature" and some "spiritual knots" which provide help on the path of inner development. Subjects touched therein are free will versus pre-destination, materialization, Being-Consciousness-Bliss, a love affair with God and rising above an organized religion.*

All these letters have been published in the *Journal of Religion and Psychical Research,* New York, at different times.

***Dear Editor***

Gough and Shacklett (*JRPR* Oct. 1993, 199-200) have rightly presented the facts about "identical twins". Notably, they have found that "similar names" are inexplicably often associated with such twins, as in the case of two adopted infants both named Jim, described on p. 199. The names in this study provide surprising evidence in support of the concept of number and letter archetypes and of their manifestation as symbols in our world.

Jenny Randles in her book, *Beyond Explanation* (1985) reported the following case:

Patricia Kern (of Colorado) and Patricia de Biasi (of Oregon) discovered this truth when a mix-up in a computer gave them the same Social Security number. This resulted in the two coming together during 1984. Both women had been born Patricia Ann Campbell, with fathers named Robert. Both had worked as bookkeepers, had studied cosmetics and loved to paint with oils. Both married military men within eleven days of each other in

1959. Both had children aged twenty-one and nineteen. And, of course, the two entirely unrelated women were born on March 31, 1941.

Marks and Spencer plc (1984) present the following case in their book *The Unexplained.*

On the evening of July 28, 1900, King Umberto arrived with his aide in a restaurant in Monza, where he was due to attend the athletics meeting the next day. With astonishment, he noticed that the proprietor looked exactly like him, and on speaking to him discovered that there were other similarities. The restaurateur was called Umberto like the King, had been born in Turin and on the same day, had married a girl called Margherita on the day the King married his queen Margherita. He had opened his restaurant on the day that 'Umberto I' was crowned King of Italy. The King was intrigued, and invited his double to attend the athletics meeting with him. But the next day at the stadium, the King's aide informed him that the restaurateur had died that morning in a mysterious shooting accident. And even as the King expressed his regret, he himself was shot dead by an anarchist in the crowd.

Yet another striking similarity concerning names and dates of birth is stated as follows:

On May 27, 1817, the 20-year-old Mary Ashford was found dead, apparently murdered, at Erdingham. On May 27, 1974, Barbara Forest aged 20 was strangled and left in the long grass near the children's home in Erdingham at which she was a nurse. That in itself is perhaps a remarkable coincidence, but no more. It is when one examines each case in detail that the identical factors begin to proliferate. Both in 1817 and 1974 Whit Monday was on May 26th. Barbara Forrest and Mary Ashford had been raped before being murdered and their bodies were found within 400 yards (360 metres) of one another, death taking place at approximately the same time of the day. It would appear (though there must be some doubt about this case of Mary Ashford), that there were attempts by the killers to hide the respective bodies. Both the coincidences do not end here. Both girls had visited a friend early in the evening of the Whit Monday to change into a new dress and then go to dance. After each murder a man was arrested —and in each instance his name was Thornton. To round off this narrative of astonishing parallels, both men were charged with murder but were acquitted. It was when the police were checking through archives after Barbara Forrest's death that they came across full reports of the murder of 1817 and noted these similarities with amazement.

Readers have before them these cases of striking similarities in the lives of persons born on the same date and given the same names. A large number of cases have been collected also by Farber (1981); Holden (1980); Lykkon (1900) and several other researchers. The study clearly suggests that the whole life of a person is fixed in advance according to the date of birth and the name given. Otherwise how can the hobbies, characteristics and events in the lives of two persons be duplicated as if they were xerox copies?

Pythagoras, the spiritual giant of Greece of the sixth century B.C., formulated the theory that every happening in the universe is related to vibrations and numbers. He assigned numbers 1 to 9 to the letters of the alphabets A to Z and described their characteristics. He is known as the "Father of numerology". The science of numbers is now so advanced that you can prepare the complete blueprint of the life of a person based on his name and date of birth. A chart is made which can be deciphered to show completely the nature, character, past, present and future of the person. I became interested in this science while I was doing some post-doctorate research in London in 1973. And now in the past twenty years, I have made thousands of charts in various countries of the world where I lived, and I am pleasantly surprised by the accuracy of the results. I compiled the principles of numbers and published them in a book form called *Secrets of Numerology* (1992). I have also written a paper arguing that most of the spiritual giants in the world were associated with the spiritual numbers 7, 9 and 11/ 2.

According to the *Bhagavad Gita,* the Tibetan Book of the Dead, Edgar Cayce, Sri Aurobindo and several other researchers, a soul in bardo state between two incarnations reviews its past lives and decides on a model for the next incarnation. Accordingly, at the appropriate time, when the vibrations in the atmosphere are in tune with the requirements of the model of the proposed life, the birth of the person takes place. The name which comes from the mother, father, priest or relative is in accordance with the divine command. Then the name and date of birth are synchronized to make a blueprint for the life, which can be interpreted for all kinds of details.

The question of free will versus predestination has been investigated at Duke University since 1920 when Prof. J. B. Rhine began his work, but the research ended inconclusively. However, accordingly to Kundalini Yoga, if the fourth centre of energy called the heart centre is awakened in a person, the consciousness is accelerated to the speed of free will and he can shape his own destiny. Otherwise, one has to submit to the pull of latent *karmas* and live a pre-ordained life.

R.K.

**Materialization of the Soul**

April, 1995.

I would like to support the ideas propagated by A. D. Holcombe in his letter to W. R. Dykes of Canton, OH (*JRPR* 10/94, pp. 227-228), that the earth-soul on "graduation" from planet earth is "permanentized" to live on any of the three-dimensional planes in the universe, yet remaining detached and uninvolved in the life there, free to move anywhere to help evolve others, under the directions of God. Many archetypes can be quoted here, such as Jesus Christ in the resurrected form after three days, and Sri Yukteshwar Giri, guru of Swami Yogananda, who materialized in a full-flesh body before his disciples several days after his death. Sri Yukteshwar Giri was touched by his disciples and showed all signs of being a fully living person. He told his students not to be sorry to lose him, since he had to do work of a higher order to help others on higher planes (*Autobiography of a Yogi* by Paramahansa Yogananda).

Other examples of flesh-body materialization here can be cited. For one example, the son of Jasper Swain described lives on higher planes as his first-hand experience several weeks after his death. He even materialized before his father and other relatives for some very short durations of time. The details can be seen in the book, *On the Death of My Son*, by Jasper Swain, a magistrate in Petermarisberg, South Africa.

There is support in theosophy for the theory that the spirit souls wandering on earth-like planes long, long ago could not move material things and finally designed bodies of solid nature, which are now called human beings. What went wrong is that most of them entangled themselves in the process, developed attachment and completely forgot their origin and the spiritual home from where they came. Some of them retained their spiritual identity and consciousness and remained free beings. They returned to higher realms but have been coming to earth to remind others of their true origin and home. Out of love for their lost fellows they have been telling them the ways and means to do so, and this is the "Journey Back to our True Home".

I talked to my grandmother through an Ouija Board, several years after her death, and found that she could travel anywhere with the speed of thoughts; she had the same desires as when she was on earth, but she did not have a physical body to activate something she might want to do. I witnessed a recent example in India. My daughter-in-law Akta, who was mysteriously sick, was taken to a "Baba" who had some ghosts in his control. Baba sent a ghost to Kanpur, a city some four hundred miles away from Delhi, to make an inquiry. Within seconds, the ghost returned with full information and correctly described the complete geography of the house and the circumstances, to the amazement of us all.

So we are all awaiting our lives in between and as souls we have the same properties as souls on the astral planes. Only those few rare ones, who have mastered the art of detachment and timelessness, have severed their links with earth while still living here, and have learned the lessons of love and selfless service, may return to the higher realms as "permanentized archetypes". This is what our God sent us here for, The Journey Back to our True Home, to multiply Himself in His own image.

*R.K.*

July, 1994.

***Dear Editor***

John F. Miller III (*JRPR* July 1993) recalled one of his past experiences several years ago. He had a girlfriend who was ready to spend the night with him. Instead he chose to go for a spiritual experience which was far more satisfying and blissful than pleasure of any other kind.

I can add to it, my experience which I had in December 1988. On one afternoon I was taking a nap after lunch on the stretched seat of my car. As I woke up, I had a vision of the ashram for quite a few seconds. I saw the Guru walking and people moving around, clairvoyantly. Right from that moment I had an experience of a blissful state for about five to six hours. The pleasure was as unique and real as if I was having a continuous orgasm with the same intensity. The situation lasted for about six hours and it was constant ecstasy.

Yvonne Kason (ARPR annual conference report, 1993) has rightly pointed out that at the developed state of transcendence the individual experiences orgasms in the mind, without any physical activity. I can vouch for it with my own experience and that of John F. Miller III. It is this state of ecstasy in which the saint or mystic lives most of the time. It is continuous and cannot be compared with any kind of temporal pleasure.

This state is indicative of the higher realm of existence called Sat-Chit-Ananda, that is Being-Consciousness-Bliss. This is the state in which a God - realized person lives with the feeling of existence, complete knowledge and continuous bliss. This is the pre-determined goal of each and every Soul in the universe, although it is different matter to consider how many lifetimes a particular Soul takes to accomplish it, and becomes a co-worker with God.

R.K.

April, 1995.

***Dear Editor***

This note is a comment on two articles by Rhea A. White, "Role Theory and EHE" (*JRPR* 4/94) & "Recalling and Recording EHE's" (*JRPR* 10/94) and the comments on the former by Rabia L. Clark (*JRPR* 10/94: 221-3).

Rhea White has emphasized the need of recording EHE's (Exceptional Human Experiences) and sending them for publication so that others can know about them. Although I agree with her that these experiences should be shared with others, at the same time I disagree in the sense that this may lead to suspension or discontinuation of the individual's spiritual development. She has herself noted that "EHE's are usually omitted from autobiographies and biographies..." (*JRPR* 10/94:196).

Rabia L. Clark has rightly said that the students on the Sufi spiritual path are "advised not to talk about their unusual experiences or miracles, and not to focus their attention on their powers...Their journey may be blocked because they inflate the ego by feeling special. Feeding the ego by 'confessional performance' of telling about one's special experiences is not denied when doing the arduous journey through the labyrinth of the spiritual path with its test and temptations which must be overcome." It is very easy to get stuck there, inflating the ego, when the more profound experiences of Truth, Beauty and Love are waiting (Hazrat Inayat Khan).

I completely agree with Rabia Clark who is talking in accordance with the Hindu path of spiritual development. Hindu saints and gurus have repeatedly warned their students against the disclosure of their experiences to others.

An EHE which takes place by accident or chance— such as an NDE, telepathy or UFO encounter—is a single event, occurrence of which may introduce the experiencer to the spiritual path. There is no harm in recording and publishing it for the benefit of others as well as for inviting explanation and help from others for the self. This should be encouraged. But once an individual takes to the spiritual path in a determined and regular way, he should guard further experiences as secrets, and of course, when the journey is complete in the sense that the subject has established a regular rapport with the infinite and he is the so-called liberated person, his biography/autobiography can be published for the benefit of others. Although the journey is never complete, since evolution is an ongoing process, even on higher realms of existence, the person is out of danger of falling back from this stage. Many saints do not disclose their experiences in full even at this stage, though they provide guidance in their own chosen words.

The spiritual journey is like a love-affair with God, an affair between the Soul and Supersoul, and it is very private and personal. Even in a human love affair between a man and a woman, the secrets of meeting and personal experiences are fully guarded for reasons of their own. Only then are they sweet, enjoyable, memorable and above all, undisturbed by others.

*R.K.*

***Dear Editor***

[A letter I addressed to Mr. W.H. Belk II of the Belk Research Foundation may contribute to our discussion of psychic and Kundalini experience.]

I am very happy to learn that you brought Peter Hurkos to USA, for a scientific study by Dr. Andre Puharich. Certainly no one would know better than you about him.

Here I want to stress the difference between psychic powers and Kundalini.

Paranormal powers were awakened in Peter Hurkos due to an injury and the powers were used exclusively for worldly purposes, for example, to locate the culprit the police failed to find. Peter did not have the evolution of inner peace in his heart or a love of God due to that particular injury, because only an external agency of the brain was evoked and not the Kundalini. That is the whole crux of the matter.

Paranormal powers automatically follow with the arousal of the Kundalini, though in varying degrees, but the practitioner never cares for them if he has a spiritual goal in mind. These powers are a hindrance in the path of God and inner peace. History is full of Yogis and Masters all over the world who acquired some of these powers on their path but they never displayed them in public and they categorically refused to surrender themselves for a laboratory test by a scientist. Scientists and governments have always failed in the pursuit of such persons for display or testing. A Yogi has already tasted the "infinite love and bliss" and has seen his future in advance; consequently, the use of paranormal powers for worldly purposes appears to be child's play and misuse of the gift of God. He has achieved this state after many lifetimes and after leading a very disciplined and hard life in his incarnation, and certainly he would not like to lose it for anything less than God-realization. I am saying this not only from reading the case histories of successful Masters round the globe but also from my own personal experiences over the years.

On the other hand, there are people who achieve paranormal powers by other means, for example, LSD, an accident or injury, a near-death-experience, or even by meditation with limited interest. These powers can be used for worldly purposes but certainly they do not bring you close to the understanding of God. The choice is yours: whether you have a limited goal in mind or an "infinite one". And in history no such person was ever happy with the use of these powers after some time: and more often than not, his downfall was imminent. As far as the powers of Kundalini is concerned, an average Hindu knows about it and that is why he lays emphasis on it. I hope that answers your question about the Hindus at present and in mythology.

You have rightly said that there is "a built-in perfection urge in a man" and this is due to the faint and subconscious memory of the true home which we left behind hundreds or perhaps thousands of millenniums ago. You have again said that the "iron curtain" of "ignorance and confusion" is raised slightly at time, and that flashes of inspiration, guidance and knowledge beyond ordinary limitations of the flesh are received which either bewilder and frighten the person, or lift him up to new heights of courage and understanding, depending upon his background and training. This is exactly the theme of "Exceptional Human Experiences" being explored today. A single EHE can be baffling but viewed through the "Integrated Path of Kundalini Yoga" it can tell where the person stands on the ladder of evolution and what he should do next.

I fully agree with Randall Verade that anyone who can rise above an organized religion and can outgrow its external observances can find the real truth about the infinite nature of God. This is what we are endeavouring to prove in our writings.

Your "Belk Research Foundation" is certainly doing a good job in exploring the human mind and I would be glad to associate myself with your work.

*R.K.*

# Bibliography

Arguielles, Jose 1987. *The Mayan Factor.* Santa Fe, NM: Bear & Co.

Asaramji, Saint 1994. *Sachha Sukh.* Yoga Vedanta Samiti, Ahmedabad, India.

———1995. *Atma Yoga.* Yoga Vedanta Samiti, Ahmedabad, India.

Assagioli, R. 1986. *Self-Realization and Psychological Disturbances.* The Quest, Winter/Spring.

Aurobindo, Sri and Mother, 1989. *The Psychic Being.* Sri Aurobindo Ashram, Pondicherry, India.

Baba, Meher 1967. *Discourses by Meher Baba* Vol. I, II, III. Sufism Reoriented Inc., San Francisco.

Bancroft, Anne 1976. *Twentieth-Century Mystics and Sages.* Arkana, William Heinemann Ltd., UK.

——— 1982. *The Luminous Vision: Six Mediaeval Mystics and Their Teachings.* George Allen and Unwin, London.

Barbara & Foster, Michael 1987. *Forbidden Journey: The Life of Alexandra David-Neel.* San Francisco: Harper & Row.

Bharti, Agehananda 1975. *The Tantric Tradition.* Doubleday, New York.

Bhattacharya, B. 1985. *The Way of Tantra.* Sterling Publications, New Delhi.

Bibb, Benjamin O. and Weed, Joseph J. 1976. *Amazing Secrets of Psychic Healing.* Parker Publishing Co., Inc., NY.

Billimoria, Purusottama 1993. *Yoga, Meditation and the Guru,* Sterling Publishers Pvt. Ltd, Delhi.

Bloom, Harold 1984. *Kabbalah and Criticism*. New York: Continuum.

Browning, Norma Lee 1970. *The Psychic World of Peter Hurkos.* Garden City, NY:Doubleday & Co.

Bucke, Richard Maurice 1961. *Cosmic Consciousness*. The Citadel Press, New Jersey.

Campbell, Bruce F. 1980. *Ancient Wisdom Revealed: A History of the Theosophical Movement.* Berkley: University of California Press.

Campbell, Joseph 1988. *The Inner Reaches of Outer Space: Metaphor as Myth and Religion.* New York, Harper & Row.

Capra, Fritjof 1985. *The Tao of Physics.* New Science Library, Shambhala, Boston.

Carter, Darlene 1986. *A Very Outspoken Interview with Dick and Tara Sutphen.* Self-Help Update Issue 31.

Cavendish, Richard 1974. *The Encyclopaedia of the Unexplained.* New York, McGraw Hill.

Chatterji, Mohini M. 1932. *Viveka-Chudamani or The Crest-Jewel of Wisdom.* The Theosophical Publishing House, Adyar, India.

Cheetham, Erika 1984. *Further Prophecies of Nostradamus.* Bantom Books, USA.

Chopra, Deepak 1990. *Perfect Health.* Harmony Books, New York.

Cirlot, J. E. 1971. *A Dictionary of Symbols*. New York: Philosophical Library.

Cooke, Grace 1966. *The Illumined Ones.* New Lands, England. White Eagle Publishing Trust.

Covina, Gina 1979. *The Ouija Book.* New York: Simon and Shuster.

Coward, H. 1985. *Jung and Eastern Thought.* State University of New York Press.

Crowley, J. 1993. *Psychic Surgery - how is such a sensational EHE to be validated.* ARPR Proceedings.

Dermenghem, Emile 1981. *Mohammed and the Islamic Tradition.* Woodstock, New York: The Overlook Press.

Evans-Wentz, W. Y. 1951. *Tibet's Great Yogi Milarepa: A Biography From the Tibetan.* 2nd. ed. London: Oxford University Press.

Edge, H.L; Morris, R. L; Palmer, J. and Rush, J.H.1986.

*Foundations of Parapsychology*. Routledge and Kegan Paul, plc, Boston.

Fisk, George W. 1993. *Response to Rhea White's Exceptional Human Experience as Vehicles of Grace: Parapsychology, Faith and Outlier Mentality*. ARPR Proceedings.

Ford, Arthur and Bro, M. H. 1958. *Nothing So Strange: The Autobiograpjy of Arthur Ford.* New York: Harper & Brothers.

Fortune, Dion 1984. *The Mystic Kabbalah.* York Beach ME: Samuel Wiser.

Frawley, David 1992. "The Wisdom Tradition of the Ancient World". *The Quest,* Theosophical Society in America, Denville, Winter 92.

Friedman, Milton 1984. *From Poland with Prana.* New Realities, no. 6, 1984.

Frost, Bede 1980. *Saint John of the Cross: Doctor of Divine Love—An introduction to his Philosophy, Theology and Spirituality.* New York: Vantage.

Fuller, John G. 1974. *Arigo: Surgeon of the Rusty Knife.* Thomas Y. Crowell Co., NY.

Garrett, Eileen J. 1949. *Adventures in the Supernormal: A Personal Memoir.* Garrett Publications, New York.

——— *Many Voices. Autobiography of a Medium.* New York, G. P. Putman's Sons.

Gauld, Alan 1968. *The Founders of Psychical Research.* Routledge & Kegan Paul, London.

Geller, Uri 1975. *My Story.* New York: Praeger.

Goel, B. S. 1985. *Third Eye and Kundalini.* Third Eye Foundation of India, New Delhi.

Gough, W.C. and Shacklett, R.L. 1993. "Physics, Parapsychology and Religion." *JRPR,* April 93.

Grant, Joan 1956. *Far Memory.* New York: Harper & Row.

Greenwell, Bonnie 1990. *The Energies of Transformation.* Shakti River Press, Cupertino, CA.

Grosso, Michael 1985. *The Final Choice.* Walpole, NH: Stillpoint Pub.

Guiley, Rosemary Ellen 1989. *Tales of Reincarnation.* Pocket Books, New York.

Gurney, Edmund; Myers, F.W.H. and Podmore, Frank 1918 & 1986. *Phantasms of the Living.* Kegan Paul, Trench, Turner & Co., London.

Hall, Manly P. 1928. *An Encyclopaedic Outline of Masonic, Hermetic, Qabbalistic and Rosicrucian Symbolical Philosophy.* H. S. Crocker Co., San Francisco.

——— 1977. *The Secret Teachings of All Ages.* Los Angeles: The Philosophic Research Society.

Hall, Trevor H. 1984. *The Enigma of Daniel Home.* Buffalo, NY: Prometheus Books.

Harding, M. E. 1971. *Woman's Mysteries.* P. Putman's Sons, New York.

Haridass, Baba 1980. *From Sweeper to Saint.* Sri Ram Publishing, Santa Cruz, California.

Hildegard of Bingen's 1986. *Scivas; Translated by Bruce Hozeski.* Santa Fe, NM, Bear & Co.

Hoeller, Stephen A. 1982. *The Gnostic Jung and the Seven Sermons to the Dead.* The Theosophical Publishing House, Wheaton, Ill.

——— 1988.*C. G. Jung and the Al Chemical Revival.* Gnosis 8 Summer 88:34-39.

Hoffman, Enid. 1976. *Huna: A Beginner's Guide.* Para Research, Rockpocket, MA.

Holcombe, A. L. 1993. *Christ Consciousness, Kundalini and Spiritual Energy.* JRPR, April 93.

Holger, Kersten 1986. *Jesus Lived in India.* Elements Books Ltd., Longmead, Dorest, England.

Hozeski, Bruce 1986. *Hildegard of Bingen's Scivas.* Bear & Co., Santa Fe, NM.

Hurst, Kenneth Thurston 1992. *F.I.N.D.'s Eights Annual Conference.* Oct. '92.

Huxley, Aldous 1970. *The Perennial Philosophy.* Harper & Row Publishers, USA.

——— 1973. *A Biography.* New York: Alfred A. Knop, Harper & Row.

Institute, The Bhaktivedanta 1986. *Interviews With Nobel Laureates and Other Eminent Scholars.*, Bombay, India.

Jaykar, Pupul 1986. *Krishnamurti: A Biography.* Harper & Row, San Francisco.

Johnson, Robert A 1987. *Ecstasy; Understanding the Psychology of Joy.* San Francisco: Harper & Row.

Jonas, H. 1958. *The Gnostic Religion.* Beacon Press, Boston.

Julian of Norwich 1961. *Revelation of Divine Love.* Translated by James Walsh, New York: Harper & Row.

Jung, C. G. 1961. *Memories, Dreams, Reflections*; recorded and edited by Aniela Jaffe. New York: Random House.

——— 1964. *Man and His Symbols.* Doubleday & Co., Inc; New York.

Kammerer, Paul 1919. *Dass Gasetz Der Serue*, Germany.

Kason, Evon 1993. *Exceptional Human Experiences, Spiritual Transformation, and Kundalini Awakening: A Clinical Perspective.* ARPR Proceedings.

Kelsey, Denys and Grant, Joan 1967. *Many Life Times.* Doubleday & Co., Garden City, New York.

Kieffer, Gene 1988. *Kundalini for the New Age: Selected Writings of Gopi Krishna.* New York: Bantom Books.

Klemp, Harold 1987. *Soul Travellers of the Far Country.* Eckankar, Minneapolis, MN:

——— 1988. *How To Find God.* Eckankar, Minneapolis, MN

——— 1989. *Child in The Wilderness.* Eckankar, Minneapolis, MN.

——— 1991. *Cloak of Consciousness.* Eckankar, Minneapolis, MN..

Kopytin, A. I. 1992. "Why Kundalini is Not Enough". *JRPR*, Oct. 92.

Krishna, Gopi 1967. *Kundalini—The Evolutionary Energy in Man.* Shambhala Publications, Boulder, Colorado.

——— 1975. *The Awakening of Kundalini.* New York, NY: Kundalini Research Foundation.

Kumar, Ravindra 1991. *On Enlightenment and God.* JRPR, Oct. 91.

——— 1992. *Secrets of Numerology.* Sterling Publishers Ltd., New Delhi.

——— 1994. *The Journey Back To Our True Home* - Part I. JRPR Jan. 94.

——— 1994. *The Journey Back to Our True Home* - Part II. JRPR April 94.

——— 1994. *Journey Back Home* - Part III. JRPR July 94.

——— 1994. *Journey Back Home - IV, Personality Transformation With Chakras.* JRPR, Oct. '94.

——— 1995. *Predestination, Psychic Sense and Free-Will,* JRPR, Oct. '95.

——— 1996. *Posthumous Personality, Reincarnation and Liberation.* JRPR, April '96.

——— 1996. *Healing Through Psychic Intervention.* Annual Conference Proceedings, ARPR, July '96.

——— 1997. *Recent Developments in Search of Truth.* Annual Conference Proceedings, ARPR, June '97.

——— 1997. *Psychic Individuation and Self-Realization* - I. JRPR, July '97.

——— 1997. *Destiny, Science and Spiritual Awakening.* Sterling Publishers Ltd., New Delhi.

Leadbeater, C.W. 1933. *The Astral Plane.* The Theosophical Publishing House, Adyar, Madras, India.

——— 1994. *The Chakras.* Theosophical Publishing House, Wheaton, Ill.

Leary, Timothy 1983. *Flashbacks: An Autobiography.* Los Angeles: Jeremy P. Tarcher.

Lemaitre, Solange 1984. *Ramakrishna and the Vitality of Hinduism.* The Overlook Press, Woodstock, New York.

Leshan, Lawrence 1974. *The Medium, The Mystic and the Physicist, Toward a General Theory of the Paranormal.* New York: Harper & Row.

Licauco, Jaine T. 1982. *The Truth Behind Faith Healing in the Philippines.* National Book Store, Metro, Manila, Philippines.

Lindgren, C.E. 1994. "Scientific Investigation and Religious Uncertainty", *JRPR*, April 94.

Litvag, Irving 1972. *Singer in the Shadows: The Strange Story of Patience Worth.* Macmillan, New York.

Locke, Steven E. and Colligan, Douglas 1986. *The Healer Within.* E. P. Dutton, New York.

Long, Max Freedom 1965. *The Huna Code in Religions.* Huna Research Publications, California.

Lutyens, Mary 1975. *Krishnamurti—The Years of Awakening.* Avon Books, U.S.A.

Maharaj, Sri Nisargadatta 1973. *I Am That.* The Acorn Press, Durham, N.C., USA.

Martin, Harvey 1991. Psychic Surgery. *The Journal of Border Line Research,* March-April '91.

Maslow, Abraham H. 1962. *Toward a Psychology of Being.* Princeton, NJ: Van Nostrand.

McAdams, Elizabeth E. and Bayless, Raymond 1981. *The Case for Life After Death.* Nelson Hall, Chicago.

McGill, Ormond 1977. *The Mysticism and the Magic of India.* A.S.Barness & Co., Cranbury, NJ.

Meek, George W. Ed. 1977. *Healers and Healing Process.* The Theosophical Publishing House, Wheaton, Ill.

Melton, J. Gordon 1986. *Enicyclopaedic Handbook of Cults in America.* New York: Garland Publishing Inc.

Mercatante, Anthony S. 1988. *Encyclopaedia of World Mythology and Media.* Frenches Forest, Australia: Child & Associates.

Miller, John Franklin 1993. "In Defence of Religion". *JRPR Oct.* 93.

Moody, Raymond 1986. *Life After Life.* Bantom Books, NY.

Mookerjee, Ajit and Khanna, Madhu 1977. *The Tantric Way: Art, Science and Ritual.* New York Graphic Society, Boston.

Morimitsu, Phil 1987. *In The Company of Eckmasters.* Eckankar, Minneapolis, MN.

Motoyama, Hiroshi 1978. *Tony Agpaoa's Psychic Surgery and its Mechanism.* Institute for Religious Psychology, Tokyo.

Muktananda, Swami 1972. *Chitshakti Vilas* (The Play of Consciousness). Gurudev Siddhapeeth, Maharashtra, India.

Myers, W. W. Fredric 1954. *Human Personality and Its Survival After Death.* Vol. 1 & 2, Longmans, Green & Co., New York.

O'Brien, Stephen 1989. *Visions of Another World.* The Acquarian Press, London.

——— 1992. *In Touch With Eternity.* A Bantom Book, Great Britain.

Paul, Irwin 1981. *Santa Teresa de Jesus de Avila.* JRPR, Oct. '81.

Paramahansa, Ramesh 1990. *Shabda Brahma*; Shanti Prakashan, Kanpur, India.

Playfair, Guy Lyon 1975. *The Unknown Powers*. Pocket Books, New York.

Ponce, Charles 1973. *Kabbalah: An Introduction and Illumination for the World Today*. Wheaton, II: The Theosophical Publishing House.

Pond, Paul 1993. *The Road Home*. JRPR, Jan 93.

——— 1993. *What is the Purpose of Exceptional Human Experience* ?. ARPR Proceedings.

Prabhavananda, *Swami and Isherwood*, Christopher 1995. Bhagavad-Gita. Barnes & Noble Books, New York.

Prabhupad, Swami 1969, 1972. *Bhagavad-Gita As It Is*. Bhaktivedanta Book Trust, New York.

——— 1980. *An Easy Journey to Other Planets*. International Society for Krishna Consciousness, West Virginia.

Prophet, Elizabeth Claire 1984. *The Lost Years of Jesus*. Summit University Press, Livingstone, MT.

Prince, Walter Franklin 1972. *The Case of Patience Worth*. Boston Society for Psychical Research, Boston.

Radha, Swami Sivananda 1992. *Kundalini Yoga*. Motilal Banarsidass Publishers, Delhi, India.

Reich, Wilhelm 1942. *The Discovery of the Orgone: The Function of the Orgasm; Sex-Economical Problems of Biological Energy*.

——— 1948. *The Cancer Biopathy*.

Reichenbach, B. A. 1993. *Empirical Accounts of Spiritual Reality: The Enclosed Garden* of *Bo Yin Ra*. JRPR July 93.

——— 1994. "Hypnosis: An Empirical Evaluation". *JRPR*, Oct. 94.

Reichenbach, Karl Von 1968. *The Odic Force: Letters on Od and Magnetism*. University Books, Secaucus, NJ. (Originally published in Germany in 1926).

Roberts, Jane 1972. *Seth Speaks: The Eternal Validity of the Soul*. Englewood Cliffs, NJ: Prentice Hall.

Robinson, Edward 1977. *The Original Vision: A Study of the Religious Experience of Childhood*. Religious Experience Unit, Oxford.

Rogo, D. Scott 1987. *The Infinite Boundary*. Dodd, Mead & Co., New York.

Rossman, Martin L. 1987. *Healing Yourself: A Step-by-Step Program for Better Health through Imagery*. Pocket Books, New York.

Sahai, Chaturbhuj 1987. *Sadhana ke Anubhava*. Ramashraya Satsang, Mathura, India.

Saraswati, Swami Satyananda 1984. *Kundalini Tantra*. Bihar School of Yoga, Munger, Bihar, India.

Shan, Idris 1971. *The Sufis*. Garden City, NY: Anchor/Doubleday.

Shepard, A. P. 1983. *Rudolph Steiner: Scientist of the Invisible*. Rochester, VT: Inner Traditions International.

Sherman, Herald 1967. *Wonder Healers of the Philippines*. De Vorss & Co., Los Angeles, CA.

Siegel, Bernie S. 1986. *Love, Medicine and Miracles*. Harper & Row, New York.

Simpson, William J. 1930. *St. Augustine's Conversion: An Outline of his Development to the Time of His Ordination*. New York: Macmillan.

Sivananda, Swami 1991. *Kundalini Yoga*, The Divine Life Society, Shivanandanagar, Tehri-Garhwal, India.

Smith, A. J. 1985. *John Donne*. New York: Mettwen.

Smith, Houston 1976. *Forgotten Truth*. Tosch-Books, Harper & Row, Publishers, New York.

Sparrow, Lynn Elwell 1988. *Edgar Cayce's Wisdom for the New Age-Reincarnation*. Harper & Row Publishers, San Francisco.

Spangler, David 1984. *Emergence: The Rebirth of the Sacred*. Dell, New York.

Steinberg, James 1991. *Divine Distraction*. The Dawn Horse Press, Clearlake, California.

Sutphen, Dick 1978. *Past Lives, Future Loves*. Pocket Books, New York.

Swain, Jasper 1974. *On The Death of my Son*. Turnstone Books, London.

Swedenborg, Emannuel 1894, 1963. *Divine Love and Wisdom*. American Swedenborg Printing and Publishing Society, New York.

——— 1972. *Divine Providence.* The Swedenborg Foundation, New York.

Symonds, John and Grant, Kenneth 1979. *The Confessions of Aleister Crowley; An Autobiography.* London: Routledge and Kegan, Paul.

Talamonti, Leo 1974. *Forbidden Universe.* The Grandstone Press Ltd., London.

Teilhard De Chardin 1968. *The Future of Man.* New York: Harper & Row.

Thompson, Keith 1990. *Stormy Search for the Self.* Yoga Journal, July/August 90.

Thurman, Robert A.F. 1984. *The Tibetan Book of the Dead.* Bantom Books, U.K.

Tirtha, Swami Vishnu 1993. *Divine Shakti Kundalini.* Yogshree Peeth Trust, Muni-Ki-Reti (Rishikesh), India.

Trungpa, Chogyam 1986. *Shambhala; The Sacred Path of the Warrior.* New York: Bantom Books.

Twitchell, Paul 1967. *The Tiger's Fang.* Menlo Park: California; IWP Publishing Co.

——— 1969. Eckankar: *The Key to Secret Worlds.* San Diego, Illumined Way Press.

——— 1971. *The Spiritual Notebook.* Menlo Park, California, IWP Publishing.

Umen, Samuel 1988. *The World of the Mystic.* New York: Philosophical Library.

Walker, Claire G. 1992. *Annual Conference Proceedings.* ARPR

——— 1993. *The Question of Validation in Psychic Surgery.* ARPR Proceedings.

Watts, Alan 1972. *In My Own Way: An Autobiography* 1915-1916. New York: Pantheon Books/Random House.

Weber, Renee 1991. *Dialogues with Scientists and Sages.* London: Routledge and Kegan Paul.

Wechseler, Rob. 1987. "A New Prescription: Mind Over Melody." *Discover*, Feb. '1987.

White, Rhea A. 1993. *Exceptional Human Experiences as Vehicles of Grace: Parapsychology, Faith and the Outlier Mentality.* ARPR Proceedings.

White, Steward Edward 1969. *The Betty Book: Excursions into the World of Other Consciousness.* Berkley Medallion Books, New York.

Whiting, Joshua C. 1987. "Sources of Spontaneous Mystical "Experience. *JRPR* 10 No. 3, July 87.

Whitton, Joel L. and Fisher, Joe 1986. *Life Between Life.* Grafton, London.

Wilhelm, Richard 1931. *The Secrets of the Golden Flower.* Harcourt Brace Jovanovich, Publishers, New York.

Willson, Terrill 1987. *How I Learned Soul Travel.* Eckankar, Minneapolis, MN.

Winterhalter, Robert 1993. "New Thought and Vedanta". *JRPR* Jan. 93.

Wood, Earnest E. 1948. *Practical Yoga - Ancient and Modern.* NY: Wilshire Book Co.

Woodroffe, Sir John 1981. *The Serpent Power.* Ganesh & Co., Madras, India.

Worrall, Ambrose A. and Worrall, Olga N. 1965. *The Gift of Healing: A Personal Story of Spiritual Therapy.* Harper & Row, New York.

Yogananda, Paramahansa 1986. *Autobiography of Yogi.* Jaico Publishing House, Bombay, India.

Zemke, LeRoy E. 1996. *Thoughts For Transformation.* Emberlight Publishers, Florida.

Zohar, Danah 1983. *Through the Time Barrier.* Granada Publishing Ltd., London.

# Glossary

| | | |
|---|---|---|
| Advaita | : | Non-duality. |
| Ahankara | : | Ego, pride. |
| Ajna or Agya Chakra | : | Sixth energy centre midway between the eyebrows, the Centre of Command. |
| Akashik records | : | Library at the Causal (upper Mental) plane. |
| Amrit | : | Nectar. |
| Anahat | : | Unstruck or unbeaten (sound). |
| Anahat Shabda | : | Unstruck Sound, heard by yogis through inner ears. |
| Anahat Chakra | : | Fourth centre of energy located near the heart. |
| Ardhanaarishwara | : | Half male/half female form of Lord Shiva. |
| Asampragyata | : | Absorption without awareness. |
| Asana | : | Yogic posture. |
| Ashram | : | Centre of yoga where the Guru imparts knowledge to disciples. |
| Atman | : | Soul or spirit, the pure self, beyond body and mind. |
| Atman Swarup | : | The form of Atman. |
| Bangle | : | Round ornament made of glass, gold or a metal worn by females in India. |
| Bardo state | : | Life between two incarnations (Tibet). |

| | | |
|---|---|---|
| Bhagatji | : | Spiritually devoted person. |
| Bhajan | : | Devotional song. |
| Bhakti Yoga | : | The path of devotion. |
| Bindu | : | Point. |
| Bindu Visarga | : | The source (point) of creation. |
| Chaitya Purusha | : | Psychic Being or High Self. |
| Chakra | : | The centre or vortex of energy. |
| Chanting | : | Repetition of a mantra. |
| Chintamani | : | Jewel of correct and positive thinking. |
| Chitta | : | The subconscious mind. |
| Devas | : | The pious celestial beings. |
| Dharna | : | Determination. |
| Dhunatmak | : | God in the form of Sound Current. |
| Dhyana | : | Meditation. |
| Dhyana Yoga | : | The path of meditation. |
| Divya Chakshu | : | Divine eye. |
| Durga | : | The benevolent female deity, representing wisdom and power. |
| Eckankar | : | The religion of Light and Sound, Minneapolis, MN. |
| Eckmaster | : | Spiritual leader of Eckankar. |
| Gross world/body | : | The physical world/body of earth, on which we live. |
| Hatha Yoga | : | The path of physical yogic practices, which includes *asanas* (postures), *pranayama* (breath control), *kriyas* (cleansing practices), *bandhas* (locks) and *mudras* (seals). |
| Huna | : | The religious code of ancient Polynesians, extending from Hawaii islands to New Zealand. |
| Ida | : | A nerve-canal running on the left side of *Sushumna* from the base of spine to the eyebrow centre. |
| Jeevan Mukta | : | Liberated while still living on earth. |
| Jnana Yoga | : | The path of knowledge. |

|  | |  |
|---|---|---|
| Kaal | : | The angel of death. |
| Kalpataru | : | Wish-fulfilment tree. |
| Kali | : | The ferocious female deity, representing newly awakened Kundalini. |
| Kama | : | Lust. |
| Kanyadan | : | Donation of an unmarried girl. |
| Karma | : | Action or the effect of action. |
| Karma Yoga | : | The path of selfless actions, without attachment to the results. |
| Kaurava brothers | : | One hundred sons of Dhritrashtra, the eldest one being *Duryodhana (Mahabharata).* |
| Kirtan | : | Repetition of *mantras* set to music. |
| Kriya Yoga | : | A set of yogic exercises, including *tapas* (austerity), *svadhyaya* (study) and *Isvara pranidhanam* (self-surrender). |
| Krodh | : | Anger. |
| Kumaris | : | Unmarried girls/women. |
| Kundalini | : | Also known as the serpent power or Shakti, it is the creative Cosmic Energy, the female counterpart of God Unmanifest. It belongs to the Causal Plane, hence it is invisible on the Physical Plane. It lies dormant at the base of the spine. When awakened, it is responsible for evolution and Self/God realization. |
| Kundalini Yoga | : | The yoga system specially designed for the awakening of Kundalini. |
| Lobh | : | Greed. |
| Mahabharata | : | The famous war epic at the time of Lord Krishna. |
| Mahasamadhi | : | The state of final absorption with God. |
| Manipura Chakra | : | The third centre of energy at the naval region. |

|  | |  |
|---|---|---|
| Mantra | : | A set of words repeated continuously for God-Realization. |
| Mental bodies | : | Bodies belonging to the mental plane, made of the finer material of that plane. |
| Moha | : | Attachment. |
| Moksha | : | Liberation. |
| Mooladhara Chakra | : | The first centre of energy at the base of the spine. |
| Nirvikalpa Samadhi | : | Absorption without any fluctuation. |
| Niyama | : | Religious observances. |
| Ouija board | : | A board and pointer used for divination, and for contacting the spirits or entities by some. |
| Oversoul | : | Absolute God. |
| Pandava brothers | : | Five sons of Pandu, namely, Yudhishthar, Bhim, Arjuna, Nakul and Sahdev (*Mahabharata).* |
| Paramatma | : | The Supreme Soul, God. |
| Pashupati | : | Master of all animal instinct, another name of Lord Shiva. |
| Patanjali | : | Famous saint and author of the book *Patanjali Yoga Darshan.* |
| Pingla | : | A nerve-canal running on the right side of *Sushumna* from the base of spine to the eyebrow centre. |
| Prana | : | Quantam Cosmic Energy. |
| Pratyahara | : | Withdrawal of the senses from external objects. |
| Pyanayama | : | Control of breathing. |
| Prarabdha | : | Collective or accumulated (from past lives). |
| Raja Yoga | : | The "royal path", including concentration and meditation based on ethical discipline. |
| Rajo guna | : | The principle of creative activity in humans. |

| | | |
|---|---|---|
| Ramayana | : | Biography of Lord Rama. |
| Ravana | : | The demon-king of Sri Lanka at the time of Lord Rama. |
| Sahasrara | : | The thousand-petalled lotus, as the seventh centre of energy at the crown of the head. |
| Samadhi | : | A state of union with God. |
| Sanskars | : | Deep-rooted sense-impressions from previous lives in the mind. |
| Sanyas | : | Formal renunciation of the world. |
| Sari | : | A garment to cover the whole body, used by women in India. |
| Sat Karma | : | Good actions. |
| Satguru | : | The Inner Guru or Teacher. |
| Satsang | : | Joining the band of people whose activities concern only God-realization, and listening to the Guru. |
| Savikalpa Samadhi | : | Absorption with fluctuations. |
| Shakti/Sakti | : | Creative Energy of God, the feminine aspect of unmanifest Absolute, responsible for all manifestations in the universe. |
| Shaktipat | : | Direct transmission of spiritual power by a guru. |
| Shabda/Shabad | : | Cosmic Sound, Om or Word, the materially creative principle. |
| Shoonyata | : | Void, a huge nothingness. |
| Siddhis | : | Occult or paranormal powers. |
| Soma Rasa | : | Nectar. |
| Subtle planes | : | Planes finer than the physical plane, such as astral, mental, causal, soul/atma etc. |
| Sukshma sharira | : | Astral or subtle body. |
| Sushumna | : | The central of the three nerves—*Ida, Sushumna* and *Pingla*—connecting the root of spine to the eyebrow centre. |

| | | |
|---|---|---|
| Swadhishthan Chakra | : | The second centre of energy near the root of the sex-organ. |
| Swami | : | The Lord, the Guru. |
| Tantra | : | The ancient science of expansion and liberation of the consciousness from its limitations, using specific techniques. |
| Tantra Yoga | : | The path leading to the union of Shiva and Shakti, or the masculine and feminine forces, using ritual, worship, discipline, meditation and attainment of powers. |
| Tantric | : | Someone having achieved certain supernatural powers through the practice of *Tantra.* |
| Tat-Tvam-Asi | : | That-Thou-Art, meaning, *Atman* is the same as *Brahman.* |
| Urdhva-reta | : | A person in whom the direction of flow of the semen has been reversed, i.e., upwards rather than downwards. |
| Varnatmak | : | The descriptive form of God, e.g., Krishna, Christ, Allah. |
| Vishuddhi Chakra | : | The fifth centre of energy in the throat region. |
| Yama | : | Moral conduct. |
| Yoga | : | Union of Soul with Supersoul; the "path" leading to it. |
| Yogi | : | One who takes to the discipline of yoga. |
| Yogic | : | Pertaining to yoga. |

# Index

# BOOKS OF RELATED INTEREST FROM NAB

**ASHTANGA YOGA**
*Gregor Maehle*
ISBN: 3292

**AYURVEDIC YOGA THERAPY**
*Mukunda Stiles*
ISBN: 3438

**DEEP YOGA**
*Bhava Ram*
ISBN: 3711

**DIVINE LIGHT**
*S.K. Das*
ISBN: 0970

**HEALING POWER OF YOGA**
*Julie Friedeberger*
ISBN: 1816

**HEALING THE FUTURE**
*Deepak Kashyap*
ISBN: 0393

**KUNDALINI YOGA**
*M.P. Pandit*
ISBN: 0768

**PRACTICAL PSYCHOLOGY OF YOGA WISDOM**
*Reinhard Kowalski*
ISBN: 3308

**TRANSFORMING SELF THROUGH YOGA**
*Tom Pilrzyk*
ISBN: 3704

**YOGA FOR MEN**
*Thomas Claire*
ISBN: 2974

**YOGA FOR YOUR TYPE**
*David Frawley & Sandra Summerfield Kozak*
ISBN: 1113

**YOGA IN MODERN INDIA**
*Joseph S. Alter*
ISBN: 3247

## MEDICINE AND SPIRITUALITY SERIES

The primary goal of the series is to explore and study the relationship between spirituality and health. It will seek to integrate spirituality into medicine on a scientific basis. It is aimed at general readers with interest in health-spirituality interaction. The different volumes in it will be informative, objective, meaningful, relevant and interesting to them.

1. **Anatomy and Physiology of Yogic Practices**: Understanding of the Yogic Concepts and Physiological Mechanism of the Yogic Practices —*Dr. M.M. Gore* **ISBN: 391-9**
2. **Making Health Care Whole**: Integrating Spirituality Into Health Care —*Cristina M. Puchalski & Betty Ferrell* **ISBN: 377-3**
3. **Healing Our Hormones Healing Our Lives**: Solutions to Common Hormonal Conditions—*Linda Crockett* **ISBN: 395-7**

***General Editor***

Dr. V. K. Nigam, *M.S. Laparoscopic Surgeon*

***Editorial Board***

Dr. J. K. Sharma, *M.D., Diabetes/Cardiology*

Dr. A. S. Puri, *M.D., Gastroenterology*

Dr. M. M. Gore, *Ph.D., Ayurveda/Naturopathy*

Dr. N. A. Gaur, *Ph.D., Spirituality*

Dr. K. S. Charak, *M.S., F.R.C.S./Surgery*

## AYURVEDA, HEALTH & WELLNESS SERIES

The primary goal of the series is to provide a comprehensive understanding of Ayurveda as a way of life. It will show how Ayurveda's ancient principles of health can help achieve the highest levels of physical, emotional and spiritual well-being. It will provide a profound but practical testament to the healing power of balanced living. It will also bring every feature of Ayurveda back to its true source—the health of the spirit.

The series is aimed at general readers with interest in the art of balanced living. The different volumes in it will be authoritative, informative and interesting.

***General Editor***

Dr. David Frawley *(Vamadeva Shastri)*

***Editorial Board***

Dr. G.C. Jain

Dr. Shekhar Annambhotla, *BAMS, MD-Ayurveda, LMT, RYT*

Dr. Sunil V. Joshi, *MD-Ayurveda*

Dr. Suhas G. Kshirsagar, *BAMS, MD-Ayurveda*

1. **Ayurvedic Diet** :The Ancient Way to Health, Rejuvenation and Weight Control—*Dennis Thompon & Susan Tinkle* **ISBN: 014-8**
2. **Tibetan Ayurveda**—*Robert Sachs*
3. **Vedic Health Care System**—*Ram Lal Shah, Binod Kumar Joshi & Geeta*
4. **Neti**—*David Frawley*
5. **Ayurvedic Healing**—*David Frawley*
6. **Soma in Yoga & Ayurveda**—*David Frawley*